Clarence K. Streit's

The Unknown Turks

Mustafa Kemal Paşa, Nationalist Ankara & Daily Life in Anatolia, January - March 1921

Clarence K. Streit's

The Unknown Turks

Mustafa Kemal Paşa, Nationalist Ankara & Daily Life in Anatolia, January - March 1921

Revised, Edited & Annotated

by

Heath W. Lowry

Bahçeşehir University Press
İstanbul, Turkey

Clarence K. Streit's

The Unknown Turks

Mustafa Kemal Paşa, Nationalist Ankara & Daily Life in Anatolia,
January - March 1921

Revised, Edited & Annotated

by

Heath W. Lowry

Cover Design by Serdar Şenel (Best Image)

Text composition & Photo layout by Faruk Özbey & Heath Lowry

Published by: Bahçeşehir University Press
Çırağan Cad. Osmanpaşa Mektebi Sok. No: 4-6 Beşiktaş/İstanbul
Tel: 90 (212) 381 05 60 Fax: 90 (212) 381 05 50
www.bahcesehir.edu.tr • e-mail:info@bahcesehir.edu.tr

Distributed by: Uğur Eğitim Pazarlama ve Yayıncılık A.Ş.
İncirli Cad. No: 99 Bakırköy-İstanbul
Telephone: 90 (212) 660 58 41 Fax: 90 (212) 660 58 42
www.uguryayincilik.com.tr • e-mail: info@uguryayincilik.com.tr

Printed by: Promat

ISBN: 978-605-5461-05-8

Dedicated to

the memory of all

The Unknown Turks

who perished in the years 1914 - 1922

Table of Contents

Editor's Foreword xi

Clarence Streit's 1921 Foreword xv

Acknowledgments xvii

Chapter I: Isolated Turkey

Many warn me to stay out of Nationalist Turkey: 'Impossible' 3

Finding a reliable interpreter, Mehmed Ali Mehmedoff 4

Transferring from one destroyer to another in a storm at Samsun 5

Landing at Samsun; get permission to go to Ankara; meet Dr. Pomeroy 7

First entry into a harem; the waning seclusion of women 9

Visiting a Greek family; see a Bolshevik diplomat; I dine in a babel of languages 11

Chapter II: Winter Travel in Turkey

First day with Russian chauffeur; blizzard; first night with snowbound camel caravan 17

First contact with U.S. missionaries; from Turkish chaos to order; from Russian improvidence to ingenuity 19

My gendarme İhsan returns home after five years; describes weddings in Turkish village 22

At Çorum's only night spot we hear Turkish troubadours sing Muslim version of the Sacrifice of Isaac; I interview an eighteen year old Turk 23

From motor transport to covered wagon pulled by Turkish 'reindeer' 25

Chapter III: Living with Turkish Peasants

Traversing an area as bleak as the 'Badlands' of Montana 31

An overnight stay in adobe-hut village, peopled mainly by women and children; barefoot in the snow 32

Chicken à la Turkish peasant 34

The adobe village that wanted to be like Vienna 36

Tagore's wisdom; lunch à la Greek; baksheesh banned; an Islamic sect that permits wine 40

U.S. Prohibition seen as a step toward Islam; a land without family names 43

A 'thirsty' locomotive and a 'sparkling' freight train ride atop a load of oats 44

Chapter IV: Ankara – The Nationalist Capital

Centuries of conquerors of Ankara 51

Mustafa Kemal Pasha [Paşa], the latest conqueror of Muslim minds; in other ways, however, they are willing and anxious to help Muslim countries 52

Our stay at Constitution Hotel where a Greek woman kept all keys 53

Turks ask for accuracy only, not praise; never did I see a Turk treat a woman without respect 56

I am the only American and first Western newsman to be here in nine months 58

Only two Ambassadors in Angora [Ankara] – one for Bolshevik Moscow, one for Menshevik Georgia – brothers who do not speak to each other 58

Hamlet in Turkish, an effective prince and a very realistic grave digging scene 63

I interview and am charmed by three Turkish guerrilla veterans, ages 12, 13, 13 65

Beginning of a long friendship with Ahmet Chukri [Şükrü] Bey; Dutch correspondent George Nypels shares my view of the Turks and new government; I see a good omen for it in the crescent moon and stars 73

Chapter V: The Government of the Grand National Assembly

The Government of the Grand National Assembly 79

A unique wartime democracy 80

How President Mustafa Kemal 'dictated' democracy in 1920 80

The Constitution of the National Government 81

The government in operation 82

An Armenian evaluation of the Ankara leaders 83

Democratic army officers and civilian leaders 84

From Grand Viziers [Vezir] and Sheikhs [Şeyh] to Presidents and Commissars 84

I Hear a typical Assembly debate 85

Open diplomacy in Ankara 86

Wartime restrictions on the press and political parties 87

Self-determination within Nationalist Turkey 88

Chapter VI: Mustafa Kemal Paşa

The Turkish George Washington 93

I interview Kemal Paşa on religious and other issues 95

'Rebel,' 'dictator,' and 'demagogue?' 106

The rise from obscure birth to a position of God-given opportunity 112

A central Anatolian city to replace İstanbul as capital 114

Chapter VII: A Pay-As-You-Go War

From insolvency to a balanced budget in two years 117

The Nationalist Leaders: not 'dreamers' but 'practical men' 119

Concrete proof of women's liberation 120

Mustafa Kemal Paşa favored naming a woman ambassador to the United States 120

Madam the General: Halide Hanoum [Hanım] 124

'The Rise Of Women In The New Turkey' by Halide Hanım 125

Ankara trusts United States more than European Allies 126

Ankara: a city at war 128

Chapter VIII: Russo-Turkish Relations: New Style

Moscow - Ankara alliance: Russia cooperates with but does not dominate Ankara 133

Bolsheviks accept Ankara's policy on Straits 134

Chapter IX: Outward Bound

I meet İsmet Paşa, Chief of the Nationalist General Staff; he has just won the important Battle of İnönü 139

Eskişehir greets me with 'Committee of 3' –2 officers and local editor– to be my guide 141

Hailed by 'Hello!' in unison from Turkish troops; Turkey Red Wheat in native home; meerschaum galore; fine faience 142

Sacred tombs; Jewish, Russian, Greek, Armenian and Turkish prostitutes; rugs made by young girls 145

Preparing the Turks of tomorrow; A sound basic principle for education 146

"Where is my cavalier?" "Here I am my lady," is heard in Turkish kindergarten 148

Tell America "We are doing all we can" 150

A day on the 16,000 acres farm of Hasan Bey, a progressive entrepreneur; his 19-year-old son is among the waiters serving us at banquet where I am given an entire leg of lamb 151

Chapter X: From Eskişehir to Antalya

On troop train to the Black Tower of the Opium Region 157

My second truck ride leads to disappearing and reappearing river 158

Delightful Antalya where streams cascade into harbor; and we embark for Istanbul 159

Editor's Postscript 163

Timeline of Clarence K. Streit's 1921 Visit to Anatolia & Map Showing his Route 164

Appendices

Appendix I.: Nationalist Leaders met by Streit in Ankara (1921-1923) 169

Appendix II.: The victorious Nationalist forces enter İstanbul (October 6, 1923) 183

Appendix III.: Paul William's interview with Mustafa Kemal Paşa on April 26, 1920 189

Appendix IV: Clarence Streit's questions & Mustafa Kemal Paşa's answers (February 26, 1921) 193

Appendix V.: Clarence K. Streit's article in the Philadelphia ***Public Ledger*** (March 28, 1921) based on the answers to questions he submitted to Mustafa Kemal Paşa 211

Appendix VI.: Streit's dispatch to the ***Public Ledger*** following his February 3, 1921 interview with Mustafa Kemal Paşa 217

Appendix VII.: Robert Steed Dunn's July 1, 1921 interview with Mustafa Kemal Paşa at his Ankara (train station) residence 221

Appendix VIII.: Streit's first dispatch from Anatolia (sent from Samsun), January 24-26, 1921 229

Appendix IX.: Clarence K. Streit's dispatch of March 25, 1921 predicting defeat of Greek invasion of Anatolia 231

Appendix X.: Miscellaneous documents & photographs related to Streit's trip 235

Bibliography 243

Index 257

Editor's Foreword

Plate 1: Clarence Streit in Anatolia[3]

In 1983, while living in Washington, D.C., I received a telephone call from a former student named Uğur Doğan, who was then serving as a young diplomat at the Turkish Embassy.[1] He told me that he had recently met a most interesting man, who not only had traveled to Ankara and interviewed Mustafa Kemal Paşa [Atatürk] in 1921, but had also written an unpublished manuscript about the seven weeks he spent in Anatolia during the winter of that year. This was Clarence K. Streit, who was one of the very first foreign journalists to visit Ankara at the height of the Turkish War of Independence, and the first foreign correspondent to personally interview Mustafa Kemal Paşa after he was elected President of the Grand National Assembly.

In January of 1921, Clarence K. Streit,[2] [**Plate 1**] then a twenty-five year old American journalist with the Philadelphia ***Public Ledger*** newspaper, set sail from İstanbul to Samsun, on what was to be the first leg of a rather perilous journey to the Ankara headquarters of the Turkish Nationalist movement in central Anatolia.

In later years, Streit was to become a well known figure as the founder and proponent of Atlantic Federalism, an idealistic plan to form a confederation of the world's democracies. The blueprint for this idealistic dream was set down in his book: ***Union Now,*** which would ultimately sell several hundred thousand copies.

When I expressed an interest in meeting Streit, Uğur Doğan kindly arranged a luncheon, in the course of which Streit shared with me his impressions of Mustafa Kemal Paşa. Impressions based on an extensive interview he conducted with the Nationalist leader on March 3, 1921, as well as his having had the opportunity to observe several sessions of the Grand National Assembly which Mustafa Kemal had addressed. In the course of his visit he had filed several stories from Ankara which appeared in the ***Public Ledger.*** One such

---

1 **Note**: Today, Ambassador Uğur Doğan is a former Deputy Foreign Minister in the Turkish foreign service and currently the Turkish ambassador in the Netherlands [HWL].

2 **Note**: Clarence Streit (1896-1986), who had just completed college, after serving in U.S. intelligence in France during the war, would subsequently have a distinguished career, as journalist, author and lecturer. Best known for his book ***Union Now***, a manifesto calling for an 'Atlantic Alliance' of Western democracies, Streit died on July 6, 1986 in Washington, D.C. [HWL].

3 Library of Congress [Hereafter: LC] Catalogue #: DLC/PP 1994: 064.184.

dispatch read: *"And so well has he labored that history will recognize in Mustapha Kemal Pasha* [*Paşa*] *the founder of the new Turkish State."* Remember, he wrote this in 1921 when the Turkish forces were in retreat, not after their victorious march to the Aegean Sea in 1922.

When Streit returned to France, in the Spring of 1921, he drafted the manuscript of a book he tentatively titled: ***The Unknown Turks,*** in which he predicted the success of the Turkish nationalist movement spearheaded by its charismatic leader, Mustafa Kemal Paşa. His prescient message fell on deaf ears. For he was unable to find a publisher in the United States or in Europe (it was his view that this stemmed from the fact that he presented the Turkish Nationalists in a particularly positive light at a time when generally they were viewed as rebellious brigands), and today, almost ninety years later, his work has yet to appear in print.

In the course of several later meetings, Streit gave me a copy of his original manuscript, together with a revised version he had completed in 1982. It was his desire to see the work finally printed in both English and Turkish, and I agreed to edit it to that end. Other projects intervened, and over twenty-five years were to pass before I returned to the task of preparing ***The Unknown Turks,*** for publication. I did so after learning that Streit's papers (and photographs) were now accessible in the collection of the Library of Congress in Washington, D.C.[4] Streit (who died in 1986) had taken numerous photos in the course of his Anatolia trip. These photographs, together with the text of his original 1921 manuscript, form the basis of the present study. It consists of an abridged and heavily edited and annotated version of Streit's heretofore unpublished 1921 manuscript, together with over 100 of his previously unpublished photographs (including a number of heretofore unknown photos he took of Mustafa Kemal Paşa in Ankara).[5]

---

4 Streit's papers are housed in the Library of Congress [Hereafter: LC] in Washington, D.C. There is a useful 49 page finding aid (in two parts) with the title: Clarence K. Streit – A Register of his Papers in the Library of Congress. Part I.: Prepared by Connie L. Cartledge in 1989 & Part II.: Expanded and Revised by Connie L. Cartledge with the assistance of Sherralyn McCoy in 1994. The papers are accessible in the LC's Manuscript Division. Part I of the Streit papers was given to the LC by his wife, Jeanne Defrance Streit in 1987-1988; while Part II was presented to the LC as a series of gifts between 1992-1994. On September 8, 2007 the copyright to the materials, which had been held by the family, reverted to the public.

Streit's photographs were separated from the papers and presented to the LC's Prints & Photographs Division. Some idea of their scope may be gained from a 3 page document entitled: Container List for Streit (Clarence K.) Papers [PR 13 CN 1994:064], which was prepared in December 2008.

5 **Note**: Streit's visit to Ankara and his interactions with the Nationalist leadership have gone largely unnoticed in the secondary literature. None of the standard biographies of Mustafa Kemal Paşa, such as: a) Lord Kinross: *Ataturk: A Biography of Mustafa Kemal, father of modern Turkey.* New York (William Morrow and Company), 1965; b) Şevket Süreyya Aydemir: *Tek Adam: Mustafa Kemal* (*1919-1922*). Volume II. İstanbul (Remzi Kitapevi), 1967; and, c) Andrew Mango: *Atatürk.* London (John Murray), 1999, mention Streit. Even standard bibliographies fail to mention his visit, see: a) Abraham Bodurgil: *Kemal Atatürk: A Centennial Bibliography* (*1881-1981*). Washington, D.C. (Library of Congress), 1984; and, b) Bilal Şimşir: *Dış Basında Atatürk ve Türk Devrimi.* Cilt I. (1922-1924) *Bir Laik Cumhuriyet Doğuyor* [Atatürk & the Turkish Revolution in the Foreign Press. Volume I (1922-1924) The Birth of a Secular Republic]. Ankara (Türk Tarihi Kurumu), 1981. Şimşir's decision to begin his survey of the foreign press in 1922 rather than in 1920 is strange. Indeed, the only study to discuss his visit at all is Stanford J. Shaw's *From Empire to Republic*: *The Turkish War of National Liberation.* 5 Volumes. Ankara (Türk Tarihi Kurumu), 2000. See: Volume III., Part I.: pp. 1066-1068, where Shaw republishes a Streit dispatch which appeared in the ***Public Ledger*** on February 9, 1921, in which he described his overland trip to Ankara [HWL].

It does so in an attempt to open a narrow window, to provide a snapshot if you will, into the nascent Turkish nationalist movement during the opening months of 1921, i.e., at a key point in its evolution. By retracing Streit's travels from the Black Sea port of Samsun, across Anatolia to Ankara, the center of the newly formed nationalist government; by reliving his contacts with the peoples he met in the course of travels, as well as with the nationalist leadership in Ankara, and, in particular with its charismatic leader, Mustafa Kemal Paşa; and, finally by examining life as he experienced it, following his departure from Ankara, in the provincial town of Eskişehir (while enroute to Antalya where he embarked for Istanbul), it seeks to sketch a portrait of life in Anatolia as it actually was in the harsh winter of 1921. To the extent it is successful, it is designed to cast light on an otherwise obscure period, a juncture in time, where the ultimate fate of the Turkish nationalist movement was still very much in the balance.

Streit's connection to Turkey did not end with his 1921 visit. At the end of the following year he covered the Lausanne Treaty negotiations in Switzerland, after which he returned to İstanbul as the ***Public Ledger***'s correspondent for the Near East and the Balkans, a position he held for the next two years.

Heath W. Lowry
İstanbul, 2011

Clarence K. Streit's 1921 Foreword

The West has tried again and again to solve the perplexing 'Eastern Question.' It has never succeeded, and its failures have been written in blood not only in the Near East but also throughout the Western world. This book is written in the belief that if we are to find the road to solution to that problem, the prejudice which has so long distorted our views of the Turks must first of all be replaced by a more humane, sympathetic and realistic attitude toward them. In the hope of promoting this, I have sought to acquaint the Occident with the Turkish people as I saw them during the trip across Asia Minor which I made in 1921 as correspondent of the Philadelphia ***Public Ledger*** [See: **Map I** below]. I will also examine the democratic government of the Great National Assembly of Turkey - the first Turkish republic in history,[6] which I found the Turkish Nationalists had established there and were maintaining while fighting for their very existence.

I am indebted to the ***Public Ledger*** for permission to reproduce some photographs and portions of articles which have appeared in its columns. My thanks are also due to Monsieur and Madame Fernand Payen for the pleasant surroundings of their island home, Le Gueric, where most of this book was written.

C.K.S. Paris
September 2, 1921

Map I: Clarence Streit's Itinerary in Anatolia (January - March 1921)

---

[6] **Note**: Here, Streit's prescience is apparent. He may well have been the first individual to ever refer to developments in Ankara as "*the first Turkish republic in history*," i.e., almost two years before the Republic was actually proclaimed on October 29, 1923 [HWL].

Acknowledgments

It gives me great pleasure to express my gratitude to two institutions with which I am affiliated: First, to Princeton University, my academic home for the past eighteen years, and in particular to my colleague there, Professor Şükrü Hanioğlu, who, in his capacity as Chairman of the Department of Near Eastern Studies, made funds available from the NES Publication Fund, for the purchase (from the Library of Congress in Washington, D.C.), of copies of the photographs which comprise such an important part of this work; and, second, to my friend Enver Yücel, Founder and Chairman of the Board of Trustees of Bahçeşehir University in İstanbul, Turkey, the institution where I currently serve as a visiting professor and am honored to serve as an Advisor to the Chairman of the Board of Trustees. Bahçeşehir University has recently published a number of my books, of which the present study is the eighth.[7] Enver Bey and Bahçeşehir University have most generously underwritten the publication costs of all these studies. No words of thanks I might express could ever adequately express the gratitude I feel for these acts of generosity.

My efforts at identifying individuals in the Streit photographs (a task made difficult by virtue of the fact that at the time of his 1921 visit, surnames were still not in use in Turkey), were assisted by Yılmaz Büyükerşen, Mayor of Eskişehir, Dr. Şaduman Halıcı of Anadolu University, Sinan Kuneralp and Professors Mete Tuncay and Haluk Oral.

A special word of appreciation is due to Barbara Orbach Natanson of the Library of Congress' Prints & Photographs Division, whose many kindnesses greatly facilitated my acquisition of the photographs which are so important to this study. In addition, the staff of the Manuscript Division's Reading Room graciously assisted my utilization of the Streit Papers.

---

7 These studies (all but one of which has appeared in both English & Turkish editions) are: Heath W. Lowry: *The Shaping of the Ottoman Balkans, 1350-1550: Conquest, Settlement & Infrastructural Development of Northern Greece*. İstanbul (Bahçeşehir University Press), 2008. pp. xii + 286 + 10 Maps + 220 Photos - *Osmanlı Döneminde Balkanların Şekillenmesi, 1350-1550: Kuzey Yunanistan'ın Fethi, İskânı ve Altyapı Gelişmesi*. İstanbul (Bahçeşehir Üniversitesi Yayınları), 2008. pp. xii + 286 + 10 Maps + 220 Photos; Heath W. Lowry: *In the Footsteps of the Ottomans: A Search for Sacred Spaced & Architectural Monuments in Northern Greece*. İstanbul (Bahçeşehir University Press), 2009. xvi + 231 + 350 color photos - *Osmanlıların Ayak İzlerinde: Kuzey Yunanistan Mukaddes Mekânlar ve Mimarî Eserleri Arayış Yolculukları*. İstanbul (Bahçeşehir Üniversitesi Yayınları), 2009. xvi + 231 + 350 color photos; Heath W. Lowry: *Ottoman Architecture in Greece: A Review Article With Addendum & Corrigendum*. İstanbul (Bahçeşehir University Press: Occasional Papers in History #1), 2009. viii + 79 + 8 photos; Heath W. Lowry & İsmail E. Erünsal: *The Evrenos Dynasty of Yenice-i Vardar: Notes & Documents*. İstanbul (Bahçeşehir University Press), 2010. pp. ix + 184 + 90 Photos - *Yenice-i Vardar'lı Evrenos Hanedanı: Notlar & Belgeler*. İstanbul (Bahçeşehir Üniversitesi Yayınları), 2010. pp. ix + 184 + 90 Photos; Heath W. Lowry: *The Evrenos Family & the City of Selânik (Thessaloniki): Who Built the Hamza Beğ Câmii & Why? / Evrenos Ailesi ve Selânik Şehri: Hamza Beğ Câmii Niçin ve Kimin Tarafından Yapıldı?* İstanbul (Bahçeşehir University Press: Occasional Papers in History #2), 2010. pp. viii + 102; Heath W. Lowry & İsmail E. Erünsal: *Remembering One's Roots: Mehmed Ali Paşa of Egypt's Links to the Macedonian Town of Kavala (Architectural Monuments, Inscriptions & Documents)*. İstanbul (Bahçeşehir University Press), 2011. pp. x + 274 + 96 Photos + 5 Appendices – *Aslına Dönüş: Mısır Valisi Mehmed Ali Paşa'nin Kavala Kasabası ile Bağlantıları (Mimari Eserler, Kitabeler ve Belgeler)*. İstanbul (Bahçeşehir Üniversitesi Yayınları), 2011. pp. x + 274 + 96 Photos + 5 Appendices & Heath W. Lowry: *Historical Vestiges of Niyâzî Mısrî's Presence on the Island of Limnos / Niyâzî Mısrî'nin Limni Adası'nda Bulunan Tarihi İzleri*. İstanbul (Bahçeşehir University Press: Occasional Papers in History #3), 2011. pp. ix + 142 + 36 Plates.

The design and outlay of the work was undertaken by the author and Faruk Özbey of Uğur Yayımcılık. At an early stage it was assisted by Clive Crook and John Scott. I am deeply indebted to both, and to my old friend John Scott in particular, who put aside his own work to assist the project. In addition, Hande Alpay and Arman Güneysucu of Uğur Yayımcılık have been unstinting with their help and assistance in the preparation of this work.

At Bahçeşehir University my all too short sojourns have been made pleasant by the many kindnesses extended me by the entire community of scholars and staff. In particular Canan Ergin, Dean of the Faculty of Arts & Science, and, the University's General Secretary Ziya Alpay, have gone out of their way to assist me at every step of the process.

As always I owe unending thanks to Demet, my wife and companion of the past thirty-seven years, whose willingness to put her life on hold to meet my seemingly unending work schedule, has made not only this study possible, but all those which have preceded it (and hopefully all those to follow) as well.

The book has also benefited from careful readings by our daughter Ayşegül, son-in-law Doug Dreyer, and our eleven year old granddaughter, Alizé. The latter spotted one egregious typo. Thanks Alizé.

That said, this work, as all such studies, is entirely my responsibility. While gratefully acknowledging all those who have contributed to it, I just as willingly absolve them from any responsibility for the final product.

Heath W. Lowry
İstanbul, 2011

CHAPTER I

ISOLATED TURKEY

JANUARY - FEBRUARY 1921

MANY WARN ME TO STAY OUT OF NATIONALIST TURKEY: 'IMPOSSIBLE'

Impossible. That is the word I invariably heard in Constantinople [İstanbul] whenever I told anyone of my intention of going to Angora [Ankara][8] to see what was really taking place in the land of mystery, which Anatolia East of the Greek front had become. Impossible to get permission from the government of Sultan (Muhammad VI) [Mehmed VI] to enter the territory which the so-called 'Kemalist' government at Ankara controlled. Impossible, if I did succeed in landing at Samsoun [Samsun] as I planned, to leave the country when I wished. Impossible to travel through the mountains at that time because of the deep snow; unsafe to travel because of the numerous bandits and the 'terrible' Turks and most uncomfortable because of the insect life which flourished in Turkish taverns and because of the lack of fuel and food. So I was informed, with the additional warning that the 'Kemalists' had become very hostile to Americans.

This was in January, 1921. In March of the preceding year, when the Allies occupied İstanbul, the Turkish Nationalists under Mustapha Kemal Pasha [Mustafa Kemal *Paşa*] had rebelled and prepared to defend Turkey against the humiliating and unbearable peace terms which, it was even then evident, the Allies meant to impose upon it. They had severed railway and telegraphic communication between Anatolia and the Western world, and had set up a new government at Ankara. They had deported practically all of the nationals of the Entente Powers [Great Britain, France and Russia], and had closed their frontiers to Europeans. American missionaries and Near East Relief workers were allowed to remain, but of the few who came out of Anatolia from time to time, none had been in Ankara.

Asiatic Turkey, in short, was almost completely cut off not only from the Occident but also from İstanbul. The Sultan, who was practically a prisoner in the hands of the Allies in his own capital, had outlawed the Nationalists in an official proclamation. His court martial had condemned Mustafa Kemal Paşa, Halideh Edib Hanoum [Halide Edib *Hanım*] and other Nationalist leaders to be hanged. Turkish newspapers were suppressed for adding the title of 'Pasha' [Paşa][9] to Mustafa Kemal's name. While most of the Turks in İstanbul were Nationalists at heart, few of them, because of the censorship maintained by the Allies and the slowness of communication with Ankara, knew the real state of affairs in Anatolia. The Allied authorities in the city were in the dark as far as the strength and character of the so-called 'Kemalist government' were concerned. They had succeeded in having the Sublime Porte [office of the Grand Vezir or Prime Minister] send a mission with the ex-Grand Vezir, Izzet Pasha [İzzet Paşa],[10] as its chief, to Ankara in December [1920] in the hope that it would succeed in bringing the Nationalists to terms.

Nearly two months had passed, nothing had been heard from the mission, yet the Allies were still hoping that it would return with at least some first-hand information as to the Nationalists. İzzet Paşa afterwards told me that his mission had completely failed because neither he nor the Allies had understood the real situation in Asiatic Turkey. A recent attempt by the British to land an intelligence officer in the country had been repulsed

---

8 **Note**: Throughout this study, I have used Streit's spellings in the first instance when a place or proper name is given, followed by the present day Turkish spelling in brackets [ ]. Thereafter, I have used the present day spellings [HWL].

9 **Note**: A title given to both high-ranking civilian and military officers in the Ottoman Empire. Today it is used exclusively for generals and admirals in the Turkish military [HWL].

10 **Note**: Ahmed İzzet [Furgaç] Paşa (1864-1937): Ottoman statesman. Appointed Minister of War in 1913 by the Unionists; during the armistice he formed a government (which lasted only twenty-five days) and served as Grand Vezir (October 14 – November 8, 1918). While serving as Minister of the Interior in Tevfik Paşa's cabinet, he was sent to Anatolia to mediate with the Nationalists over issue of representation at the 3rd London Conference. He was forcibly taken to Ankara and released only upon resigning his ministerial post. Shortly thereafter, he agreed to serve once again in Tevfik Paşa's cabinet, this time as Minister of Foreign Affairs [HWL].

by the Turks all along the coast of the Black Sea, while a Frenchman who had tried to go from Samsun to Ankara to obtain a coal concession had been deported.

Although no authentic information concerning the new Turkish government could be obtained in İstanbul, it was plainly evident that it was growing stronger. It was not only successfully defying the Allies, but, the previous autumn, it had defeated the Armenian Republic and just recently it had checked a Greek offensive. A trip through Anatolia offered the traveler a unique opportunity of seeing the Turks under a purely Turkish government of their own making, free from foreign influence or restraint. The story of the 'Kemalist' government was the one story in the Near East which had not been told. No foreign correspondent had been to Ankara since the new government had become firmly established. Despite the warnings I received, I thought the trip might be made, and I was determined to at least try. America had never declared war on Turkey. We had simply severed diplomatic relations with the Sublime Porte. We were known to have no political ambitions in Turkey.

I felt that if I could once get in telegraphic communication with Ankara and bring before the Nationalists the advantages of allowing an American correspondent to visit their territory, I could gain their permission. I armed myself with a couple of letters of introduction [**Note**: and a *kartvizit* (business card in Ottoman Turkish identifying him as a correspondent with the Philadelphia ***Public Ledger***) [**Plate 2**] HWL] to Nationalist leaders which I obtained from influential Turks in İstanbul. These Turks told me that it would probably take a couple of weeks before I got an answer from Ankara, and so I obtained a visa for Georgia with the intention of stopping in Samsun only long enough to send my telegram and then proceeding to Batoum [Batum] and visiting the Caucasus while awaiting results.

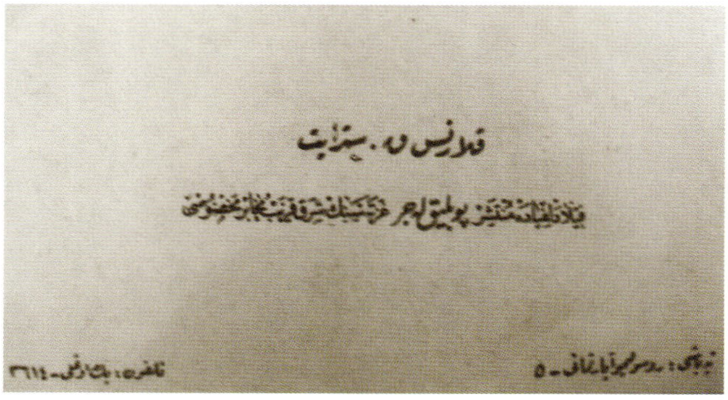

Plate 2: Business card identifying Streit as a correspondent with the Philadelphia ***Public Ledger***[11]

Finding a reliable interpreter, Mehmed Ali Mehmedoff

While I could talk directly with the educated Turks in French, I wanted to get to know the common people as well, and for that purpose an interpreter was essential. It was even more essential that he should be reliable and as unbiased as possible. Greeks and Armenians, who usually act as interpreters, were clearly out of the question, and so, of course were the few Turks who speak English. It is unfortunately true that most foreigners see the Turk through the eyes of Greek and Armenian interpreters who often are prejudiced against him. One cannot often get the Muslim point of view from a Christian, least of all from an Oriental Christian.

I decided that the best man for the job would be a Persian Muslim. I sought advice from Mr. Laurence Moore, with whom I had served in the Army Intelligence Service in France during the war, who was then Secretary of the American Chamber of Commerce in İstanbul and for years had been a member of the faculty of Robert College, the famous American institution on the Bosporus, if he knew any such man.

Through him, I found Mehmed Ali [**Plate 3**], who was not only a Persian but was also a graduate both of Robert College and of Michigan Agricultural College.[12] Mehmed Ali had spent seven years in the United States, held a certificate to teach in the Michigan high schools and had taken out his first citizenship papers in America. He had the American point of view, and his neutrality in the many questions regarding the Near East could be

[11] LC Catalogue #: DLC/PP 1994: 064.

Plate 3: Streit's Persian Interpreter Mehmed Ali [Mehmedoff][13]

relied upon. He was highly recommended by Mr. Moore who had known him a long time.

Mehmed Ali was a dealer in antique rugs. He had never before acted as interpreter but was willing to go with me because he wanted to visit Anatolia. For my purpose of obtaining the truth about the situation in Asiatic Turkey, a better man than Mehmed Ali, I believe, could not be found.

Transferring from one destroyer to another in a storm at Samsun

We left İstanbul on January 21st (my 25th birthday) on the American destroyer-dreadnought, 'Barker [DD.213],' and, after visiting the Bulgarian port of Varna and the Rumanian port of Constantza [Köstence], arrived on the 24th at Samsun. The sea was running so high that the 'Barker' could not send a boat ashore. The 'John D. Edwards,' the destroyer-dreadnought [DD.216], which was stationed in Samsun harbor to look after the interests of American relief workers and missionaries scattered through Turkey

Plate 4: The American Destroyer 'John D. Edwards' at Anchor in Samsun[14]

[**Plate** 4], attempted to send a boat to us. The sailors lowered it from the davits, and we could see it stand almost vertical as it would shoot up on the crest of a huge wave. Then it would plunge out of sight. Finally, they abandoned the attempts and hauled up the boat. It seemed that my hopes of telegraphing to Ankara were doomed to failure, as the 'Barker' intended to proceed that evening to Batum.

---

12 **Note**: It is unclear as to why Streit refers to Mehmed Ali as a 'Persian.' The name, as he gives it is clearly Turkish (with a Russian ending). It appears more likely that he was an Azeri Turk, but conceivably from the large Azeri element in Persia (Iran). Even today, Iranian Azeris in the North of the country often use the Russian: '*off*' ('son of') ending on family names [HWL].

13 LC Catalogue #: DLC/PP 1994: 064.247 [Red Album: Turkey, 1920-1921 by C. K. Streit].

14 LC Catalogue #: DLC/PP 1994: 064.247 [Red Album: Turkey, 1920-1921 by C. K. Streit].

The sea calmed slightly a little later, however, and the captain told me that if I wanted to take a chance on getting wet I could go over to the 'Edwards' on the motor dory he was sending to that ship with the mail. The sailors who were to make the trip had put on life preservers and one was tied about me. We got into the dory, and it was lowered into the sea. For a landsman, the short trip was exciting enough, especially the jump for the ladder of the 'Edwards' when we came alongside of it.

I intended only to ask the 'Edwards' to send my telegram to Mustafa Kemal Paşa for me, and to return to the 'Barker,' receiving the answer of the Turks, when it came, by wireless at Batum. But Captain Alexander Sharp of the 'Edwards' [**Plate 5**] pleasantly surprised me by saying that he thought the Turks would welcome an American correspondent and would send me the permit immediately. Consequently, I had Mehmed Ali join me with our baggage.

Plate 5: Captain Alexander Sharp & Officers of the 'John D. Edwards[15]

[15] LC Catalogue #: DLC/PP 1994: 064.247 [Red Album: Turkey, 1920-1921 by C. K. Streit].

As a harbor, Samsun has its drawbacks. Ships must anchor in the open roadstead. Just how open it is may be seen from the fact that I had to remain on the 'Edwards' three days before the sea calmed sufficiently to permit a boat to land. Of the twelve kinds of winds listed in the naval log, Lieutenant Royal, the executive officer, selected 'strong breeze' [22-27 knots] as the one correctly describing the weather. The narrow destroyer during this time was rolling only twenty-six degrees on her anchor chains and in the wardroom the chairs and dishes had to be fastened down. The shore was obscured much of the time by a fine snow which the wind was driving before it. If this were merely a nautical 'breeze,' I had no desire to see it develop into the next gradation in the list, a 'fresh gale.'

On the third day, Mehmed Ali and I went ashore with Captain Sharp, an officer of the type which makes one proud of the men in the American navy, a personification of the 'square deal' and a tactful diplomat. For these qualities especially, I found that he was highly respected by the Turks in Samsun. He was in a delicate position as we had no official relations with Turkey, but he filled the place admirably.

Captain Sharp had told me that nothing in English was allowed to enter or leave Anatolia, the only languages permitted for correspondence being Turkish and French. This was a war measure taken by the Nationalists and aimed, not at the Americans but at the British, and intended to make it easier to keep hostile propaganda out of their territory. If Americans spoke a language of their own, it undoubtedly would have been exempted from the general prohibition, for the Turks, despite all the ill that has been said of them in America, have the friendliest feeling toward us. A curious instance of this occurred during the World War. English at that time also was prohibited, but among the languages permitted 'American' was included.

LANDING AT SAMSUN; GET PERMISSION TO GO TO ANKARA; MEET DR. POMEROY

As the rule was to search anyone who landed, except Captain Sharp, I carefully divested myself of every scrap of paper containing a word of English. Only a few weeks before Colonel Coombs,[16] head of the Near East Relief, had landed in Samsun with the intention of going to Ankara. In the relief supplies which he brought with him, the Turks discovered Greek propaganda for the Pontus Republic which had doubtless been placed there by some Greek employees of the commission in İstanbul. Colonel Coombs was unaware of the presence of this literature, but it was sufficient to make the Turks suspicious of Americans, especially since many of the relief workers and missionaries were openly partial to the Greeks and Armenians and treated the Turks, under whose government they were working, as if they were dogs. The Turks had finally accepted Colonel Coombs' word that he was not trying to aid the Greeks along the Black Sea to rebel, but they had not allowed him to proceed to the interior. It was with some trepidation that I set foot on the soil of Asiatic Turkey, for after this incident and from all that I had heard, I was far more likely to be forced to remain in Samsun indefinitely then to be permitted to leave it when I wished.

But I had no more than arrived in Samsun than the gloomy warnings I had received in İstanbul began to prove to be groundless. The Turkish harbor police when Captain Sharp explained to them why I had come, allowed me to pass on my word, without being searched, although they went through the pockets of Mehmed Ali. Captain Sharp then introduced me to İbrahim Edhem Bey, the mutasarrif [*mutasarrıf*] or civil governor of the sancak or district.[17] When I told him of my desire to go to Ankara as an American journalist, far from being opposed to the project, he was so favorably inclined that

[16] **Note**: Colonel J. P. Coombs, Director of the American Commission for Relief in the Near East, at Samsun, was (according to a report which appeared November 9, 1920 in the ***New York Times***), later arrested and held by the Nationalists in Samsun [HWL].

[17] **Note**: İbrahim Edhem Bey had been Governor (*mutasarrıf*) of Samsun when Mustafa Kemal Paşa landed there on May 19, 1919, on the first leg of what was to become the founding of the Turkish Nationalist movement. He is not to be confused with the Avcı İbrahim [Akıncı] Bey, who served as Governor of Samsun in 1930-1931 [HWL].

he immediately sent a telegram to the Commissar for the Interior[18] recommending that permission be granted.[19] He also telephoned to the harbor police to allow me perfect freedom in going to and from the destroyer. I was thus the only man aside from Captain Sharp who had the privilege of not being subjected to search. The seven Americans in Samsun had to go to the destroyer to read and answer their mail and were searched both going to and returning from the ship.[20]

Instead of having to wait a couple of weeks for a reply as I had feared would be the case, special permission for my interpreter and me to go to Ankara came in two days. The quickness with which the permit arrived confirmed the impression I had already, and which was to grow stronger - that the Turkish Nationalists were confident that they would get a square deal from Americans, and that they wanted to get their case before the American public.

Samsun is a city with a population of about 25,000 and is the center of the best tobacco district in Asia Minor. It is from this port that much of the leaf for our Turkish cigarettes comes. The seven Americans in the city consisted of three tobacco buyers, three Near East Relief workers and Dr. G. T. Pomeroy. The prohibition of English had made it impossible for the tobacco men to carry on their business and for several weeks, they and Dr. Pomeroy had been waiting for permission from Ankara to leave for İstanbul. The permission came just before I left Samsun. At the same time the Turks raised the ban on English for the Americans in the city to allow them to carry on business correspondence in that language.

Despite the annoyance from which they had suffered, I found the sympathies of the Americans at Samsun were with the Turkish Nationalists. The present government, the tobacco men told me, was superior to the old regime. Dr. Pomeroy, who was on the friendliest terms with everyone -for a year he had been caring for the sick of all races and religions in the district- was also a Turkophile, told me:

> If I had come here from another planet and knew nothing of Christianity and Islam except what I've had ample opportunity to observe in this region, I could choose the Muslim religion. For one thing, though it may seem strange to you, the Muslim women are much better treated by their husbands than are the Greeks and Armenians. They have more rights and are more respected by their husbands.

[18] **Note**: While the use of the term 'Commissar' in place of 'Minister,' sounds strange today, it was the term which was still in use in 1921. Streit, provides the following explanation: "*Some of the Turks, in their anxiety to remove any trace of Bolshevism from the Nationalist Government, even object to the members of the Cabinet being called 'People's Commissar.' They prefer that the Turkish word be translated: 'People's Mandataire' or 'Steward' or 'Minister. But because the government, in its diplomatic correspondence, which is written in French, still uses the term 'Commissaire du Peuple' I have followed this usage.*" The Turkish term used in Ankara at the time of Streit's visit was: *Halk Komiseri*. That this was the case is confirmed by Halide Edib: *The Turkish Ordeal*. New York (The Century Co.), 1928. pp. 144-, where in discussing the Nationalist government in 1920-1921, she consistently refers to its Ministers as Commissars, and their ministries as: Commissary for Foreign Affairs, Commissary for the Interior, etc. [HWL].

[19] **Note**: LC: Streit Papers II: 75 – Folder 2 contains the text of the telegram İbrahim Edhem Bey forwarded on Streit's behalf to Ankara, which reads: "*His Excellency Mustapha Kemal Pasha, Angora: As correspondent of Philadelphia* ***Public Ledger*** *and its syndicate of forty American newspapers respectfully ask your permission to visit Angora for not more than one month.* ***Ledger*** *is one most influential organs of Republican party which will control American foreign policy for next four years. It believes American public may have been misinformed by its present sources of information in Near East which seem prejudiced against Turks. Interested only in getting truth and being fair to all sides* ***Ledger*** *wishes me to get in direct contact with Turkish leaders at Angora and offer them opportunity to put their case before American public. As credentials have confidential sealed letter from Grand Vizariat to Minister Foreign Affairs Angora and note from Hamid Bey member executive Board Imperial Ottoman Bank.* ***Ledger*** *instructs me not to enter your territory however unless assured of freedom to leave within one month. I ask same safe conduct for my interpreter Mehmed Ali, Persian graduate Roberts College. Please address reply to me care American destroyer at Samsoun. Respectfully submitted. Clarence K. Streit*" [HWL].

FIRST ENTRY INTO A HAREM; THE WANING SECLUSION OF WOMEN

It was in company with Dr. Pomeroy while he was making his professional visits that I first entered that place of mystery known as a Turkish harem. The harem, as we think of it, is practically non-existent in Turkey today. While polygamy is legally permitted, in practice it is confined to some of the Paşas in İstanbul and to the villages where, because of the many wars, there are more women than men. The Turkish home is divided into two parts, the *selâmlik*, where the men live and where visitors are received, and the *harem* which is given over to all the women in the family. The word harem simply means 'inside'[21] and to Turks does not necessarily suggest, as it does to the Westerner, dancing girls, slaves and eunuchs. The seclusion of women is an old custom in the Orient and was not introduced by Muhammed, who, as a matter of fact, did much to better the status of women. Before his time, unrestricted polygamy was the rule in the Orient. The Prophet limited the number of wives a man might have to four and specified that he must treat each one of them equally. The Turks are said to be the least polygamous of the Muslims. The heavy expense of maintaining more than one wife, the fact that in normal times there are no more women than men, the discord and jealousies which polygamy, whether permitted or not, inevitably causes, and sentiments of romantic love have combined to make monogamy the rule in Turkey.

Even the seclusion of women carries with it some right. The principle of the harem is extended even to the street cars in İstanbul; for instance, a curtain sets aside a certain part of each car for the use of women only. As for the veils and the lattice work in front of the windows of the harem, it seems to me that they work perhaps as great a hardship upon the men as upon the women. The women, at least, can see the men, but a man can only see his wife, his daughters, his sisters and his mother. He cannot even see his wife before he marries her although she can see him. Imagine the disappointment of many a Turkish bridegroom when he lifts the veil of his bride! And if he is lucky enough to have drawn a pretty wife in this veritable lottery, the poor Turk has not the pleasure of showing other men how fortunate he is, as Western husbands have. Yet, strangely enough, the belief persists in the West that the social customs in Islam are entirely favorable to the men.

The seclusion of women, however, is dying out in Turkey. Veils now rarely are to be seen in İstanbul, nor in the other large cities of the country, though in the provinces they are yet the custom. The homes of the advanced Turks are much like ours. Several times I had the pleasure of being received in them by the women of the family who were clad in European dress. But, in the conservative Turkish families the separation of the home into the masculine and the feminine parts still exists, and it is very seldom that a male stranger is allowed to enter the harem.

Dr. Pomeroy's professional duties, however, enabled him to go into Turkish harems as freely as into Christian homes. He was trusted and adored by people of all races and religions in the district. The family which we visited was of the conservative Turkish middle class. Dr. Pomeroy had been treating the mother for some time. Mehmed Ali and I accompanied him to her bedside. None of the male members of the family was present.

The two sisters of the sick woman, refugees from the zone occupied by the Greeks, were living with her. She had two daughters, one Saadet, a sweet little girl of twelve, whom I photographed inside the harem with her loom [**Plate 6**], the other a shy, pretty girl of nineteen, with whom I talked in French. She was engaged to her cousin, Munir Kiamil [Münir Kâmil], a lieutenant in the Nationalist army. They were all quiet, gentle mannered women, whom one could not help but like.

---

[20] **Note**: In the original 1921 text of his manuscript, Streit added and then crossed out the following sentence: "*The Press, indeed, is literally one of the Great Powers, and its representatives often obtain privileges which diplomats cannot gain*" [HWL].

[21] **Note**: It literally means 'women's apartments' [HWL].

Plate 6: Saadet at Her Loom[22]

"*Do you find us Turks as barbarous as they say we are?*" the mother plaintively asked me. When I told her that such was not the case, she said "*I hope that you will tell your readers then that we are not such inhuman monsters as some people say we are.*"

While I was drinking the cup of delicious Turkish coffee they offered me in the sickroom -no visit of any character in Turkey, I was to find, was complete without a cup of coffee- Münir Kâmil was announced. His fiancée immediately left us and remained in another room during his visit, for custom decreed that he was not to see her until they were married. And separation is even more strictly enforced after betrothal than before it. He seemed slightly surprised to find us in the sickroom but was cordial enough. He was typical of many of the Turkish officers I was to meet from then on: handsome, intelligent, modest, courteous, and gentlemanly. I photographed Saadet and him in the drawing room, which was furnished in European style and contained a piano, and also outside the house [**Plate** 7]. Mehmed Ali was amazed at my boldness in asking permission to take these photographs in the house. He insisted that it "*wasn't done.*" But the Turks seemed glad to have the pictures taken and asked me to send them copies.

Plate 7: Münir Kâmil & Saadet[23]

[22] LC Catalogue #: DLC/PP 1994: 064 [Red Album: Turkey, 1920-1921 by C. K. Streit]

[23] LC Catalogue #: DLC/PP 1994: 064 [Red Album: Turkey, 1920-1921 by C. K. Streit].

I took pictures everywhere in Turkey from then on and had no trouble at any time. In fact, nearly all my subjects were very willing, and those who weren't were too polite to object. I scandalized Mehmed Ali another time by asking for and getting permission to take the picture of the interior of a sacred Muslim tomb. At Ankara, one day, while I was interviewing Fevzi Paşa,[24] Commissar for the National Defense and President of the Council of Commissars, the members of the cabinet assembled in the room for their daily meeting. I at once asked to be allowed to take their picture. Mehmed Ali told me later that he nearly sank through the floor when he heard my request. He laughed and added, "*They were so surprised that they could not say 'No.' The people here, you know, aren't accustomed to Western newspaper methods. You've been educating them and making the road easier for any journalists who follow you.*"

Visiting a Greek family; see a Bolshevik diplomat; I dine in a babel of languages

After leaving the Turkish home, I went with the doctor to visit a Greek family which occupied one of the best houses in Samsun. Only the mother and her four daughters were at home. They received Dr. Pomeroy as affectionately as had the Turks. Samsun has a large Greek population. It is in the territory which formerly constituted the Greek Kingdom of the Pontus. It was at Sinope [Sinop], not far from Samsun, that Diogenes is said to have begun his famous search for an honest man. After the Armistice, there developed in this region a strong propaganda for the establishment of a Greek Pontus Republic. The Allies had aided this separatist movement, and British troops had occupied the town. The Pontus Greeks thought that they were already masters and began to treat the Turks in a lordly fashion. The large Greek church, which almost dominates the town, was even painted blue and white, the national Hellenic colors.

Then the Turkish Nationalists had forced the few British troops to evacuate the district and had regained control of it. The Americans who had been in the city all the while were surprised at the lenience with which the Turks had treated these Greeks. Most of the Pontus agitation, Dr. Pomeroy said, was due to the efforts of the Greek priests. Yet the priest continued to occupy one of the best houses in Samsun, his church remained open and still flaunted its provocative colors in the eyes of the Turks. Dr. Pomeroy thought that if it were not for the activities of the Greek priests, the Greeks and Turks would get along together without trouble.

Many of the Greeks, to escape military service with the Turks, had fled to the mountains. They had received arms from the British. They became brigands and preyed upon the Turkish villages and upon the caravan route which was one of the military lines of communication. The Greek peasants, who live in villages separate from the Turks, protected them. The Turks, while they were fighting the Greeks in the West, could not afford to leave such a dangerous situation in their rear. The Greeks naturally would not betray their countrymen. The result was that the Turkish gendarmerie burned to the ground several of the villages suspected of harboring brigands before they succeeded in establishing order and security in the district.

We went to a Greek hotel that afternoon for tea where Dr. Pomeroy introduced me to Valdemar Ingall, whose card, in French, described him as 'Assistant to the Chief of the Bureau of Information of the R.S.F.S.R. in Turkey.' The imposing array of letters, of course, meant the 'Federated Socialist Republic of the Soviets of Russia.' Ingall, who spoke both English and French, was a laughing, agreeable young man and an enthusiastic communist. He immediately ordered tea for three, insisting that since Russia was closer than America, he should be the host. He appeared to be well-satisfied with the progress of the Bolsheviks in Turkey, although he admitted that it would take a long time to introduce communism in the

[24] **Note**: Mustafa Fevzi [Çakmak] Paşa (1876-1950). Turkish soldier, who later became Field Marshall and Prime Minister. Close associate and friend of Mustafa Kemal Paşa [HWL].

country. He left the next day for Russia on one of the small Bolshevik boats then in the harbor.

That night Mehmed Ali and I dined with Mr. and Mr. Robert McDowell, who were in charge of the Near East Relief work in the city. The other guests were a young Turkish doctor and his wife. The doctor was an idealist, very intelligent and wide awake. Like most of the educated Turks, he was very embittered against England, whom he held responsible for the Greek War, and he keenly resented the fact that foreigners considered the Turks to be barbarians.

I cannot but sympathize with this bitter feeling of resentment on the part of the Turks. One had only to talk with the average Westerner to realize what social outcasts the Turks are. They are considered to be beyond the pale, someone quite apart from the rest of humanity. Of course, their history is stained with crimes, but so is that of every other nation with whose history I am acquainted. What arouses my indignation especially is that all the good qualities in the Turks are entirely overlooked in the West, and their effort to better conditions in their country are not only ignored by the more advanced nations, but are criticized.

This wholesale indictment of a nation is as stupid as it as unjust. It is calculated to arouse the worst side of anyone's nature. It is a commonplace in the army that the lieutenant who is unjustly treated by his superior officer is inclined to vent his injured feelings upon someone subordinate to him, 'to pass the buck.' A mother angered by an altercation with her husband, often gives her child a slap if the son or daughter happens to give her the slightest pretext at the moment. Similarly, the Turks would only be human if they let loose their pent up bitterness, at the injustice they receive, upon the minorities within their power.

The doctor's wife was a pretty girl of good breeding, as most Turks seem to be by nature. She was almost Parisian in her appearance, wearing a black silk dress with a small fur around her neck and silk stockings and French heels. She wore no veil, the only vestige of the usual Turkish costume being the black silk scarf which was bound tightly over her hair. She could speak only a little French, although her husband was quite fluent in this language. At one time the conversations were going on in English, French, German, Turkish and Persian.

Another day when I had tea with the McDowells, the guests included Ahmed Ruchdi Bey [Ahmed Rüşdi Bey], the Turkish director of the *Régie* [government tobacco monopoly] tobacco plant in the city; Th. Constantinidi, a Greek, who was the manager of the plant; and a Turk, the chief of the gendarmes in the district, whose son had been educated in America. The father, however, spoke only Turkish although the other two men spoke French. The two Turks and the Greek were evidently on the friendliest terms - one would never have guessed that a few hundred miles to the West, war was going on between the two peoples, and that the Greeks in Samsun had only recently revolted and attempted to set up a separate government.

Before I left Samsun I visited the *Régie* [tobacco] plant where I found Greek, Armenian and Turkish women and children working side by side [**Plates 8 & 9**]. It is only since the war that the Turkish women have begun to work outside their homes - another instance of how the seclusion of women is disappearing.

Mr. McDowell was one of the Near East workers who dispensed relief without asking whether the needy person was a Christian or a Muslim. He was, indeed, strongly pro-Turkish in his sympathies and declared that the United States should recognize the new government at Ankara.

Plate 8: Greek, Armenian & Turkish Women Tobacco Workers[25]

Plate 9: Streit (center) Visiting the *Régie* Tobacco Plant in Samsun[26]

[25] LC Catalogue #: DLC/PP 1994: 064 [Red Album: Turkey, 1920-1921 by C. K. Streit].
[26] LC Catalogue #: DLC/PP 1994: 064 [Red Album: Turkey, 1920-1921 by C. K. Streit].

CHAPTER II

WINTER TRAVEL IN ANATOLIA

FIRST DAY WITH RUSSIAN CHAUFFEUR; BLIZZARD; FIRST NIGHT WITH SNOWBOUND CAMEL CARAVAN

There is no railroad leading from Samsun into the interior, although the Turks are planning to build one to Sivas. The usual means of travel is a light, covered, spring wagon called the 'yaili' [*yaylı*]. One must count on two weeks in a yaylı, to go from Samsun to Ankara. Fortunately, the Near East Relief Commission allowed me to use one of their light Reo trucks [**Plate 10**] to go as far as Tchorum [Çorum]. Beyond that city the roads were said to be impassable for an automobile.

I had for a chauffeur a Russian refugee, Georges Krennikoff, employed by the Near East Commission. He took with him another Russian, Andros, as assistant. Georges was a university student, a most intelligent fellow and a driver used to roughing it on the roads of Anatolia. As a special courtesy, the Turkish officials sent a 'gendarme' [Tr.: *jandarma*][27] Ihsan [İhsan], with me to facilitate my travels.

The weather at Samsun was deceptively warm, but as the road climbed directly into the snow clad mountains I soon began to realize that this was to be no pleasure excursion. The car had neither windshield nor top and a bitterly cold wind was blowing directly in our faces. With four blankets wrapped around me I still was chilled. The farther we went the worse conditions became. We had a chain on but one rear wheel, and the result was that we were continually getting stuck in the deep snow, which had drifted over the road [**Plate 11**].

We had expected to reach Mersivan [Merzifon], seventy-five miles distant, that night. At 4:00 p.m. we had gone but a third the distance, and we were stuck in the snow in a lonely stretch of mountains without a house or village in sight. For two hours we shoveled snow and pushed the car. The sun went down, and it seemed that we would have to spend a night in the open. None too pleasant a prospect, for there were no trees, or fuel with which to make a fire. But finally when we had about exhausted our ingenuity and strength we got the car out of the drifts.

Plate 10: Krenikoff, Mehmed Ali & Streit (left to right) Preparing to Depart Samsun[28]

Plate 11: The Near East Relief 'Reo' Truck Enroute to Merzifon[29]

27 **Note**: *Jandarmas* are soldiers deployed as police in rural areas [HWL].
28 LC Catalogue #: DLC/PP 1994: 064 [Red Album: Turkey, 1920-1921 by C. K. Streit].
29 LC Catalogue #: DLC/PP 1994: 064.74.

Plate 12: Camels in Front of the Snow Covered Doruk Han[30]

Plate 13: Camel Drivers at the Doruk Han[32]

It was dark then, and I discovered to my consternation that we had no lights. Andros, however, produced a coal oil lantern. He lay down on one of the front mudguards and held this flickering light in front of the car. He had no gloves and would not take the woolen sock I offered him. How he endured the intense cold I cannot imagine. I had a pocket electric lamp and used it to illuminate the other side of the road until my hand, covered only by a wet kid glove, became unbearably cold and I had to take shifts with Mehmed Ali. Thus, we slowly proceeded through the night. The speedometer had the effrontery to register only two miles per hour. And then - Allah be praised! We came upon a lonely tavern, Torook Han [Doruk *Han*][31] [**Plate 12**].

The proprietor assured us that all his rooms and beds were taken, and that he had nothing to give us to eat except bread and tea. "*This is in the mountains*," he apologized. A caravan had preceded us to the tavern, and the road was filled with camels squatting in the snow. The ground floor of the han was divided into two parts; the larger of which was used as a stable, and it too was occupied by camels. In the smaller part there was a tiny stove, and some boards were laid on the ground. Here the camel drivers were gathered to spend the night and made room for us. Fortunately we had brought some food with us, and as we had our blankets, we did not suffer.

The camel drivers fell to work late at night kneading dough with which to make their next day's bread. Occasionally, a camel in the next room would stick his head through the half doors and with curious eyes watch his masters [**Plate 13**].

The next day it was even colder - so cold in fact that Georges, though his hands were protected by heavy gloves, had to stop again and again to keep them from getting numb. Our troubles with the snow drifts continued, but finally by reversing the car we backed our way through to Merzifon.

Note: From Doruk Han, Streit and his party proceeded to Merzifon via the town of Havza, which (while he does not describe it in his account) his photographs contain a picture labeled simply: 'Khavsa' [**Plate 14**], i.e., Havza [HWL].

[30] LC Catalogue #: DLC/PP 1994: 064.78.

[31] **Note**: Hans are inns for travelers. This is the one site visited by Streit in Anatolia which is not clearly identifiable today. It may possibly be the present-day Doruk Han; or, conceivably, that of Çakallı Han, both of which are in the general area described by Streit [HWL].

[32] LC Catalogue #: DLC/PP 1994: 064 [Red Album: Turkey, 1920-1921 by C. K. Streit].

Plate 14: Main Street in Havza[33]

FIRST CONTACT WITH U.S. MISSIONARIES; FROM TURKISH CHAOS TO ORDER; FROM RUSSIAN IMPROVIDENCE TO INGENUITY

There we stopped at Anatolia College, an American missionary institution founded some forty years ago [**Plate 15**]. I found on the campus a colony of twenty-five American missionaries and Near East Relief workers, both men and women, who, because of the Turkish regulation prohibiting the use of English in correspondence, had received no letters from their homes and very little news from the outside world in the past five months.[34]

Plate 15: Merzifon American College[35]

---

[33] LC Catalogue #: DLC/PP 1994: 064.80.

[34] This facilitated censorship because at that time more Turks knew French than any other foreign language [CKS].

[35] LC Catalogue #: DLC/PP 1994: 064 [Red Album: Turkey, 1920-1921, C.K.Streit]. **Note**: LC Catalogue #: DLC/PP 1994: 064 [Red Album: Turkey, 1920-1921 by C. K. Streit]. This is a photograph of the 'Alumni Library Museum' (built: 1911) on the campus of Anatolia College in Merzifon. Compare with: George E. White: *Adventuring with Anatolia College*. Grinnell, Iowa (Herald-Register Publishing Company), 1940. p. 161 [HWL].

They besieged me with questions as to what was going on in the world and greedily devoured the contents of a copy of the ***Public Ledger***, three months old, I had with me. Because our motor was not working well, I spent the next day at Merzifon while Georges repaired it.

The college has an excellent hospital, equipped in a most modern way, and is doing a great deal of good in the community. Some of the students are Turks, most are Greeks and Armenians. Though the college authorities try to be impartial, I should say that their sympathies are with the Christians. They did not seem to realize fully that they were living under a Turkish government which was not recognized by the United States and which was at war with Greece, and that the Greeks in that region had carried on openly, and were still carrying on secretly a propaganda campaign against the Turks for the establishment of a Pontus Republic. A month later the Ankara government, after the assassination of the Turkish professor in the college, decided to close the institution, and expel all its American personnel except the hospital staff, while the war with Greece lasted.

We obtained from the college a chain for the other rear wheel of the car and from then on had no more difficulty with the snow. From Samsun to Çorum we followed the main highway, and all along this route we encountered an almost continual stream of camel, packhorse and donkey caravans [**Plate 16**].

The Anatolian camels, it seems, work better in the snow than in the heat of summer with which we are accustomed to associate them. They usually go in groups of ten, single file, often with a donkey leading each string of camels [**Plate 17**]. Several times we passed yaylıs flying the Turkish flag and escorted by two mounted gendarmes. These yaylıs were in the postal service. I was surprised at the number of people who were travelling on foot through the snow. Time and again we passed columns of conscripts plodding along the road and led by a couple of officers.

In view of the heavy traffic along this road [**Plate 18**] which, it had been reported, was infested with Greek brigands, I was struck by the fact that we met only a few armed patrols, and they nearly always consisted of four of five gendarmes on foot. While at Doruk Han I asked one of the camel drivers if travel were safe: "*A couple of months ago you could not travel over this road,*" he said, "*but now, thanks to our father Mustafa Kemal Paşa, there is no longer any danger from the brigands. May Allah give him a long life!*"

Certainly, everywhere I went in Anatolia, I found perfect order being maintained without any unusual display of

Plate 16: Camel, Packhorse & Donkey Caravans Enroute to Çorum[36]

Plate 17: Camels on the Road[37]

[36] LC Catalogue #: DLC/PP 1994: 064 [Red Album: Turkey, 1920-1921 by C. K. Streit].
[37] LC Catalogue #: DLC/PP 1994: 064 [Red Album: Turkey, 1920-1921 by C. K. Streit].

And, in some of the villages, it is true, little attention is paid to the custom of wearing the veil.

Once İhsan is satisfied, the next thing is to send the local religious teacher or hodja [*hoca*] (he is hardly a priest in our sense of the word, for there is no real priesthood in Islam) and two witnesses, one for the boy and one for the girl, to Fatima's home. There they find her alone in a room behind the door, which is slightly open.

The hoca asks, "*Do you wish to marry İhsan, the son of İsmail?*" He receives no answer. A girl must not be too quick to respond to so important a question. He repeats the same question. Still no answer. Once more he asks - and now Fatima must give her decision. And it is for her alone to decide whether the answer will be yes or no. Her parents cannot force her to marry against her will, although, of course, as in any other country, they can bring pressure to bear on her. But it seems that it is no rare event for a Turkish girl to upset the plans made for her future by rejecting the offer made to her through the door.

But Fatima has found İhsan attractive, and her answer is a low affirmative. The hoca, however, is not yet satisfied. "*Is this decision made of your own free will?*" he inquires. As Fatima assures him that it is, we are now ready for the betrothal. İhsan's mother calls again, this time accompanied by twenty or twenty-five of the village women. She puts a gold ring on Fatima's third finger. It does not matter upon which hand the ring is worn. Rosewater is served and there is music, feasting, dancing and perhaps a bonfire. The festivities may last for several days for the betrothal is the chief ceremony. İhsan and Fatima are now kept even more strictly apart than before their engagement.

The wedding takes place a year later. Fatima is then taken on horseback or in a yaylı, accompanied by the village fife and drum corps and a flag, to her new home and they are now man and wife. Feasting and dancing by the men accompany the wedding ceremony and the bridegroom, at least in some places, is required to give presents to his guests. It is the custom in other places for the friends of the bridegroom to beat him on the back when he enters the harem to see his bride for the first time. The marriage ceremonies, I found from talking with other Turks, differ slightly in the various villages. All marriages do not take place at so youthful an age, and often a man has recourse to a woman marriage-broker in order to obtain a wife.

AT ÇORUM'S ONLY NIGHT SPOT WE HEAR TURKISH TROUBADOURS SING MUSLIM VERSION OF THE SACRIFICE OF ISAAC; I INTERVIEW AN EIGHTEEN YEAR OLD TURK

After dinner in a Turkish restaurant for the ridiculous price of fifteen cents, Mehmed Ali and I set out to see if there was any night life in Çorum. There were lights in only one building but from it came attractive sounds of Oriental music. We entered, and, in crossing the door still, left centuries behind us. For within was the old, old Orient. It was a coffee house, crowded with Turks (all men) sitting cross-legged on the raised platform, which ran around the room, or on little stools in the center, smoking water pipes [Tr.: *nargiles*] and cigarettes and drinking coffee or tea. At one end of the room sat a swarthy Turk playing a sort of mandolin, while a boy with a tambour [*tanbur* or *tambur*] (lute) accompanied him. He was a professional storyteller [Tr.: *meddah*], one of the troubadours or ballad-singers of such towns in the East, which knew neither movies nor books.

When we entered he was just beginning with an invocation in praise of [the Prophet] Muhammed. Then he launched into his story, the old Biblical tale of the sacrifice of Isaac. But it was the Muslim version which he gave, the chief difference being that Ishmael instead of Isaac plays the role of victim (The ***Qur'an*** contains much of the substance of the Old and New Testaments and recognizes Abraham and Christ as Prophets).

It was a tale of the Islamic East told in an Eastern fashion, in the way it has been handed down through the centuries. I could catch only the words 'Ibrahim' and 'Ishmael' from time to time, and had to depend on Mehmed Ali to translate the story for me during the interludes - yet, despite this, never before did the tale make so vivid an impression on me.

The troubadour sat back with half-closed eyes, and beginning each verse with a long drawn-out "*Ah - ayeeee!*," he would sing with considerable expression, then stop and play a few appropriate chords on his mandolin. As he approached the tragedy his voice alone was enough to make tremors run along one's spinal column. His audience with close interest listened to him in dead silence. When he got to the part: "*And Ibrahim went into the inner room and got a knife and all alone wept bitter tears* (twang went the mandolin) *and then, leading his beloved Ishmael by the hand set out for the mountain,*" I saw old men near me with tears in their eyes. Others were visibly affected, as well.

The story ended, another man sang some love lyrics in a high, strained falsetto, while holding his fingers in his ears. Then the proprietor, who had refused to let us pay for our coffee, saying that we were his guests, for our special benefit, had the three of the musicians sing and play a lively air. This, he said, was Europeanized Oriental music from 'Stamboul,' the Turkish quarter of İstanbul. They were trying to improve their music. It was much more Oriental than European, however. On the other hand, the music written by Turkish composers, which later in Ankara and Eskişehir I heard the military bands of the Nationalist Army playing, and the tunes of the patriotic songs I heard the troops marching to, and the songs I listened to children singing in the schools, all were distinctly European.

When I returned to the Hotel Anatolia, Mehmed, the eighteen year old son of the Turkish proprietor was making a fire in my room. I used the opportunity to talk with him. Our conversation will throw some interesting sidelights on the Turkish character.

"*Have you a theater here?*" I asked.

"*No, we would never allow such a thing. They do more harm than good.*" "*Why*", and there was a twinkle in his eye, "*if there was a theater here, I'd be there, instead of here making your fire, and you'd be freezing! Once there was a circus here for a week and nobody did any work.*"

"*Well, have you a movie?*"

"*No. There was one here for a while last year. Everybody went to it for a week, but we saw it was showing the same old lies over and over again each night, and so it was run out of town.*"

It was easy to see that their movie house had had, unfortunately, only a very limited number of films which it had been forced to repeat. Since the scenes it showed were so utterly different from anything the Turks, who had never been out of their country had ever seen, it was not surprising that they were skeptical.

"*What do you do for amusement, then*?" I asked.

At this, Mehmed launched into a description of the beauties of Çorum in the summer. He was very proud of his town and especially of its orchards and water. I jokingly suggested that I would have to come and settle down at Çorum.

"*If it is so written in your destiny, you will,*" Mehmed replied gravely. "*You can find bread anywhere, but nowhere else can you find such water as we have at Çorum. It is water which pulls a man to a place.*"

Mehmed went on to tell me in glowing terms of the good times they had in their orchards in the summer. Sometimes the young men would secretly bring their sweethearts to the orchards, and the girls would dance. If one man looked too much at the girl of another, there was likely to be trouble.

"*And in the winter don't you have such parties?*" I inquired.

"*Perhaps in some of the houses of the richer men. But there would be no pleasure in them then. Summer is the only time for such things - out in the orchards, where the fruit is hanging from the trees, the brook is babbling, the bees humming, and birds twittering - when the surroundings are poetical.*"

I confess I was astonished to hear a hotel boy - and a Turk - talking in poetical terms.[41] But my acquaintance with the real Turks was only beginning.

By this time the fire in the small stove was puffing merrily. The sound attracted Mehmed. "*You see*," he laughed, "*we have an auto, too*!" I shall not soon forget his roguish smile, and the picture he made as he stood there with his fez cocked at an angle on his head.

FROM MOTOR TRANSPORT TO COVERED WAGON PULLED BY TURKISH 'REINDEER'

The caravan route to Ankara does not pass by Yozgat - it takes the short cut through Sungurlu - and so we met very little traffic the next day. We stopped for lunch at Aladja [Alaca], a town of 5,000 population, almost purely Turkish. It was market day and the town was full of people [**Plate 20**]. As soon as they heard the automobile they came running to see what it was, and when we stopped, the main street of the town for a hundred feet on both sides of the car was jammed with curious Turks [**Plate 21**]. Clad, as most of the peasants were, in moccasins, baggy trousers and brightly colored calico shirts, they made a picturesque group.

A merchant from whom I bought some fox skins -furs are abundant in Anatolia and absurdly cheap - explained that this was the first automobile to come to Alaca in several years. The people here - and everywhere I went in Turkey, for that matter, were hospitable and the kaimakam [*kaymakam*] or governor of the sub-district, as usual, offered me coffee and cigarettes.

Plate 20: Market Day in Alaca[42]

[41] At fifteen at the 'Florence Hotel' in Missoula, Montana, I got my first job. I worked from 7 p.m. to 7 a.m. as the only night bellhop and elevator boy. My wages were $ 25.00 a week. My worst chore began at 2 a.m. when I had to mop the floor of the main lobby and clean the some twenty big brass cuspidors placed beside each of the leather chairs in the room. In short, there was nothing to stimulate my own love of poetry [CKS].

[42] LC Catalogue #: DLC/PP 1994: 064.79.

Plate 21: People of Alaca Examine the Truck[43]

That afternoon in a lonely stretch of the road we were stopped by four armed horsemen. They turned out to be gendarmes, however, and not bandits. They said that the kaymakam of Alaca had telegraphed to their post for them to accompany me to Yozgat if I so wished. But by this time I had seen enough of Turkey to agree with the Samsun mutasarrıf's statement that travel was safe, and declined their services with thanks. Later, I found that Yozgat, a few months before, had been the scene of an uprising of the old Turks against the Nationalists and in the city itself I saw the streets patrolled at night by a few soldiers - a display of military force which I observed in no other Turkish town. Doubtless this was the reason why the extra gendarmes had been offered, but we had no trouble.

Yozgat is a city of perhaps 10,000 inhabitants, well situated on both sides of a ravine. Here, as in Merzifon, the best building was the school. Some effort was being made to beautify the city - pine trees had been planted on both sides of the main street. The town boasted a one-page newspaper.

I called upon the mutassarıf, who told me the roads were good enough to continue in the automobile to Ankara. He had the town searched for us for benzine [*benzin*] (gasoline) but as there was only a small quantity to be had, I decided to send the car back and continue in a yaylı. The mutassarıf, accordingly, sent for a livery stable proprietor who assured me he could give me a team of horses that were as "*fleet as jaylan* [*ceylân*]." I hired them

43 LC Catalogue #: DLC/PP 1994: 064 [Red Album: Turkey, 1920-1921 by C. K. Streit].

for the five-day trip to Ankara, for 'ceylân,' Mehmed Ali told me, meant "*reindeer in Turkish*"[44] [**Plate 22**].

The mutassarıf insisted that I was a guest of the city and had my baggage removed from the han where I had taken lodgings to the mayor's reception room in the city hall where good bedding had been provided. Here I came acquainted with the Turkish method of washing. A pitcher of water and a basin were brought in. I started to wash in the basin, but Mehmed Ali corrected me. It seems, in Turkey and the Muslim world one must wash in running water. He poured the water over my hands, letting the waste fall into the basin. It was just as if one was washing from an open faucet - but as there were few faucets in Turkey, one generally requires a friend to assist him in performing his ablutions.

Dinner, which was served in courses, as is usual in Turkey, consisted of soup, eggs fried in butter, roast mutton, potatoes, rice and beans and a Turkish dessert. It was served to me in my room by the members of the fire department, who had been detailed to wait on me.

Plate 22: Streit's Yaylı and his driver Ahmed[45]

[44] **Note**: Actually: gazelle or antelope [HWL].

[45] LC Catalogue #: DLC/PP 1994: 064.189. **Note**: On the back of this photo Streit wrote: "*My 'Yayli.' I spent six days in such a carriage*" [HWL].

CHAPTER III

LIVING WITH TURKISH PEASANTS

TRAVERSING AN AREA AS BLEAK AS THE 'BADLANDS' OF MONTANA

The yaylı, to this Montanan,[46] was really an undersized version of the covered wagons by which our 'West was won.' Though slower than our light open truck, it was more comfortable for we rode lying down on blankets and pillows. True, the canvas covering the top, sides and back gave me no view of the countryside. I did not complain of this obstruction for the scenery was desolate. For two days we went through a rock salt desert, meeting little traffic and seeing few villages. This district, which greatly resembles the Badlands of Montana, had been terrorized by a band of four hundred brigands. Three weeks before my arrival, however, the government had succeeded in removing them by granting them a general amnesty and sending them to the front. I whiled away the time en route in sleeping or in discussing the ***Qur'an***, Muslim customs and Omar Khayyam with Mehmed Ali. We enjoyed ourselves, too, in talking with Ahmed, the lad who drove the yaylı. We asked him so many questions that his favorite answer became a despairing, "*Oh, master, in the name of Allah, I don't know.*"

Plate 23: Streit's Gendarmes Corporal Edhem Çavuş & Hacı[47]

Two mounted gendarmes accompanied me through the desert, Corporal Edhem Tchavoosh [*Çavuş*] and Hadji [*Hacı*], a private [**Plate 23**]. Their appearance in their huge black capes was striking. They were both fine looking men, genial and goodhearted. Hacı seemed to think it was his duty to unlace my shoes at night. There was no servility, however, in his manner. Evidently it was only a part of the respect to be shown a stranger. There is a strange mixture in the character of the Turks of a sense of personal dignity, of fraternity and equality, with an Oriental respect for authority.

[46] **Note**: Streit, who was born in the state of Missouri, grew up in the state of Montana, in the Northwestern United States [HWL].

[47] LC Catalogue #: DLC/PP 1994: 064.181. **Note**: On the back of this photo Streit wrote: "*Corporal Edhem and Hadji who accompanied me for several days. Typical Turk gendarmes*" [HWL].

Plate 24: The Village of Sekili[48]

AN OVERNIGHT STAY IN ADOBE-HUT VILLAGE, PEOPLED MAINLY BY WOMEN AND CHILDREN; BAREFOOT IN THE SNOW

After having traveled about fifty miles - we rarely made more than that distance in a day in our yaylı - we came to Sekili,[49] one of the most impoverished villages I have ever seen [**Plate 24**], where we spent the night. Most of the young men had gone away to the World War, and, as usual, few of them had escaped with their lives. Other villagers had fled because of the bandits. Most Westerners seem to think that the brigands in Turkey prey simply upon the Christians and that the Turks themselves never suffer.

The peasants who remained in Sekili were living in poverty and rags. I saw two girls walking through the snow in their bare feet, carrying water from the river [**Plate 25**]. One of them was so frightened when I took her picture that she burst into tears. In several other places, I should add, I saw women and children walking in their bare feet in the snow.

Plate 25: Barefoot Girls Carrying Water in the Snow[50]

[48] LC Catalogue #: DLC/PP 1994: 064.72.

[49] **Note**: The village of Sekili is located in the *Kaza* (Sub-Province) of Yerköy in the *Vilâyet* (Province) of Yozgat [HWL].

[50] LC Catalogue #: DLC/PP 1994: 064.201.

Conditions in Sekili were worse than in other villages in the territory which I visited, but in the best of them the peasant leads so hard a life and has been so cruelly exploited by the Sultan's government and by Greek and Armenian merchants that one cannot help feeling sorry for him. Especially, when one has lived with him, and found him to be an honest, hospitable, industrious and kind-hearted man who wants to improve his methods of farming and better conditions for his children. He is tolerant and peaceable when left to himself - he does not fight for the love of fighting as does the Arab but rather from habit and ignorance. He wants nothing more than to farm in peace, but war has for so long been the normal condition in Turkey that he is inclined to accept soldiering as inevitable.

The peasants own their land but do not live upon it. They live together in these villages and from 'time immemorial' they say, they have run the village affairs themselves through a council elected each year, having at its head one of the peasants as *reis* or mayor. The government fixes the amount of taxes the village is to pay, and the council is held responsible for their payment in a lump sum. When the villagers cannot themselves settle their disputes, they appeal to the governor of the district. Their lands are not fenced off, except where there are orchards and vineyards. Their methods of agriculture are nearly the same as they were centuries ago.

All the villages I saw were much the same - a group of low, flat-roofed houses clustered together by no particular plan. The houses are strongly built of sun-dried mud bricks, the walls of the house in which I spent the night in Sekili being nearly two feet thick. The room had two windows, but it was impossible to open them as they were securely cemented with mud [**Plate 26**].

Apparently, there are neither chairs nor beds in these village houses. The ground is used as the floor. It is excavated to a depth of eight or ten inches in the center, leaving a raised platform three or four feet wide around the walls of the room. This is covered with rugs upon which one sits cross-legged. Quilts and perhaps a feather-bed are spread on the rugs at night and there the peasant sleeps without springs or mattresses.

Wood is scarce in much of Turkey and houses are heated by mongols [*mangals*]. Imagine the ash pan of a stove standing on legs about ten inches from the floor and filled with glowing coals or charcoal embers, and you have the mangal. I found mangals everywhere I went in Turkey, including some of the government offices in İstanbul, though here they were more ornate, being made of brass.

Plate 26: The Village of Sekili[51]

[51] LC Catalogue #: DLC/PP 1994: 064 [Red Album: Turkey, 1920-1921 by C. K. Streit].

CHICKEN À LA TURKISH PEASANT

There were plenty of chickens and eggs in Sekili but no vegetables or cereals, not even rice. Rice, mixed with other vegetables or meat, pilaff [*pilav*] as the Turks call it, forms the standard dish of most of the peasants.[52] Their usual meat is mutton, which they have in abundance as they are great sheep-raisers. Many of the sheep are of the fat-tailed breed. The peasants use this fat altogether too much in their cooking to suit my taste. They do not seem to like beef, and pork is prohibited by their religion. They have a large number of ways of preparing mutton, however, some of which are quite good. As I am not fond of this meat, chicken and turkey formed the principal meat items of my diet while in Turkey.

At Sekili, I had chicken à la peasant. They did not pluck the fowl. They simply skinned and boiled the meat, thus depriving the meat of most of its taste. Elsewhere, however, I found the Turks prepared chicken and turkey much as we do. The bread in Sekili was the most curious and unpalatable food served to me. It was made of very coarsely ground whole wheat flour mixed with water and baked in round thin sheets about eighteen inches in diameter and less than a quarter of an inch thick [Tr.: *lavaş*]. It was not crisp but of the consistency that the sheet - I refuse to call it a loaf - could be folded without breaking it. As they apparently had no knives, forks or spoons in Sekili, we ate our eggs by putting them on this bread and folding, or rather, wrapping it around them to form a sandwich. From the time I left Merzifon until I reached Ankara I was never given a knife with which to eat. Nearly always, however, I had a fork, and always, except in Sekili, a spoon. The spoons in the villages were made of wood.

A little cheese, made from the milk of water buffalo, which forms the chief dairy animal and beast of burden of the peasant, ended the meal. There was neither coffee nor tea in this village, a most extraordinary thing, for the Turk is very fond of these two beverages. Sekili was the only place in Turkey where I did not find coffee and tea in abundance. When a Turk cannot offer you one of these drinks you may be sure that he is in the worst way financially. But even so, I had to insist before the peasant with whom I stayed would accept payment for his hospitality.

The next day Ahmed decided to take a shortcut and the result was that we got on a very bad road. In crossing a small stream covered with thin ice the yaylı nearly turned over, the front wheels were almost submerged and the horses, in trying to pull us out, broke the tongue. This was in the midst of the desert where no help was to be found [**Plate 27**].

Plate 27: Streit's Yaylı in the Stream[53]

[52] **Note**: On this point Streit was clearly misled by the fact that, with the exception of Sekili, he was generally fed pilav in each of the villages he visited. In point of fact, then, as now, pilav and meat for villagers are a delicacy and it was his status as an honored guest that led his hosts to serve him these items which he mistook as their standard fare [HWL].

[53] LC Catalogue #: DLC/PP 1994: 064.195. **Note**: On the back of this photo Streit wrote: "*Our accident in the Salt Desert*" [HWL].

Ahmed, the driver, and Hacı, the gendarme, took off their shoes and socks, waded into the icy water and unloaded the yaylı and then, while the horses pulled, they pushed it up the steep bank.

My respect for the hardiness of the Turks was considerably increased by this incident. The broken tongue was mended with some rope and we continued [**Plate 28**].

We had intended to reach the town of Madan [Maden] that night. To do this we had to climb a steep hill, but the poor 'reindeer' were worn out and could not ascend it. But it was a lucky accident which had delayed us and fatigued the horses. It forced me to spend a most pleasant and interesting evening at the village of Djerid Muminli [Ceritmüminli],[54] which was near the bottom of the hill.

Plate 28: Repairs Underway on Streit's Yaylı[55]

[54] **Note**: The village of Ceritmüminli is located in the *Kaza* (Sub-Province) of Keskin in the *Vilâyet* (Province) of Kırıkkale [HWL].

[55] LC Catalogue #: DLC/PP 1994: 064.205. **Note**: On the back of this photo Streit wrote: "*An accident in the 'Salt Desert' – my carriage 'yayli' gets stuck in icy stream, tongue breaks. Note the hardy Turk gendarme, bare-legged, in icy water*" [HWL].

THE ADOBE VILLAGE THAT WANTED TO BE LIKE VIENNA

Djerid Muminli [Ceritmüminli], which means 'Strong in Faith,' with its eighty families, was five times larger than Sekili, though its population, too, had been depleted by the war. Its some six hundred inhabitants before the war had furnished the government one hundred fifty soldiers -almost one fourth of the entire population - and of these, seventy had been killed and most of the remainder had either been taken prisoner and had not yet been able to return or were serving in the Nationalist Army [**Plate 29**]. It is this frightful drain on the population as much as anything else which has made the Turkish leaders so anxious for a durable peace and so bent upon conserving the health of the people.

Ceritmüminli, however, was fairly prosperous, as prosperity goes in Turkish villages. The best house in town was the 'guest house,' but that I found to be the case in most Turkish villages. It gives a good illustration of the hospitable nature of the Turks. These houses are built entirely on the initiative of the peasants in order to provide lodging for 'the stranger within the gates' [**Plate 30**]. They expect no payment for their hospitality. "*It is our duty,*" they say, and if you insist, they quote some verse from the ***Qur'an***. The stranger cannot help but compare the followers of Muhammed with those of Christ and this is not the only instance in which he decides that the Muslim comes closer to Christian standards than the average Christian.

Mustapha [Mustafa], the reis (village headman), showed me about the village. Then we went to the guest house

Plate 29: Boys in the Village of Ceritmüminli[56]

[56] LC Catalogue #: DLC/PP 1994: 064 [Red Album: Turkey, 1920-1921 by C. K. Streit].

where tea was served. The room was much larger than the one in Sekili and the windows could be opened - otherwise its interior was much the same. I sat down Turkish fashion in one corner, near me sat Mustafa, and some twenty-five peasants occupied the opposite sides of the room. They were nearly all old, gray-bearded men. They were sober and reserved - that I found to be characteristic of the Turks [**Plate 31**]. There is something grave and judicious in the bearing of the Turks, in the measured tone in which they say "Evyet, effendi!" [*evet efendi*] ("Yes, Sir") which makes one think: these are men of parts, well poised, dignified, true elders. They listened attentively to the conversation I carried on with Mustafa through Mehmed Ali, at first seldom making any comment themselves. I offered cigarettes several times and for my part smoked the ones which the reis rolled for me. Thus, the ice was broken.

Plate 30: The Ceritmüminli *Misafir Evi* (Guest House)[57]

Plate 31: The Elders of Ceritmüminli (Mustafa Reis in Fez)[58]

57 LC Catalogue #: DLC/PP 1994: 064.196. **Note**: On the back of this photo Streit wrote: "*'Guest House' where I spent the night in village of Djerid-Muminli*" [HWL].

58 LC Catalogue #: DLC/PP 1994: 064.183. **Note**: On the back of this photo Streit wrote: "*Mustapha, the 'reis,' and peasants of Djerid Muminli*" [HWL].

"*You must excuse us for not being able to offer you all that you are accustomed to,*" Mustafa said at the beginning. That apologetic remark I heard everywhere in Turkey. Those who are educated or who have traveled - and many Turk peasants 'saw the world' in the army - are keenly aware of the backwardness of their country and are desirous of progress. That is one of the most encouraging characteristics of the Turks. In so old a country one would not expect civilization to encounter, more difficulty than it does from the dead weight of custom, from the 'what was good enough for father' spirit.

These peasants had heard of America as a humanitarian nation and they wanted our help. They were very much interested in machinery and their curiosity covered a wide field. I had to explain to them how an American daily newspaper was published, and the questions they asked showed a quick intelligence. I used my Corona [typewriter] with carbon copies to demonstrate to them the utility of machinery. They had never seen a typewriter before and were amazed by it. I asked Mustafa to tell me what the peasants wanted from America, saying that I would write the message as Mehmed Ali interpreted it. What Mustafa said was: "*We want America to help us improve our schools and send us farming implements.*"

I passed the carbon copies around, and the peasants kept them as souvenirs. Then I wrote a letter on the machine to the reis thanking him and the village for their hospitality to me. Mehmed Ali translated it to them, and my hosts smiled with delight and each of them gravely saluted. Mustafa at once asked for a sheet of paper and with a pencil wrote a letter to me in Turkish peasant fashion. He held the sheet doubled in his hand and wrote with the hand on his knee - a writing desk certainly not lacking in simplicity. He read the letter, and the peasants again smiled and showed their approval, and it was my turn to salute. Then Mehmed Ali translated the letter to me, and once more I saluted - I had got accustomed to Oriental politeness, a most necessary thing if one is to gain the confidence of the Turks. And I replied with the three Turkish words I had made it a point to learn: "Teshakurrederim, effendim, tchok teshakurrenderim," [*teşekkür ederim, efendim, çok teşekkür ederim*] meaning, 'Thank you, Sir, thank you very much.' I used that phrase on many occasions and found that it made my road much smoother. The Turk at once warms to one who treats him politely and as a friend.

Mustafa's letter, literally translated, follows:

Feb. 7, 1337

To His Excellency Mr. American Correspondent:

Your accidental visit to our village has very much pleased us, who have wished for an eternity to have friendly relations with America; and the modesty you have displayed but emphasizes your generosity and intelligence. We request that we should join hands with America on questions of industry, commerce and agriculture and should help each other in the defense of our countries.[59]

From the Elders of Ceritmüminli
Mustafa

Dinner was then announced by one of the sons of the reis bringing in a huge platter, at least three feet in diameter, which he placed before me on the upturned legs of a small stool. He decorated the rim of the platter with the same sort of bread that I had eaten at Sekili and placed a bowl with some eggs fried in butter in the center. I invited the reis and the two gendarmes to eat with Mehmed and me. They were rather surprised, especially the gendarmes who at first said that they would wait until I had finished, but on my pressing them they accepted. The invitation made a good impression on the crowd of peasants who remained in the room and watched us as we ate.

[59] The last sentence in the letter was written at my request that he mention what he wanted from America [CKS].

We all ate out of the same bowl, using wooden spoons to take out the eggs and place them on bread, eating them sandwich fashion. There were not even spoons for the next course which consisted of a special Turkish dish called beurek [*börek*]. This was made of the same coarse flour, but baked this time to a crisp and it was rather good. Fingers were used for knives and forks. Then came a bowl containing little balls of ground meat cooked in a sort of soup. Each used his spoon to fish out his meat from the common bowl. Next a plate of haviz [*havız*], which looks and tastes something like fudge and is made of grape molasses, was placed before us. This was eaten by taking a bit of bread between the fingers and scooping up some of the succulent dish. I thought that it was the dessert - but no, the meal could not be complete without pilav, and, sure enough, it received the honor of being the last course. All the food was good, but the rice was especially well cooked. It was served with a bowl of sweet unfermented liquor made from grapes and called *pekmez* [sic. *hoşaf*] by the peasants, though the usual pekmez is solid. Mustafa set the fashion by taking a spoonful of rice and then dipping the spoon into the pekmez and washing down his pilav with it. When I praised the taste of the drink they gave me a small bowl of it. I drank to their health, but then I had to explain the courtesy, for they do not have that custom.

I could not forget the spectators at our 'banquet,' for such the dinner was for the villagers, and wishing to return in some measure, the peasants' hospitality, I opened a can of California peaches which I was lucky enough to have with me. It gave me the opportunity of giving a little talk on the benefits of civilization - how I could not only prolong summer into winter but also enjoy the fruits of my country in a distant land. I gave Mustafa, as reis, half a peach. But as there was not enough to go around on that basis, I cut the other slices in thirds and gave each peasant a piece.

They were quite overcome with astonishment and delight. One bearded old man just behind Mustafa could not retain his stoical impassiveness and whispered to the reis, "*tell him that we are all very happy that he came.*" I mention these little things to show by what methods I was able to break through the ordinary reserve of the peasants and get their confidence and their point of view.

The party showed no signs of breaking up, and we continued to smoke and talk. But in an hour or so the peasants one by one saluted and left, until only Mustafa and his two sons remained [**Plate 32**]. His oldest son, Mustafa told me, had been wounded in the World War. The government had informed him that his son was in an İstanbul hospital. Mustafa remarked that the old regime had never taken this trouble and then said : "*Oh, I wanted to go and see him, but,*" he added with the stern pride of a warrior race, "*I couldn't let the village think a Turkish father could not bear to have his son wounded.*" He spoke simply with no attempt at making an effect but rather as if explaining once more to himself his

Plate 32: The Ceritmüminli Reis Mustafa & Sons[60]

[60] LC Catalogue #: DLC/PP 1994: 064 [Red Album: Turkey, 1920-1921 by C. K. Streit].

course of action. The Turkish peasant has the virtue of all undeveloped peoples - language to him is a means of conveying his real thought instead of concealing it.

I asked Mustafa if the boys who had returned from the war were dissatisfied with their former life in the village.

"*Yes, they are,*" he replied, "*My son, for instance, fought with the Austrian armies in Galicia. He went to the big city there -Vienna- once. He told me how splendid the houses were and how clean were the streets and toilets.*" And with touching simplicity he added, "*We want to make the village like that.*"

When one considers the thousands of other peasants who have come back to their villages as the propagandists of Western civilization, one begins to understand the ferment that is now going on in Turkey.

I don't know how long Mustafa and his sons would have remained, despite the lateness of the hour, if I had not told them that I was tired and had a letter to write to my fiancée. But then I had to satisfy their curiosity as to our marriage customs, which they agreed were simpler and better than theirs. To illustrate the difference in our customs, I showed them some photographs I had of my fiancée, my mother and my sisters. Mustafa was greatly interested. The gendarmes and the sons, I could see, were consumed with curiosity.

One of the former, after explaining that their religion would not allow a woman to show her face, asked, "*Did you show him the picture because he is an old man?*" I told him that we had no such custom, explained to him the status of women in the West, and showed him and the others the pictures.

A bed, which must have been part of the dowry of some village bride, was then spread on the floor for me. Despite the lack of springs, it was comfortable enough and I turned to Mustafa and said, "*Why, I'll sleep like a king tonight!*"

The remark evidently went to his heart, for he put his hand on my shoulder and said, "Tchoke teshakurrederim, bey effendi!" [*çok teşekkür ederim, bey efendi*]. 'Bey efendi' is the term of address used by the Turks when they wish to be more than usually polite and respectful.[61]

TAGORE'S WISDOM; LUNCH À LA GREEK; BAKSHEESH BANNED; AN ISLAMIC SECT THAT PERMITS WINE

I left Ceritmüminli the next day with considerable regret and a very warm affection for the Turkish peasant. With such people as this to work with, a Westerner who had the welfare of the Turks at heart could accomplish wonders in raising the standard of life in the villages. But all the West sends the Turks is the missionary, and he is sometimes a narrow-minded bigot who approaches the Turks from the wrong angle, that of religion.[62]

How much wisdom there is in those words of Rabindranath Tagore, "*Men forget their humanity when they consider their gods.*" What the Near East needs above all to bring it up to the plane of Occidental civilization are men and women who will forget the different gods and remember only humanity.[63]

[61] **Note**: This footnote is taken from Streit's revised 1982 manuscript [HWL]: "*Even the rereading of this passage, 61 years later, I am deeply moved even to the point of tears by my one-day-and-one-night visit to the 'village that wanted to be like Vienna.' When I returned to Constantinople in 1923 as* ***Public Ledger*** *correspondent for the Near East and the Balkans I sent Djerid Muminli [Ceritmüminli] a gift of a John Deere steel plow* [See: **Appendix X.**, p. 237], *for the peasants were still limited to wooden plows. I also sent them other gifts to help them a little realize their dream of a better life. I have, alas, never been able to return to Turkey since 1925 when I was transferred to the* ***Ledger****'s Paris bureau, but I still hope to return to see the waters of Tschorum* [Çorum], *the progress of the great revolution begun in Ankara and the village which I hope is still 'strong in Faith*'" [CKS].

[62] I found the missionaries most Christianly in their giving much needed medical treatment to Muslims, as well as Christians [CKS].

There is much of good in the Muslim religion. It has been a great civilizing force, not only in the Orient but also in the Occident. We should not forget that it is to Muslim doctors that we owe the conservation of much of the wisdom of the ancients which might otherwise have perished, for the Dark Ages then hung over Europe. H.G. Wells[64] considers Islam even superior to both Christianity and Judaism. However, true that may be, the Occident certainly has nothing to fear from Islam, if rightly interpreted, and has much to gain.

Our aim should be to help the advanced Turks in their policy of using the ***Qur'an*** to promote liberalism. It would even pay American exporters to send a few missionaries, not of Christianity, but of civilization (farming experts, engineers, teachers, etc.) to Turkey in response to the call for help which the Turks are making. They could thus gain the undying friendship of the Turks (Persia has never forgotten Morgan Shuster[65] and is even now asking for him to return) and at the same time by promoting the welfare of the country, they could increase its value as a market.

The next day we stopped for lunch at Madan [Maden],[66] a town of about 8,000 inhabitants, where I ate at a Greek restaurant. One street was lined with blacksmiths and

Plate 33: Typical Anatolian Shops[67]

[63] While a Rhodes Scholar at Oxford in 1921, I had the privilege of meeting this Nobel prize poet. He held an open seminar there. Only a half-dozen students attended it; I was the only American. The seminar inspired me to write a poem immediately afterward [CKS].

[64] **Note**: Herbert George Wells (1866-1946), English author, best known for his work in the science fiction genre [HWL].

[65] **Note**: William Morgan Shuster (1877-1960). American lawyer and civil servant. Appointed by the Iranian Parliament (*Majlis*) in May 1911 as the 'Treasurer-General' of Persia to assist in managing the country's finances [HWL].

[66] **Note**: Maden appears to be a shortened version of the name Keskin Madeni. Today the name has been shortened to Keskin. It is a *Kaza* (Sub-Province) of the *Vilâyet* (Province) of Kırıkkale [HWL].

[67] LC Catalogue #: DLC/PP 1994: 064 [Red Album: Turkey, 1920-1921 by C. K. Streit].

coppersmiths, most of whom were Armenians, though the shops of Turkish artisans were mixed in with them. The stores and shops in Turkey are all much alike - a single small room, with the side facing the street entirely open [**Plate 33**].

At Maden, our two gendarmes left us. In the past baksheesh [*bahşiş*] or tipping has been the curse of Turkey. After two days riding in the bitter cold weather and after wading barefoot in the icy water when our yaylı broke down, these two men, however, certainly deserved something. I could hardly believe my ears, then, when both of them absolutely refused to accept the generous tip I offered them. "*It is forbidden. The government pays us. We did only our duty,*" they said.

The fact that the government paid them was in itself passing strange which showed that a new order had evidently begun. For years, the Sultan's government has been habitually behind in paying the salaries of many of its employees.

The Nationalists deserve credit for the steps they have taken to lessen the evils of bahşiş. Not once during my travels in Turkey did I have need to resort to bahşiş to get anything done. Nor was I the only one who observed this phenomenon in Asiatic Turkey. Several Americans on the S.S. Milano, on which later I left Anatolia at Adalia [Antalya] for İstanbul, went ashore to see the town while they were in port. They, too, had been warned that they would not be allowed to leave Nationalist territory if once they set foot upon it. They had no trouble in returning to the ship. While they were on shore, a Turkish policeman accompanied them as a guide. They told me they were much pleased with his services and were astonished when he refused the customary tip they offered him.

I gave my two gendarmes in lieu of the tip a letter to their chief, expressing my satisfaction of them. This pleased them immensely.

In the afternoon, we descended into the valley of the Kizil Irmak [Kızıl Irmak] (Red River), the most important stream in Central Anatolia. Here we came to the village of Hasan Deh-Deh [Dede],[68] founded 450 years ago by a man of that name who was one of the leaders of the Alevi sect of Muslims. The village is remarkable for its well-built mosque and minaret of red sandstone and for its tomb of Hasan Dede [**Plate 34**], which make it one of the shrines of the sect. The Alevis resemble the Shiite sect, to which Persians and some Arabians belong. In that they do not recognize the first three caliphs who succeeded Muhammed, as do the Sunnite sect which includes the vast majority of Muslims. The once bitter hostility between the Turkish Sunnites and the Persian Shiites is now dying out, apparently, for the Turks paid no attention to the fact that my interpreter was Persian. Other peculiarities of the Alevis are that the drinking of wine is permitted, and the priests are not allowed to marry, the exact opposite being true for the orthodox Muslims.

Plate 34: Mosque & Mausoleum in the Village of Hasan Dede[69]

[68] **Note**: Hasandede is today a village located in the Merkez *Kaza* (central Sub-Province) in the *Vilâyet* (Province) of Kırıkkale [HWL].

[69] LC Catalogue #: DLC/PP 1994: 064.247 [Red Album: Turkey, 1920-1921 by C .K. Streit].

U.S. prohibition seen as a step toward Islam; a land without family names

The religious sanction, however, has not proved sufficient to stop the drinking of alcoholic beverages among the Turks. Their chief drink was rakki [*rakı*], a sort of absinthe, which is also the popular drink in Athens. The saloon keepers in Turkey were Christians, chiefly Greeks. Rakı was having a bad effect on the health of the Turks and one of the first acts of the Grand National Assembly [*Büyük Millet Meclis*] was a prohibition law. The penalties imposed seem severe enough - a fine of fifty Turkish pounds for selling alcoholic drinks and a sentence of eighty days in prison for buying them. The hocas, I was told, were greatly pleased when they heard that America had gone dry. They thought that at last we had begun to accept the teachings of the Prophet and were on the road to joining the 'true believers.' The Turkish doctors whom I met were very much interested in knowing the methods we had taken to enforce prohibition. They were concerned with the physical welfare of the people and had done much to secure the passage of the dry law over the opposition which developed in the Assembly, based partly on the fear that the government's revenues would be diminished and partly on the love of drink which some of the Deputies had. The law seems to be fairly well enforced. I saw no drunkenness anywhere in Turkey and no drinking, though no doubt it is still going on to some extent in private.

Ahmed, when we were approaching Hasan Dede had told me that the Alevis drank wine and that this was the only place where I could still get a drink. I asked Ba-Ba [*Baba*], a hoca, who was head of the village (who received me in the guest house), and as usual served coffee and rolled me a cigarette, if they had any wine, suggesting that I was thirsty. After some hesitation, he sent a man to look for some. He brought back a small bowl half filled with a sweet wine made in the village. It was the only fermented drink I found anywhere in Turkey, although doubtless there are other oases.

Hasan Baba had a grievance. The Ankara government, it seems, had not paid the village the fifteen hundred Turkish pounds due it from the vakouf [*vakıf*] or pious foundations. When Hasan Baba heard that I was a newspaper correspondent, he hastened to tell me of the grievance for he was convinced that if the outside world knew of the wrong which was being done the village it would be speedily remedied. He had another complaint to make. The government had quartered in the mosque recruits and troops who happened to reach the village at nightfall. This is nothing unusual. The Turks, in time of need, do not hesitate to make use of the mosques as hospitals and as temporary barracks. But in this case, the soldiers had used most of the woodwork within the mosque for fuel (there is little wood in this part of Turkey). Hasan Baba showed me through the mosque and made no objection to my taking pictures inside. In fact, he seemed pleased when I took a picture of him standing behind the sacred tomb of Hasan Dede [**Plate 35**]. On the wall back of the tomb was a curious

Plate 35: Hasan Baba (center) & Associates [70]

[70] LC Catalogue #: DLC/PP 1994: 064.247 [Red Album: Turkey, 1920-1921 by C. K. Streit].

genealogical table which traced the founder of the village back to Adam.

The genealogist in Turkey, I imagine, has an exceedingly difficult task, for only the advanced Turks have family names. The wife of Ali Kemal, for instance, is not called Ali Kemal Hanım (Hanım meaning either miss or madam, though usually the latter). But she goes by her maiden name, Fatima Hanım. (Fatima, to digress again, is not pronounced Fa-tee-ma, but Fatima.) Neither will the children take Ali Kemal's name; they use simply the ones given them. Thus, one of his sons may go through life as Ahmed Ferid, another as Towfik [Tevfik], while the grandson of Ali Kemal may be known to the world as Djelal [Celal]. Most Turks have but one name and where they have two, as Mehmed Ali, Mustafa Kemal, the second is not a surname.

There seems to be a paucity of names in Turkey and one gets the impression that most of the male population are named Mehmed, Ali, Mustafa, Kemal, Ferid, Djemal [Cemal], Djelal [Celal], Djevad [Cevat] or Tewfik [Tevfik], for these are as common as Tom, Dick and Harry in the West. Many of these names go back to the early heroes of Islam and it is a common practice to give a child one of Muhammed's many names. Mahmoud, Mehmed, Mehmet are all corruptions of Muhammed, and Mustafa is one of his other names.

Mehmet Ali is the most popular combination for it includes the name of the Prophet and of his famous son-in-law, Ali. There are often a dozen or twenty men in a Turkish company of soldiers each of whom has no other name than Mehmed Ali. The confusion which this system causes is not hard to imagine. It is apparently a survival of early days in the Orient. Thus, in the first chapter of Matthew, one reads that Abraham begat Isaac and Isaac begat Jacob and so on down to Joseph - exactly the same as Mehmed begat Ferid and Ferid begat Kemal, as a Turkish genealogical table runs today.

To return to Hasan Baba and his complaints against the government: I asked him if it were worse than the previous regime.

"*No, it is much better,*" he answered, "*Formerly when the mutasarrıf visited the village he would send gendarmes ahead to arrange for his reception. We would have to spread our best rugs before him and provide him with the choicest mutton at his meals. Now, when the mutasarrıf comes here, he comes just as you did today. He sits down just as you are sitting in the guest house and takes his coffee as any other visitor.*"

A 'THIRSTY' LOCOMOTIVE AND A 'SPARKLING' FREIGHT TRAIN RIDE ATOP A LOAD OF OATS

That night we reached Yakshi Khan [Yahşihan],[71] the present terminus of the narrow-gauge railway [**Plate 36**] which the Turks are building to Sivas (in Eastern Central Anatolia) from Ankara. Luckily, a freight train was leaving the next day for Ankara, fifty miles distant. We made our baggage in the form of a windbreak atop a carload of oats and traveled lying down behind it. The day was full of incidents. Something was wrong with the

Plate 36: The Railroad Terminus of Yahşıhan[72]

[71] **Note**: The town of Yahşihan is today the center of a *Kaza* (Sub-Province) bearing its name in the *Vilâyet* (Province) of Kırıkkale [HWL].

[72] LC Catalogue #: DLC/PP 1994: 064 [Red Album: Turkey, 1920-1921 by C. K. Streit].

Plate 37: Streit's Thirsty Engine Stopped for a Drink[73]

water pipes of the tiny locomotive, and a bucket brigade had to be formed to fill the boiler before we could start. That locomotive was nothing if not 'thirsty.' We had to stop at nearly every stream and irrigation ditch we came to, let down a hose and give the engine a drink [**Plate 37**]. The train consisted of six cars of oats and one of wood; the latter being used as fuel for the locomotive. Its hunger was as keen as its thirst, and we had to replenish our supply of wood twice before we passed the divide and could coast into Ankara.

We had not gone five miles before the grade of the track became too steep for the locomotive despite all of its energetic snorting and puffing [**Plate 38**]. The train crew, a happy lot, decided that the proper strategy would be to take a running start. We backed down, the engineer opened his throttle, and by this device we gained perhaps a hundred feet on the previous attempt before the locomotive came to a panting stop. The crew tinkered a bit with the engine and tried the same plan of attack twice again, but with no better results. It was evident that the load was too heavy. Finally, the conductor cut off the two last cars and thus we achieved the hill.

But what was to be done with the two cars? The conductor was perplexed. Then an idea came to him. He assembled the other members of the crew and they

[73] LC Catalogue #: DLC/PP 1994: 064.202. **Note**: On the back of this photo Streit wrote: "*Our locomotive takes a drink*" [HWL].

Plate 38: Streit's Ride to Ankara[74]

walked back to the two cars and attempted the hopeless task of pushing them up the hill one by one. They ended by leaving the cars temporarily in the care of Allah, and we continued on our way for ten miles until we came to where the Turks were building a new bridge over the Kızıl Irmak. Here there was a switch, and we waited while the locomotive went back and picked up the two cars [**Plate 39**].

The Turks have encountered considerable difficulty in building their railroad through the mountains. We passed through twelve tunnels in twenty-five miles. Most of the road was constructed during the war. The narrow-gauge track is only temporary, as the grade and the tunnels have been made for a standard gauge railway. The tunnels and stone culverts built by the Turks, and one of the stations near Ankara show good workmanship.

Plate 39: Streit's Locomotive Returns to Pick up Cars[75]

[74] LC Catalogue #: DLC/PP 1994: 064 [Red Album: Turkey, 1920-1921 by C. K. Streit].
[75] LC Catalogue #: DLC/PP 1994: 064 [Red Album: Turkey, 1920-1921 by C. K. Streit].

I mention this because of the curious impression abroad that the Turks are incapable of doing such work. Yet the ***Encyclopedia Britannica*** speaking of the Hedjaz [Hicaz] Railway says. "*The line was designed, surveyed and constructed by Turkish engineers -employing Ottoman navies and laborers- in a highly efficient and economical manner.*" The Nationalist government intends to push the construction of this railway to Sivas this summer. When I passed over it workmen were building a new tunnel. The grade has been constructed nearly as far east as Yozgat.

Those tunnels burnt themselves into my memory - via my heavy raincoat. The asthmatic locomotive threw up a continual stream of sparks which rained down on us in the tunnels, leaving numerous little holes in our clothing as a souvenir of the trip [**Plate 40**]. All in all, however, it was the most comfortable day's travel I had of the nine I spent en route to Ankara. 'Day's travel' is no exaggeration, despite the distance being but fifty miles, for we left Yahşihan at 7:00 a.m. and did not arrive in Ankara until 5:00 p.m.

At one of our numerous stops en route, I visited one of the primitive flour mills which abound in Turkey. Water power is used to run them, not by vertical wheels as in the Occident but by a horizontal wheel or turbine attached directly under the mill stone, which is similar to those to be found in old mills in the West. It is a rather ingenious contrivance. The water is carried in ditches along the hillside and at intervals a portion of it is diverted by wooden flumes leading to the various mills. The grain is ground into coarse whole wheat flour.

Plate 40: Streit's Open-Air Ride to Ankara[76]

[76] LC Catalogue #: DLC/PP 1994: 064.197 [Red Album: Turkey, 1920-1921 by C. K. Streit].

Chapter IV

Ankara the Nationalist Capital

Centuries of conquerors of Ankara

The route by which I came gives the stranger the most striking impression of Ankara of any of the approaches to the city. The train suddenly leaves a narrow canyon and the panorama of the celebrated metropolis of ancient Galatia, spreads before one's eyes. The city is situated on the summit and lower flanks of a volcanic butte which stands 500 feet above the valley. Near the summit its sides are precipitous. Minarets relieve its silhouette. Around the top of the hill runs an old wall which is in a remarkably good state of preservation, and gives a medieval aspect to the city [**Plate 41**]. On the summit of a bare and rocky hill which is cut off from the butte by a deep canyon, stands an isolated dome covering the tomb of a Muslim saint. The wide valley which stretches around most of Ankara throws the butte into sharp relief. What a natural fortress it must have been, one thinks, in the old days when it went by the name of Ancyra.

Celebrated in geography for the goats and cats to which its name has been given, Ankara is hardly less famous in history. The city is first mentioned as the place where Alexander the Great received the delegation of Athenians who had come to congratulate him on his victories. Later, in 278 B.C., the wandering Gauls conquered and settled in this section of Asia Minor, hence, the name, Galatia. Then came the Romans. It was on the plains of Ankara that Mithridates the Greek, King of the Pontus, was decisively defeated by Pompey in a memorable battle. The Romans made Ankara one of their provincial capitals and built many things in the city -a hippodrome, baths, temples, aqueducts- whose magnificence, it is said,

Plate 41: The Approach to Ankara *Kalesi* (Fortress)[77]

[77] LC Catalogue #: DLC/PP 1994: 064.

were not exceeded even in Rome. The city abounds in fragments of their ruins and the Nationalist government plans a museum in which they may be collected. One of the most striking of the ruins of Roman Ankara is the lone 'Column of Augustus' which stands near the present National Assembly buildings, and is now crowned with the immense nest of a stork. The walls of the city, which have been destroyed and rebuilt many times, contain many blocks of marble, sculptured or bearing inscriptions in Greek and Latin which rehearse the ancient history of the fortress.

Later, Ankara was ravaged successively by the Persians, the Arabs and the Seljuk Turks. The last named lost the city to the Crusaders under Godfrey de Bouillon who occupied the citadel for eighteen years. Then Ghengis Khan swept through Asia Minor, leaving Ankara under the control of his brother, Hulagu Khan. It is at this strategic point that the Ottoman Turks in 1260 started their victorious career by aiding the Seljuks to inflict a crushing blow on Hulagu Khan. Nearly a century and a half after the Mongols, this time under the mighty Timur, obtained their revenge on the plains of Ankara by the decisive battle in which the Ottoman forces were overwhelmed and their sultan, Bayezid I, was taken prisoner. After the death of Timur, Ankara once more passes into the hands of the Ottoman Turks who have held it ever since, except for the temporary conquest of the city in the early nineteenth century by the Egyptians.

After a lapse of five centuries, Ankara is again playing a leading role in the history of the Ottoman Turks, a role, indeed, which is likely to prove to be the most important in its long record. For Ankara today, as the capital of the Turkish Nationalist government, is the new Mecca, not only of the Turks but also of Islam. The dominating sentiment in the East today is not religious but political. The peoples of Islam, living under foreign domination, have made the doctrines of self-determination and nationalism their own, and they look to Mustafa Kemal Paşa as their new prophet. Muslims everywhere are following with the keenest interest the success of the Ankara government. The Turks, despite the schisms in Islam, have the prestige of centuries of power in the East. It is but natural that Muslims should look to them for leadership and help. Delegations from all parts of the Islamic world come to Ankara to obtain aid in overthrowing the rule of foreigners in their countries and establishing their independence.

"*Send us an army of only twenty thousand men and we will drive the English from India,*" Indian Muslims have told the Turkish Nationalists. The Turks, however, have no intention of going on such a Nationalist Crusade. They laugh at the idea of the millions of Indians needing a few thousand Turks to liberate them.

"*Our progress too long has been held back by anxiety as to the political effect liberal reforms would have on our position in Islam. We want to see the other Muslim peoples have the right of self determination, but we are not in a position to fight their battles for them. We must have a durable peace ourselves.*" That is the point of view given to me by Nationalist leaders.

Mustafa Kemal Paşa, the latest conqueror of Muslim minds; in other ways, however, they are willing and anxious to help Muslim countries

In other ways, however, they are willing and anxious to help Muslim countries. At the request of the Emir of Afghanistan, Mustafa Kemal Paşa has sent a commission of Turkish officers to Cabul [Kabul] to reorganize the Afghan army on modern lines. The Arabs of Mesopotamia have asked him for a leader and he has sent them the Sheik of the Senussi. Of course, such actions are to the advantage of the Turks for they help keep the Allies occupied elsewhere and thus increase the chances of victory for the National Assembly government.

But it is especially to the Turks in İstanbul and in the zones occupied by the Greeks that Ankara has become a veritable Mecca. Ankara is filled with Turks from these districts, many of whom had never before penetrated so far into Asiatic Turkey. Every day of the three weeks in February which I passed in Ankara saw more of them arrive. Poets, artists, architects, writers, officers - young men on fire with enthusiasm for the new Turkey. They had left their comfortable homes in İstanbul and braved the hardships of a two-week's journey through the snow-covered mountains of Anatolia in order to help the movement for Turkish independence.

However, Ankara was not selected by the Turkish Nationalists for their temporary capital, because of its history but because of its central location and its rail connection with the Western Turko-Greek front. The choice has little else to recommend it. About one third of the city was burned during the war -the part situated on the Western slope of the butte- and none of this has been rebuilt. The burned portion included part of the Christian and part of the Turkish quarters of the city, and they accuse each other of having caused it. As likely as not, it was of accidental origin, for disastrous fires are all too common in Turkish cities. The general use of mangals is one cause of them. Another is the Turkish habit of leaving a small lamp burning all night in a bedroom. This curious custom, I was told, comes from the fear of the dark which Turkish children share with others the world over. The parents are so soft-hearted that they leave a lamp lit in the room. The Turks thus get into the habit of sleeping in a lighted room and even when they become mature, some of them, it seems, cannot sleep well in complete darkness.

Whatever caused the Ankara fire, the result is that the influx of people which has followed its being chosen as temporary capital, has made it almost impossible to obtain lodging. Another disadvantage of Ankara as the seat of a liberal government is that the city is so far from being progressive in spirit that the Nationalists continually poke fun at it. They play on the pronunciation of its name, calling it sometimes Engheri [*en geri*], which means 'most backward,' and sometimes Enkara [*en kara*] which means 'blackest.' The city has a population of about twenty five thousand and is the *vilâyet* or province of Ankara.

But to get back to our narrow-gauge train. A policeman met us upon our arrival and conducted us to the office of his chief, in the station which serves the standard-gauge railway running to Eski-shehr [Eskişehir]. It was with genuine pleasure, after my nine days of slow travel through the mountains, that I again saw a real railway, with real locomotives, passenger and freight cars. It was a return to civilization. In the station the chief, after a telephone conversation, told me to go to the city police office. The town is about half a mile from the station.

The city police seemed rather surprised that an American should have arrived in the city and appeared somewhat suspicious of me. After they had telephoned to the Commissariat of the Interior and verified my pass their manner changed, and they said they would try to find me a room. The best they could do was to get me a little cubbyhole in the Liberty Hotel. The room was only large enough to hold two single beds with a narrow passageway between them. It faced the North and most of that wall was taken up by two windows containing several broken panes.

Our stay at Constitution Hotel where a Greek woman kept all keys

A few days later I was lucky enough to get a room in the Constitution Hotel, the best hotel in town [**Plate 42**]. It was slightly larger and afforded a little more protection from the wind. The window in this room was also badly in need of repair. Glass was hard to obtain and so I made the best of it and on windy days and nights I kept a rug hung over the window.[78] Had that room been a yacht we could have competed with Sir Thomas Lipton,[79] I believe, for the wind kept the heavy rug bellied out like a sail. Despite this protection the snow would sift through and fall upon our beds on stormy nights. For heat we had two mangals and kept our hands warm part of the time by hovering over them [**Plate 43**].

[78] **Note**: This footnote is taken from Streit's revised 1982 manuscript [HWL]. This was my first purchase of an Oriental rug. Later we bought many Persian rugs from Mehmed Ali and his brothers, who were rug dealers based in Constantinople, with a branch in New York City. Over the years, the rugs have made homes of the furnished apartments in the cities (Rome,

Plate 42: Ankara's Taşhan[80]

The first newspaper I saw contained a warning against the Spanish influenza, which had broken out in the city. I contracted a cold almost immediately which soon developed into a bad attack of ordinary grippe. Fortunately, the weather then became warmer for a few days and I recovered without difficulty. My feet were almost frozen the first two days in the automobile and they became numb at the slightest drop in the temperature thereafter. Usually I slept in this well-ventilated Ankara room not only with my clothes on but also with a sweater and an extra pair of woolen socks.

Plate 43: Mehmed Mehmedoff Huddled Next to the Mangal[81]

My room was in the han part of the hotel, which, it must be said, was much more badly furnished than what was called the 'hotel' section [**Plate 44**]. The Turkish hans I have seen are all built on the same model - square, with an open courtyard in the center and an open veranda running around the second story where the rooms are.

Constantinople, Paris, Vienna, New York and now Washington, D.C.) in which my family and I have lived during my career as a journalist [CKS].

79 **Note**: Sir Thomas Lipton (1848-1931). Scottish merchant, creator of the Lipton tea brand and yachtsman (sailor) [HWL].

80 LC Catalogue #: DLC/PP 1994: 064 [Red Album: Turkey, 1920-1921 by C. K. Streit].

81 LC Catalogue #: DLC/PP 1994: 064 [Red Album: Turkey, 1920-1921 by C. K. Streit].

Plate 44: The 'Han' Part of the Constitution Hotel[82]

The ground floor is used as a stable. Cheap padlocks served to lock all the doors in our han, and as the same key fitted them all, the guests had no keys to their rooms.

The Greek woman servant, whose room was next to mine and only two doors removed from that of Hazim Bey [Ebu Bekir Hâzım],[83] ex-Minister of the Interior in the İstanbul cabinet, kept the key and whenever any of us wanted to enter our room we would first have to find her. At all hours of the day and night the courtyard rang with cries of "*Madame*! *Madame*!" the term by which she was addressed.

Note: Streit's arrival in Ankara was noted by the *Anadolu Ajans* (Anatolian Agency), the official press office of the Nationalist government in the French version of their Daily Bulletin No. 64, of February 14, 1921, with the following item:

Agence D'Anatolie Angora le 14 février 1921
No. 64 Un journaliste Américain a Angora

Angora 13 février 1921 - Mr. Clarence K. Streit, correspondant de The Public And Ledger Syndicate de Philadelphia est arrive à Angora via Samsun. Mr. Clarence renseignera la presse Américaine, sur la vraie sitnation d' Anatolie. L' Agence d'Anatolie souhaite la bienvenue à Mr. Clarence et un plein et loyal success dans la tâche delicate qu'il s'est chargé

Anatolian Agency, Ankara, February 14, 1921. No. 64: An American Journalist in Ankara.

Mr. Clarence K. Streit, a correspondent of the Public Ledger and Syndicate of Philadelphia has arrived in Ankara via Samsun. Mr. Clarence will inform the American press about the actual situation in Anatolia. The Anatolian Agency extends its welcome to Mr. Clarence and wishes him success in honestly fulfilling the delicate task with which he is charged[84] [HWL].

---

[82] LC Catalogue #: DLC/PP 1994: 064 [Red Album: Turkey, 1920-1921 by C. K. Streit].

[83] **Note**: Ebu Bekir Hâzım [Tepeyran] Bey (1864-1947), who served as the Ottoman Minister of the Interior, from February 8 - April 8, 1920 [HWL].

[84] LC: Streit Papers II: 75 - Folder 2.

Turks ask for accuracy only, not praise; never did I see a Turk treat a woman without respect

It will be seen from these facts that the Turkish authorities made no special effort to prejudice me in their favor by looking after my physical welfare. It was quite different while I was in Athens when King Constantine[85] returned to his throne. There the Greeks made every attempt to gain the favor of the correspondents by entertaining them. We received so many invitations to teas, banquets, concerts, theaters, automobile rides and sightseeing trips that had we accepted them all little time would have been left to find out what was going on in the city. Except later when I was at Eskişehir, the Turkish officials, during my stay in Asia Minor, and particularly in Ankara, left me free to do as I pleased. They were very cordial to me, however, and gave me whatever help they could when I asked them for it. Their attitude pleased me for I did not want my tour to be a personally conducted one. Another thing which struck me was the modest, not to say humble, spirit which many of the Turks with whom I talked displayed. All they ever asked me to do was to report just what I had seen [**Plate 45**].

In this connection some notes I took of a conversation I had with a Turkish lieutenant and four civilians in an Armenian restaurant in Ankara will be of interest. When they heard that I was an American correspondent they appeared pleased. All the Turks I met seemed glad that a foreign correspondent had come to see what was going on in their country, especially one from America, for they trust us to give them a square deal. They complained of the distorted news the world was getting of the situation in Turkey. One of them said that their government was at fault in not having made any effort to counteract

Plate 45: Ankara Street Scene[86]

[85] **Note**: Constantine I. (1868-1923), King of the Hellenes from 1913-1917 and again from 1920-1922. Forced to abdicate by a Greek military revolt in the wake of the defeat at the Battle of the Sakarya (September 18, 1921) [HWL].

[86] LC Catalogue #: DLC/PP 1994: 064 [Red Album: Turkey, 1920-1921 by C. K. Streit].

hostile propaganda abroad. Another replied that they needed all the money they had now for their army.

When I mentioned my experiences with the peasants they were genuinely pleased. Said one, "*That's just what we would wish a correspondent to do - and what we would expect from an American. Other correspondents pay no attention to the common people but get most of their information from officials.*"

"*We don't want you to praise us, but we want you to describe things just as you saw them - not more nor less than that,*" another said.

I asked them what they thought of the project of sending Halide Edib Hanım, the famous Turkish authoress and feminist leader, as ambassador to the United States. They were strongly in favor of it, for "*the very fact that she was named for the position would help dispel some of the false ideas held about us.*"

"*Is Mr. Correspondent married?*" one of them asked Mehmed Ali. When told that I was not, he said that it was a pity for that made it more difficult for me to become acquainted with Turkish women. "*You would find that our women are more cultured and more advanced intellectually than are we men,*" he said with pride. I remarked that I was engaged. The young officer immediately was interested and sympathetic and said, "*Then your mind isn't at peace.*"

"*You seem to speak from experience,*" I replied. "*Perhaps you too are engaged?*"

"*Something like that,*" he said with a smile.

"*You can do better work while you are single than you can after you are married,*" declared the oldest of the civilians, and smiling he added, "*I, too, speak from experience.*"

"*No, it's just the contrary,*" the officer replied. "*His mind won't be elsewhere, then.*"

"*At any rate,*" said the older civilian, "*if you come back to Turkey sometime after you are married, through your wife you will be able to meet our women and know them better.*"

"*Oh, it will be much better to have your wife with you,*" the officer added, sympathetically. "*Your mind will be at peace then.*"

The insight I got to the romantic side of Turkish character goes far to disprove the legend of the 'terrible Turk,' and to confirm Dr. Pomeroy's statement that the Turks treated their women better than did the Christians of the country. Time and again I encountered the poetic attitude toward love which the Çorum hotel boy had expressed. Love lyrics were as popular in the theaters of Ankara as in the old coffee houses in Çorum. The song which received the most applause and was encored again and again by the soldiers each time it was sung, told of a girl's longing for her sweetheart who was in the Nationalist army. Not once did I see a Turk treat a woman, whether she was Muslim or Christian, and no matter what was her station in life, with anything but respect. I noticed in the caravans I met in my travels that if there were not enough horses or donkeys for every-one, the women nearly always rode and the men walked.

But to return to my conversation with the five Turks, they made the usual complaint that the European Powers would never leave them in peace and give them time to develop their country. They were always engaged in wars. They wanted America to extend them a helping hand - but America was so far away. There was so much to be done in Turkey. They needed machinery. They needed experts from America to teach them how to farm scientifically. Even as it was, the soil was very productive.

"*Yes, the soil of the old Empire is very fertile - so many Turks are buried in it,*" the young officer interjected bitterly.

Turkey, indeed, struck me as preeminently a land of cemeteries. Not only has each village a large one, but in some cases the cemeteries have outlived their villages. In approaching almost any large Turkish town one must first pass through acres and acres of graves, for the cemeteries usually lie unfenced around the town. This is especially true of Ankara. The butte is nearly encircled with its ever-increasing graveyard.

What gives these cemeteries a peculiarly desolate appearance is that most of the graves are anonymous, being marked only by an ordinary slab of stone, such as one might pick up anywhere and which bears no inscription whatever. There are some graves with marble slabs, sometimes surmounted by a stone fez or turban, which bears inscriptions but they are in the minority. The cemeteries are almost always in a dilapidated condition, the stones leaning in all directions. Little attempt, apparently, is made to look after the graves. These characteristics of the Turkish graveyard, as I understand it, are due to the teachings of Muhammed who told his followers that they should pay attention to the living and not to the dead, and that the grave of a man should be obliterated sixty or seventy years after his death. Exception, however, was made for saints and heroes.

I AM THE ONLY AMERICAN AND FIRST WESTERN NEWSMAN TO BE HERE IN NINE MONTHS

I found that I was the only American in Ankara and the first foreign correspondent to reach the city in nine months. Larry Rue, a correspondent of the ***Chicago* [*Daily*] *Tribune***, had been in Ankara the previous April [1920] when the assembly was opened,[87] but no one had come since its government had become established. As late as July last year the Nationalists were fighting against reactionary insurrections within eight miles of their capital.

I was not, however, the only Westerner in the city as Dr. Vincenzo Fago, formerly of the Italian Foreign Office, and Signor Luigi Epifani of the Italian Colonial service had arrived the same day that I did, on a commercial mission. Later I was surprised to find that the director of the Imperial Ottoman bank in the city was an Italian, two of the inspectors were French and one was English. I also met a German woman, the wife of a Turkish official in the Commissariat of Finances. She had not adopted the Turkish costume and wore the only European hat I saw in six weeks. A number of the Turks in İstanbul, I might add, have French wives and one, at least, is married to an American.

ONLY TWO AMBASSADORS IN ANKARA – ONE FOR BOLSHEVIK MOSCOW, ONE FOR MENSHEVIK GEORGIA – BROTHERS WHO DO NOT SPEAK TO EACH OTHER

This woman was the only German I found in Turkey except for the bookkeeper in the Bolshevik Embassy. The Turks, in general, dislike the Germans as a result of the domineering attitude of German officers and soldiers in the country during the war. I do not believe there is any possibility of the Germans regaining their place of influence with the Turks.

[87] **Note**: Streit is clearly confused on this point. The only **Chicago *Daily Tribune*** journalist who interviewed Mustafa Kemal Paşa in 1920 (the interview took place on April 26, 1920 and it was published on May 10, 1920), was Paul Williams. He filed a total of six dispatches from Ankara: a) the interview itself, called: *Wilson's 14 Points Or War - Kemal Pasha*. ***Chicago Daily Tribune***. Chicago, Ill.: May 4, 1920. p. 3 [See: **Appendix III.**, pp. 189-192 for the full text of this story]; b) *Kemal Unmasks London Squeeze Play on Turkey: Nationalist Chief Evaded Trap*. ***Chicago Daily Tribune***. Chicago, Ill.: May 8, 1920. p. 3; c) *Kemal's Fear of Allies' Aims Like Prophecy*. ***Chicago Daily Tribune***. Chicago, Ill.: May 12, 1920. p. 10; d) *Secret Treaty Forced Turks to War - Kemal: Says Allies Had Pledged Porte to Russia*, ***Chicago Daily Tribune***. Chicago, Ill.: May 13, 1920. p. 7; e) *Turk Victims of Stage Setting, Kemal Charges: Says Allies Show Them in Worst Light*. ***Chicago Daily Tribune***. Chicago, Ill.: May 15, 1920. p. 6; and, f) *Free Turkey or Dead Turkey is Hope of Kemal: Cuts Adrift from Porte for Heeding British*. ***Chicago Daily Tribune***. Chicago, Ill.: May 16, 1920. p. 4. Larry Rue, a second correspondent with the ***Chicago Daily Tribune*** was also reporting from Turkey in this period, but there is nothing in his dispatches (all of which were filed from Constantinople and Smyrna) indicating that he visited Ankara or that he met with Mustafa Kemal Paşa [HWL].

"*They came as friends - they left as enemies,*" many Turks told me. "*We were forced to sacrifice fifty Turkish villages at one time to protect two German colonies,*" one officer said. Dr. Alexander McLachlan,[88] President of the International College at Smyrna [İzmir], informed me that the Turks had started a secret movement even before the Armistice to expel the Germans. Frenchmen and Englishmen who had been prisoners of war in Turkey confirmed the impression I received of the bitter hostility of the Turks toward the Germans.

The two embassies, Bolshevik and Georgian, made up the rest of the foreign colony in Ankara. The diplomatic situation in the Turkish capital was probably unique in history, for the two ambassadors were brothers, and their countries were at war. Boudou Mdivani[89] [**Plate 46**] represented Soviet Russia, Simon Mdivani[90] [**Plate 47**] represented the Republic of Georgia. The Mdivani family is of Georgian origin and includes two other brothers who have followed Simon into the Menshevik camp.

Plates 46 & 47: Boudou Mdivani (left) & Simon Mdivani (right)[91]

[88] **Note**: Alexander McLachlan was a Canadian educator, who founded, in 1891, the 'American Boy's School' in Izmir. In 1936, the school was relocated to Beirut, Lebanon, where it became the Preparatory School for the American University of Beirut. Maternal grandfather of the American Turcologist, Howard A. Reed [HWL].

[89] **Note**: Polikarp (Budu) Mdivani (1877-1937): Bolshevik revolutionary and government official. Joining the Bolshevik faction of the Russian Social Democratic Party of Workers in 1903. Mdivani established himself as an active revolutionary operating in Tbilisi, Baku, Batumi and other towns. In 1918, he became a member of the Revolutionary Military Council of the 11th Army, which three years later invaded Georgia. With the start of Stalin's purges, Mdivani was expelled from the party in 1936 and later arrested and sentenced to execution that was carried out on 19 July 1937 [HWL].

[90] **Note**: Simon Mdivani was the Chairman of the Party of Social-Federalists, which participated in the short-lived Menshevik controlled Democratic Republic of Georgia (1918-1921). On February 25, 1921 the Bolshevik Red Army reoccupied the country and Georgia became a Soviet Republic. In March of 1921, the members of the parliament and government were forced to leave the country. The fate of Simon Mdivani is unknown [HWL].

[91] LC Catalogue #: DLC/PP 1994: 064 [Red Album: Turkey, 1920-1921 by C. K. Streit].

"I split from my brother in politics twenty five years ago," Boudou Mdivani told me, *"and time has only deepened the breach. Our mother never could understand how she could have given birth to such different sons,"* he recounted. *"How do you boys expect to settle the question of world peace,"* she would ask, when she found us raising the roof with our arguments, *"since you can't keep peace even in the family?"*[92]

War between Russia and Georgia broke out just before Boudou arrived in Ankara [**Plate 48**] and Simon did not go to meet his Red brother at the train. The two had not spoken to each other when I left the city.

The Bolshevik Embassy [**Plate 49**] added greatly to the variety of the foreign colony for its twenty five members included ten different nationalities - Russian,

Plate 48: Bolshevik Envoy Boudou Mdivani's[93] Arrival in Ankara[94]

---

92 **Note**: While visiting Eskişehir in January of 1921, Halide Edib encounters Simon Mdivani in a hotel dining room. He was traveling with Bekir Sami Bey. When Halide Edib enquired about Mdivani and his companions, she was told: *"It is the Georgian ambassador, the Menshevik. The New Bolshevik ambassador of the same name, Comrade Mdivani, is a brother of his, but they are like cat and dog. The soviets may invade Georgia any moment, and this one may lose his job"* Halide Edib: *The Turkish Ordeal.* New York (The Century Co.), 1928. p. 241 [Hereafter: Halide Edib, 1928] [HWL].

93 LC Catalogue #: DLC/PP 1994: 064.150. **Note:** On the back of this photo Streit wrote: *"Boudou Mdivani, special Bolshevik envoy to Angora, upon his arrival in the city. At his right is Hikmet Bey, Director of Political Affairs, in Ministry of Foreign Affairs. Soldiers wearing star on caps are Bolsheviks. Photo by Essad Nedim."* When the Bolshevik Envoy Boudou (Budu) Mdivani arrived in Ankara (accompanied by Red Army soldiers), he was greeted by [Yusuf] Hikmet [Bayur] Bey (1881-1980), Director

Plate 49: The Bolshevik Embassy in Ankara[95]

Polish, Swedish, German, Finnish, Georgian, Lithuanian, Azerbaijan, Turcoman and Turkish. It was the sort of legation one would expect from the Internationalist Republic [**Plate 50** following page]. A spirit of equality certainly reigned in the embassy. When I interviewed the ambassador, the Turkestan Turk, who was the office boy, sat in one chair smoking a cigarette, and he addressed Mdivani familiarly as "*comrade.*" In a picture of the members of the embassy, which I bought from a Turkish photographer, I noticed that the Russian girl who acted as cook was included, as were also the servants, a local Armenian woman and her two daughters. Polakov, the interpreter, was a very intelligent and likeable young man who had studied Oriental languages in the University of Moscow before the Revolution. He spoke English and French as well as Turkish and Persian. The interior walls of the embassy were lined with propaganda placards and photographs and over the building the red flag flew [**Plate 50**].

The Bolsheviks are also endeavoring to promote their trade relations with Turkey. They have a consulate at Trebizond [Trabzon], an agent at Samsun and a consul general at Ankara. The latter was Prince Chatopski who for twenty-five years was in the Czar's consular service in Asiatic Turkey. He was not a Bolshevik -he was the only member of the legation at Ankara who was not called 'comrade.' Naturally he wasn't called 'prince.' Plain 'Chatopski' sufficed for him in the minds of the Bolsheviks who had employed him as an expert and with whom he seemed to get along well enough.

---

of Political Affairs, in the Commissariat of Foreign Affairs, who was one of the few actual Communists in Ankara. Hikmet Bey, who following the 1934 Family Name Law took the surname of Bayur, was later to author the multi-volume *resmi tarihi* (official history) of the closing decades of the Ottoman Empire, published by the Turkish Historical Association. Somewhat paradoxically, this work is titled: *Türk İnkilap Tarihi* (History of the Turkish Revolution), the name generally used to refer to the Nationalist struggle. In 1921, Bayur was sharing a house in the village of Kalaba, several kilometers outside of Ankara, with Halide Edib Hanım, her husband Adnan [Adıvar] Bey, and Hamdullah Suphi [Tanrıöver] (another Bolshevik sympathizer). I say paradoxically, because Halide Edib was widely perceived to be the chief spokesperson for the pro-American element among the Nationalists in Ankara. See: Halide Edib, 1928: p. 201 [HWL].

94 **Note**: This photo was taken by Esat Nedim [Tengizman] (1897-1980). Many of Esat Nedim's unique photos of Mustafa Kemal Paşa and the Turkish War of Independence were destroyed in a 1979 fire at his home in the Çiçekçi quarter of Üsküdar (İstanbul). Esat Nedim participated in the Independence War as a supplementary officer, i.e., he was an officer of the 'Supreme Military Command Photography.' He was entrusted with this position in response to Mustafa Kemal's command: "*Let us bring a war photographer along on this life and death struggle. Find me such a person*" [HWL].

95 LC Catalogue #: DLC/PP 1994: 064.149. **Note**: On the back of this photo Streit wrote: "*Bolshevik Embassy Angora*" [HWL].

Plate 50: The Staff of the Bolshevik Embassy in Ankara[96]

---

[96] LC Catalogue #: DLC/PP 1994: 064.247f. **Note**: On the back of this photo (which Streit states he purchased from a Turkish photographer) [See: p. 61 above] he wrote extensive notes under the general heading of '*Bolshevik Embassy Angora.*' They include the following: **Front** (*left-right*) *Georgian woman - 4 Russian women* (*woman in white is Embassy cook*) *- 3 Armenians, woman and girls* (*Embassy servants*); **2nd** [**row**]: *2 Russians - Mehmedoff* (*Azerbaijani Turk*), *Military Attaché - Oupmal* (*Lithuanian, 1st Secretary*), *Swede, 2 Russians, Azerbaijani Turk, Russian*; **3rd** [**row**]: *Crimean Tatar, 2 Russians, German* (*Book-keeper*), *Russian*; **4th** [**row**]: *2 Russians* (*second is Polakov, Interpreter*), *Husni* [Hüsnü] (*Ottoman Turk, Commander Turk Battalion in Red Army*) - with cigarette in mouth, *Turkestan Turk, Russian*. [This appears to be a unique photo of Hüseyin Hüsnü [Alibeykov], a Turkish communist, who had been an Ottoman officer in the World War, during which time he had been held as a prisoner of war in Russia. In the winter of 1921 he is known to have been working in the Ankara Bolshevik Embassy as a 'translator.' See: Erdem Akbulut & Mete Tuncay: *Türkiye Halk İştirakiyun Fırkası* (*1920-1923*). İstanbul (Sosyal Tarih Yayınları), 2007. pp. 332-340]. Streit then added the following information: *Oupmal has since been replaced but others remain in Angora.* (*Cap with star is regular cap of Bolshevik army*). For Streit's handwritten note on back of this photo, see: **Appendix X.**, p. 235 [HWL].

The coffee house and the two theaters were the only places of recreation and amusement in the city. The former were usually well filled with men drinking tea or coffee, reading the two daily newspapers of the city or playing backgammon or cards. The Turks are a sober, almost puritanical people. There was not only no drunkenness, as I have already said, but there was no gambling and there were no street walkers, although there was a small restricted district. The quiet of the night was broken only by the tapping of the watchman's stick on the pavement as he made his rounds.

The only thing I saw in the theaters, to which the most fanatical puritan might object, was a very tame 'Oriental' dance given by an Armenian girl. In fact, it was nothing more than a 'shimmy.' The performances were usually of the vaudeville order and made up of songs, dances and farces. The singers, dancers and actors were atrociously bad, except the clown, who was rather amusing, despite the fact that most of his jokes were puns which I could not appreciate.

Hamlet in Turkish, an Effective Prince and a Very Realistic Grave Digging Scene

Of the many surprises I had while in Turkey none was greater than the one I got on the first of March, when I saw posters on the street announcing that the Anatolian Stage Society that night would present that "*monumental work of art,*" that "*most famous tragedy in the world*" - 'Hamlet.' One of the posters was illustrated with a large picture showing the play scene in the drama [**Plate 51**]. Knowing as I did the bitterness of some Turks toward the English I was rather astonished to see them make such a selection to celebrate this occasion -March 1st is the beginning of the New Year according to the old Turkish calendar- but the Turks assured me that art had no national boundaries.

Plate 51: Poster Advertising Performance of 'Hamlet'[97]

Hamlet drew a record crowd of soldiers and civilians to the National Theater that night. A military band furnished music and a monologist, entertainment, while the manager of the theater tinkered with the compressed air-oil lamps which had to be used for lighting as something had happened to the electrical installation.

The Turkish translator had followed Shakespeare faithfully, though he had combined a few of the scenes for the sake of brevity. Even then the play was not lacking in length. I remained until 2:00 a.m. when the last act was just beginning. The Anatolian Society suffered from an obvious lack of necessary props. But the actors at least wore appropriate costumes, which I had hardly expected to see. Hamlet was clad in the customary black. Kamal Raza [Kâmil Riza Bey],[98] a graduate of the Turkish Conservatory, played the role. He was far superior to

[97] LC Catalogue #: DLC/PP 1994: 064.247f.

[98] **Note**: So famous was Kâmil Riza Bey's performance as Othello the Moor, that he was known throughout Turkey as 'Otello Kâmil' ('Othello Kâmil'). The world-renowned Turkish Marxist poet, Nazim Hikmet (whose stay in Ankara overlapped that of Sreit's, also recorded his impressions of the theater where Streit watched the performance of Hamlet. In a piece titled '*Oyunlarım Üstüne*,' he wrote: "*In Ankara, in the Winter of 1921, in a run-down theater, housed in a converted stable, under the light of gas lamps, in weather so cold that every few seconds I had to blow on my hands, I saw Otello Kemal perform. For the first*

the other members of the troupe, the only other actor worthy of the name being the one who played the King. Kâmil Riza had an actor's face with great mobility of expression. He showed considerable histrionic ability. He indulged in a declamatory style at times but with all of his faults, his Hamlet was a living and noble character even to me. I could not understand the language he spoke. I was told that he had made a great success as the Moor in the Turkish translation of Othello, and I do not doubt but that he was more suited to that role.

Nothing could have been more solid and material than the ghost. He was clad in a long, light blue robe trimmed with ermine and wore a crown on his head. Except for his stiffness of movement his whitened face and Hamlet's shriek when he entered at the door, there was nothing to indicate that he was a ghost. However, when one considers that the Turks had scarcely more stage properties at their disposal than had the Elizabethans, one could not expect much in the way of illusion.

If the ghost was lacking in reality, the grave digging scene was real enough. As the stage was directly above the ground all that was necessary was the removal of a few planks to allow the gravediggers to do their work. And they had plenty of incentive to do it. It was very chilly in the theater which was heated by only two stoves, around which most of the audience crowded as the play wore on. The proprietor of the theater was extremely economical with his wood, so much so that one of the Turks beside me near the stove offered to pay for some fuel to keep the fire from going out. There was no stove at all on the stage or near it, and the actors were obviously suffering from the cold, though they endured it manfully. Greater devotion to dramatic art would be hard to find. The gravediggers had a chance to get warm with their shovels and, spurred by the chill of 2:00 a.m. -for such was the hour- they fell to with a will. They said their lines, but they did not let that interfere with their exercise. Judging from the huge mound of dirt which they heaved up on the stage, they dug a hole big enough to bury two men. And into this cold earth they placed the shivering corpse of Ophelia, and there the poor girl remained until the curtain ended the long scene between Hamlet and Laertes.

The play-within-a-play scene in the third act was given more effectively than I had expected. The tragedy as a whole dragged, and it suffered from the fact that some of the actors at times forgot their cues and the prompter had to ring a bell to bring them on the stage. I remember that the king saved the situation once. He was left alone on the stage with the queen, for Polonius had failed to appear. The royal couple tried to cover up his slowness by talking to each other, but finally the king lost patience and in a regal tone said, "*Isn't there anyone there? Send in Polonius.*" That worthy then entered, looking as if he had just got out of bed. One leg of his doublet was six inches higher than the other.

Horatio reminded me of a dime-novel sleuth. The women characters were perhaps the worst. The queen was Armenian; Ophelia, a Greek girl. All the other members of the troupe were Turkish. The barriers of custom and religion which have kept Turkish women from the stage are now breaking down. A Muslim actress was playing before the İstanbul public this spring for the first time in history.

It would not be fair, I must add, to judge the Turkish theater from what I saw of it in Ankara. As New York City is our theatrical center, İstanbul is even more that of Turkey. There, one can hear Turkish operas, operettas, tragedies and comedies and translations of foreign classics given by their best actors in appropriate stage settings. The Turks are great lovers of drama and poetry.

time in my life I saw a performance of Shakespeare" ("*Ankara'da 921 kışında, ahırdan bozma salaş bir tiyatroda, gaz lambalarının ışığında ve ikide bir soğuktan avuçlarıma hohlayarak Otello Kâmil'i seyrettim. Ömrümde ilk defa Şekspir'i seyrettim*"). While there is no way of determining whether Nazim Hikmet and Streit attended the same performance of Hamlet, the similarity of their descriptions, plus the fact that in an earlier passage Streit, in describing the influx of individuals coming from İstanbul to Ankara, had mentioned: "*Poets, artists, architects, writers, officers - young men on fire with enthusiasm for the new Turkey,*" [See: p. 53 above] raises the possibility that their paths might have crossed in Ankara [HWL].

Not knowing their language I cannot judge the merits of their work. But the fact that that they are not lacking in artistic temperament is evident from the grace and piquancy of the drawings which appear in such Turkish magazines as Umid [*Ümid*] in İstanbul. When one remembers the Alhambra and the other monuments of Islam's greatness, and when one sees the marvelous work done today on a small scale by Turkish craftsmen, one cannot but desire a regeneration of the artistic East. With a durable peace in Turkey, I believe that it is bound to come. In fact, it may have already begun. The religious dogmas, which prohibit pictures of living beings, are breaking down; and if the Turkish artist can do as well in portraiture as he does in geometrical tracery, the world will be enriched indeed.

The Nationalist government, beset as it is with war, is not now in a position to give much encouragement to art, other than the indirect aid of freeing the people from some of the teachings of Muhammed. The Prophet's prohibition of pictured images of living beings, however, served a good purpose in the past. It was directed against the worship of idols and fetishes, against the superstitions which filled the East. Christianity found an easier, if more dangerous road, in replacing idols with pictures and statues of the Christ and the Virgin Mary, and, in general, in giving a Christian halo to pagan festivals.

"*There is no God but God*," cried the Prophet of Islam. And by a rigid iconoclasm from the start he succeeded far better than the Christian preachers in fixing the attention of converts upon the abstract idea of a spiritual Deity. It was centuries later that the Protestants in the West took this step and denounced the use of pictures in the Church.

As I have already mentioned, the Nationalist government is planning a museum in which to house the ruins of Roman Agora. The small but pleasing building in which the National Assembly meets was completed last year by a Turkish architect, Ali Kazim Bey [Ali Kâzım Bey].[99] It is a good example of the Ottoman style of architecture. In addition, a literary magazine and a periodical devoted to drama have been started in Ankara.

The Turks have found time, too, to adopt our Arbor Day Custom. A 'Tree Association' has been formed under the patronage of Mustafa Kemal Paşa, the purpose of which is to teach the people, especially the school children, the love of trees. As many parts of Anatolia are completely deforested, the movement is not without a utilitarian end.

I INTERVIEW AND AM CHARMED BY THREE TURKISH GUERRILLA VETERANS, AGES 12, 13, 13[100]

Among the Turks I met while in Ankara, not the least interesting were Sergeant Osman [**Plate 52**], Towfik [Tevfik][**Plate 53**] and Djemal [Cemal]. I was sitting in the restaurant of Mehmed Inaayet [İnayet], a Greek who had become a Muslim some fifteen years ago, when Osman and Tevfik came swaggering in.

"*Ah, here come the brigands*!" İnayet's Armenian waiter whispered genially to me, and he went to attend upon them with exaggerated politeness. In truth, armed as they were with swords and automatic pistols they would have had the appearance of bandits had their physical stature been more imposing. For the two 'brigands'

[99] **Note**: The construction of this site began in 1915 as the clubhouse of the *İttihat ve Terakki Cemiyeti* (Union & Progress Party aka Young Turk Party). Its plans were drawn up by the architect Hasif Bey. Due to the war and the death of its young designer it remained unfinished. When it was decided to make the site the home of the Turkish Parliament on April 23, 1920, its construction became a priority. It served as the home of the *I. Türkiye Büyük Millet Meclisi* (First Grand National Assembly) between April 23, 1920 and October 15, 1924. I am unable to confirm Streit's attribution of its design to an architect named Ali Kâzım Bey [HWL].

[100] **Note**: One of the many unique aspects of Streit's account is the following description and photos he provides of this otherwise unknown aspect of the Turkish Nationalist struggle, i.e., the existence of boy soldiers among the Nationalist forces [HWL].

Plate 52: Boy Soldier: Sergeant Osman[101]

[101] LC Catalogue #: DLC/PP 1994: 064 [Red Album: Turkey, 1920-1921 by C. K. Streit].

Plate 53: Boy Soldier: Tevfik[102]

[102] LC Catalogue #: DLC/PP 1994: 064 [Red Album: Turkey, 1920-1921 by C. K. Streit].

were boys, thirteen years of age. They took themselves seriously and carried themselves like men. And they were not mere boys - they had been matured by experiences which many an adult has never had.

"*Who are these lads? Bandits, really?*" I asked İnayet.

"*Oh, yes,*" he said. "*They are orphans. They ran away and joined the brigands* [*çeteciler*] (*the name generally given to the irregular volunteer forces which the Nationalists had to rely upon at first*). *Until these irregulars were disbanded by the government a few months ago they were fighting at the front under Edhem Bey*[103] *against the Greeks. The bandits fought better than the regulars at first. The Greeks put a price on the head of Osman.*" [**Plate 52**]

I asked the boys to come to my table and have dessert. Osman wore a Laze [Laz] cap, an American army leather coat and leather-lined riding breeches and spurs. He was quiet, reserved, and dreamy. He had lost one eye [**Plate 52**]. Tevfik wore a gray uniform. He was talkative enough and gestured in a lively fashion as he told me of their experiences [**Plate 53**]. The boys had met just before the battle of Yeni Shehr [Yenişehir].

"*It was early in the morning; we were sitting around the camp fire eating simid* [*simit*] *(a kind of bread) and drinking milk,*" Tevfik said in describing the battle. "*All of a sudden they said, 'Here come the infidels!' There they were - galloping toward us on their horses. We grabbed our rifles and bang! bang! bang! we shot. Then we jumped on our horses to run away but we saw we were surrounded. Only nine of us escaped. Osman was wounded and then bayoneted by a Greek. One of my comrades was taken prisoner. I don't know whether he's alive or dead. If he's dead, may he rest in peace; if he's alive, may his ears ring!*"

The latter phrase is literally translated. To the Turks, who use it often, it means, "*May he hear my good wishes.*"

It was strange to hear a small boy talking of 'killing' as a commonplace, and denouncing the Greeks for "*raping our women.*" The two lads had taken part in the attacks the previous year on Brusa [Bursa] and on the Bosporus. Now Mustafa Kemal Paşa had taken them under his protection; they were attached to the president's bodyguard.

"*I had three rifles, French, Greek and Bulgarian makes,*" Tevfik told me. "*I gave the Bulgarian carbine to the Paşa*" (the word he used in common with other Turks in referring to Mustafa Kemal. Paşa is of Persian origin and means, literally, 'viceroy'.[104] The term can be translated as 'His Excellency'). *"If he will put it in his belt and take fifty cartridges with him, he can protect himself when he rides in his automobile,*" Tevfik suggested with boyish enthusiasm for fighting. He illustrated his remark by pointing an imaginary rifle around the room and saying, "*Bang! Bang!*"

The Paşa, fortunately, has need of no such protection. I have never seen him armed and the mental picture which Tevfik suggested of this able general in his civilian clothes of English cut, riding through the peaceful streets of Ankara with a rifle in his belt, was highly amusing. The more so because it was exactly the picture most Westerners would expect to see. His 'bodyguard' when it accompanied him - consisted of a couple of *aides-de-camp* who are unarmed

---

[103] **Note**: *Çerkez* (Circassian) Ethem (1886-1948) was a Turkish militia leader of Circassian irregulars in north western Anatolia. He had initially gained fame for fighting against the Allied powers invading Anatolia in the aftermath of the World War I and afterwards resisted the Greek advance in Anatolia. He was instrumental in putting down various rebellions against the authority of the Grand National Assembly of Turkey. Played a key role in the establishment of the Green Army, and refused to join his forces with the regular army established under the command of İsmet Paşa. His subsequent surrender to, and alleged co-operation with, the Greek army resulted in his citizenship being revoked on the grounds of treason and his being announced a *persona non grata* by the Grand National Assembly. After the War of Independence he settled in Jordan, where he died in 1948 [HWL].

[104] **Note**: Streit was misinformed on this point. Paşa is a Turkish word, which, at the time of his visit, was the highest title granted to civilian and military authorities [HWL].

as far as one can see. There are also Policemen stationed at the gates of his house. In view of the fears which the Turks have that some agent of the Greeks or of the Allies might attempt to assassinate him (While I was in Ankara an Indian, Moustapha Saghir [Mustafa Sagir],[105] was arrested. He confessed that he was a British spy and that his purpose was to kill the Paşa). It is surprising that the Paşa is not more closely guarded.

But Tevfik had lived the warrior's life which most small boys can only dream about, and the carrying of a high-powered rifle had become as natural to him as a toy-pistol to the youth of more settled countries. There had been three of them but the other, he said disdainfully, "*was a mere kid. They sent him to school.*"

I could not help but like the little devils, and I asked them to visit me the next day so that I could take their pictures. With a snappy military salute they left me. Only Tevfik, however, came; Osman was too shy. If Tevfik smoked a cigarette like a man, he showed a small boy's delight in the Swiss milk chocolate I bought for him in the city. A few days later he came back with another boy soldier - would I not take his picture, too?

The newcomer was Djemal [Cemal], aged twelve [**Plates 54 & 55**]. He came from Adrianople [Edirne]. His mother had been killed by the Bulgars in the Balkan Wars. His father had been killed in the World War and he had been placed in an orphanage in İstanbul. After the Allied occupation of the city he ran away to Ismid [İzmid], and there worked for a while with an English cook. He had picked up a few English and French words - "*Yes, good, one, bon, monsieur.*" He asked me to put some common English words in his notebook and for Mehmed Ali to add their Turkish equivalents so that he could learn more of my language. Cemal could read and write - Tevfik was illiterate. Cemal had come to Ankara from Eskişehir on his own accord to go to school, but he had not found what he wanted and was returning. He desired to be a mechanic.

"*Would you like to go to the United States to study?*" I asked. "*Oh, yes,*" and his face brightened. His father had once been to America on business. "*But do you teach Turkish there?*" he asked doubtfully and added another question, "*Is America with us and against the Greeks?*"

He had left İzmid to join the 'brigand' troops. He gave a vivid description of the Greek shrapnel, of the "*rat-tat-tat*" of their machine guns. The Greeks scalped the Turkish irregulars, he said, and he described how they did it. From a red ribbon a medal hung on his breast. On it was written in Turkish, "*Souvenir of Djemal* [Cemal] *Bey, Commander of the Green Flag Army.*"[106] The short sword with its sheath of inlaid silver which he wore in his belt had also been presented to him by Cemal Bey. He showed me a letter written by a Turkish regular officer which commended the lad to whomsoever he might meet: "*Though young in years,*" the paper said, "*he has fought like a man and deserves well of his countrymen. He has been twice wounded, once in the head and once in the left thigh.*"

Cemal took off his calpak [*kalpak*] and showed me the groove which a bullet had cut in the side of his skull. The other bullet had partly shattered his thighbone and had lodged in his flesh. A surgeon had removed it. Apparently his wounds no longer troubled him.

In a holster on his hip, he carried a loaded 38 Belgian automatic. His familiarity with guns was amazing in one with so boyish a face. He picked up my own automatic - an English make - carelessly flipping out the shells and without any instructions took it apart and put it together again. He was well satisfied by his critical examination of it and urged me to sell it to him [**Plate 54 & 55**].

[105] **Note**: Mustafa Sagir (b. 1877 - d. May 24, 1921), a native of India, who was arrested as a British agent in Ankara and accused of plotting the assassination of Mustafa Kemal Paşa. He was tried and sentenced to death by the Independence Tribunal (*İstiklal Mahkemesi*); executed in the *Karaoğlan Meydanı* (today: *Ulus Meydanı*) on May 24, 1921 [HWL].

[106] **Note**: The 'Green Army' which was disbanded on September 29, 1920, was a guerilla force whose adherents were a rather strange mixture of Islamists and Marxists. Among its supporters was the famous leader of the National Force guerillas in Western Anatolia, Çerkez Edhem. I have been unable to identify a Cemal Bey among its commanders [HWL].

Plate 54: Boy Soldier: Cemal[107]

[107] LC Catalogue #: DLC/PP 1994: 064.151 [Red Album: Turkey, 1920-1921 by C. K. Streit].

Plate 55: Boy Soldier: Cemal[108]

[108] LC Catalogue #: DLC/PP 1994: 064.151 [Red Album: Turkey, 1920-1921 by C. K. Streit].

The boys were greatly interested in my typewriter, and I showed them how it worked. I wrote 'Cemal' in capital letters with the machine, explaining how it was done and asked him to copy his name by comparing the written letters with those on the keyboard. Cemal began with an 'L' and I then remembered that Turkish is written from right to left instead of left to right.[109] I told him that he would have to begin at the left. It was a puzzle for him, but the quickness with which he grasped the idea and found the right letters in an alphabet which was entirely strange to him spoke well for his native intelligence. Tevfik, who knew no alphabet, was slower-witted and confused the 'E' and the 'F,' the 'W' and the 'M,' and Cemal had to come to his help. To appreciate the difficulty of the feat, imagine an American boy who had never seen a typewriter called upon to copy the Chinese characters for his name.

Cemal was such a bright, manly little chap that he won my heart at once. Whoever had the good fortune of giving him or Tevfik an education and a chance in life would be amply rewarded. The lads have seen life but it has not spoiled them. There is a strange sober dignity and restraint about them. They are grown men in some ways, yet at heart, they are still little boys.

Children are much the same the world over, it seems. On warm days I saw little Turkish girls and boys skipping rope together in the streets of Ankara [**Plate 56**]. I saw the boys playing marbles. They had no 'glassies;' they had no 'potteries' (marbles made of clay) even. They used the vertebrae of sheep as substitutes[110] [**Plate 57**].

Plate 56: School Children Playing in the Streets of Ankara[111]

[109] **Note**: This footnote is taken from Streit's revised 1982 manuscript [HWL]. Not until 1928 was the Latin alphabet substituted for Arabic script [CKS].)

[110] **Note**: In Turkey the children's game of 'knucklebones' is called: *aşık atmak* [HWL].

[111] LC Catalogue #: DLC/PP 1994: 064 [Red Album: Turkey, 1920-1921 by C. K. Streit].

Plate 57: Boys Playing Marbles in the Streets of Ankara[112]

Beginning of a long friendship with Ahmed Chukri [Ahmet Şükrü] Bey; Dutch correspondent George Nypels shares my view of the Turks and new government; I see a good omen for it in the crescent moon and stars

In İstanbul bowling is popular among the Turks, and they have several soccer clubs. I have seen accounts of games they have played with Armenian and Greek teams in the city. The encouragement of sports in the Near East will do much to bring peace to that unfortunate region. The Turks are now publishing in İstanbul a weekly illustrated sports magazine, ***Spor Alemi*** (The Athletic World).

Soccer is slowly penetrating the provinces of Anatolia. Ahmed Chukri [Ahmet Şükrü],[113] a student in the Ankara high school, wanted to get a soccer ball so that he could introduce the game there. He had studied for a short time at Robert College, the American institution in İstanbul, and could speak French and a little English. He had served in the army during the war, though he was then only sixteen years old. One of his legs had been amputated below the knee as the result of a wound. Despite all my protests he insisted upon giving me a ribbon with which he had been decorated for bravery by Enver Paşa. His calling card was curiously decorated with a moonlit scene drawn in colors. The children are taught in the schools to make these sketches and to draw similar designs on their stationery.

I remained in Ankara nearly a month. During that time I attended several sessions of the National Assembly and talked with nearly all the Nationalist leaders and

[112] LC Catalogue #: DLC/PP 1994: 064.51. **Note**: Streit simply wrote '*Angora*' on the back of this photo. It appears to have been taken in the Ulus district of the city, as the mosque in the background is the: *Hacı Bayram Câmii* [HWL].

[113] **Note**: This footnote is taken from Streit's revised 1982 manuscript [HWL]. Ahmet Sukru [Şükrü] became a long-time friend and is now a university professor in Ankara. He adopted the family name of Esmer when the Turkish republic began requiring the use of surnames. He was a delegate to the 1962 Atlantic Union Conference in Paris and for years has been an ardent Atlantic Federalist. [CKS]

Cabinet members and also with Izzet Pasha [İzzet Paşa] and Salih Pasha [Salih Paşa],[114] the two ex-Grand Viziers of Turkey who headed a mission sent from İstanbul with the hopeless task of trying to reunite Ankara with the Sultan's government [**Plate 58**].

Despite the formal prohibition of English, I obtained permission to send letters and telegrams in that language to the outside world, through the good offices of Halide Edib Hanım, who was very pro-American. She acted as censor for me, though only twice did she cut out anything I wrote. My dispatches were sent by telegraph to the Black Sea port, Zungouldak [Zonguldak], and from there by boat to İstanbul. None of them arrived there in less than three weeks - a striking illustration of the extent that Ankara was then cut off from the rest of the world. In normal times a telegram takes only a few hours to go from Ankara to İstanbul.

A few days before I left Ankara, the foreign press service in the city was doubled by the arrival of Mr. George Nypels, the well-known special correspondent of the

Plate 58: The Sultan's Emissaries to the Ankara Nationalists (The Ex-Grand Viziers Salih Paşa & İzzet Paşa in the middle of the photo)[115]

[114] **Note**: Salih Hulusi [Kezrak] Paşa (1864-1939). In 1919 he served as Minister of the Navy in both the Ferit Paşa and Ali Rıza Paşa cabinets. In 1920 he served for twenty-five days as Grand Vezir. In 1920-1921 he spent three months in Ankara negotiating with the Nationalist government [HWL].

[115] LC Catalogue #: DLC/PP 1994: 064. **Note**: Streit identifies four of the five individuals in this photo as (starting with second from left): 1) Hoja Fatin Effendi, 2) Salih Paşa, 3) İzzet Paşa & 4) Djevad Bey [HWL].

Amsterdam Algemeen Handelsblad.[116] **[Plate 59]** He came by way of Adalia [Antalya] and left by the same route. We had a good laugh together at the expense of his consul in İzmir who had objected to giving him a visa for Ankara on the ground that he did not want to take the responsibility of allowing Dutch citizens to enter the territory of that "*government of brigands.*"

We both had found the situation in Nationalist Turkey far better than the Occident imagined and even the people on the shores of the Levant imagined it to be. Mr. Nypels was as favorably impressed as I by the Nationalist government. In a letter from which I have at hand he remarks: "*The Turks had and have my full sympathy and I recognize their splendid qualities. They are by all means a hundred times nobler and finer and better than all the Levantines they live with - the Armenians, Greeks and what we call the Europeans of the East.*"

Plate 59: Clarence Streit (left) & George Nypels (right) in Ankara[117]

---

[116] **Note**: Interestingly, Nypels was not afforded the same gracious access in Ankara which had been accorded Streit. See: Alexander H. De Groot: *The Netherlands & Turkey: Four Hundred Years of Political, Economical, Social and Cultural Relations.* İstanbul (The ISIS Press), 2009. In particular: pp. 186-194. Nypels himself contrasts his treatment with that given Streit (attributable in part to Nypel's having shown up in Ankara without an authorized travel permit and in part to suspicion on the part of the Nationalists that he was collaborating with the recently arrested Mustafa Sagir); and his 'reception' is reflected in his portrayal of Mustafa Kemal (based on having watched Mustafa Kemal at a session of Parliament he attended, and an interview he later obtained). He describes Mustafa Kemal Paşa as: "*a small man with a hard cold face and unpleasantly piercing eyes, without any beauty of face or attitude, wearing a kalpak and sport coat...*" The less than warm welcome he received at the hands of Mustafa Kemal also led him to refer to him as: "*a neurasthenic* (one suffering from chronic fatigue) *of 40 years old,*" although he did grudgingly concede that he was: "*as well an admirable soldier and statesman.*" While, as Streit writes, Nypels was clearly impressed with the Turkish people and the efforts of the Nationalist Government, he clearly did not share Streit's overwhelmingly positive impression of its leader [HWL].

[117] LC Catalogue #: DLC/PP 1994: 064.184. **Note**: On the back of this photo Streit wrote: "*Mr. George Nypels, Correspondent of the **Amsterdam Algemeen Handelsblad** (right); Author (left) Angora*" [HWL].

CHAPTER V

THE GOVERNMENT OF THE GRAND NATIONAL ASSEMBLY

CHAPTER V

THE GOVERNMENT OF THE GRAND NATIONAL ASSEMBLY

Plate 60: The Newly Completed Building of the Grand National Assembly[118]

The Government of the Grand National Assembly

Note: The parliamentary headquarters [**Plate 60**] were described by Streit as: "*the small but pleasing building in which the National Assembly meets was completed last year by a Turkish architect, Ali Kazim Bey. It is a good example of the Ottoman style of architecture.*"

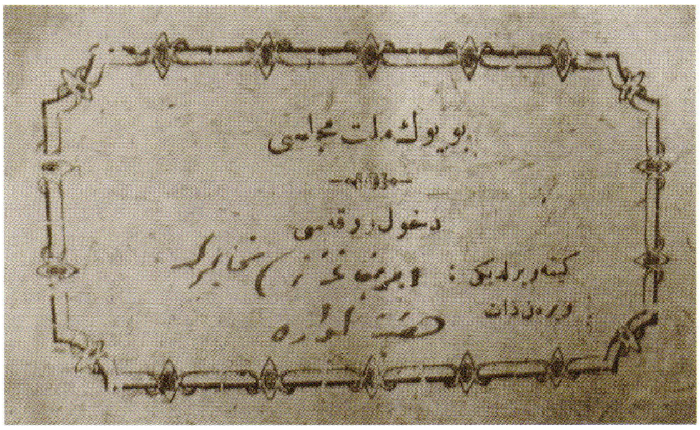

Plate 61: Streit's Press Pass for the Grand National Assembly[119]

Streit was issued a 'Press Pass'(*Duhul Fırkası*) [**Plate 61**] which allowed him to observe the workings of the Turkish parliament and availed himself of this privilege on several occasions during his three week stay in Ankara. The 'Press Pass' was issued by the Executive Board (*Heyet-i İdare*) of the *Büyük Millet Meclisi* (Grand National Assembly) and authorized the *Amerikan Gazetesi Muhabiri* (American Newspaper Journalist) to enter the newly built parliament while it was in session [HWL].

[118] LC Catalogue #: DLC/PP 1994: 064.198. **Note**: On the back of this photo Streit wrote: "*Where the Great National Assembly of Turkey meets in Angora. Built by the Nationalists. Osmanli style architecture. Note electric lights and telephone wires, foreground, installed by Nationalists*" [HWL].

[119] LC Catalogue #: DLC/PP 1994: 064. Album.

A unique wartime democracy

"*Solve your problems by meeting together and discussing them.*" [*Qur'an*]

Behind the speaker's chair in the hall where the Grand National Assembly of Turkey meets in Ankara this advice, which Muhammed gave his followers, is displayed in letters wrought in silver. It indicates at once the way in which the Nationalist leaders are emphasizing the liberal doctrines of Islam and the democratic spirit which brought the assembly into existence and has guided its labors. The success which has attended its application has done more than anything else to convince the Turks, accustomed for centuries to despotic rule, of its wisdom.

The Turkish Assembly constitutes one of the most interesting and extraordinary examples of representative government in the world. It is unique, I know of no other such body which can be compared to it. Legally, all power, executive as well as legislative, is vested in the Assembly. What is more remarkable is that in practice, despite the wars in which Turkey is engaged, it really wields this power. Moreover, it exercises the functions of the Caliph as it does those of the Sultan. The supreme authority in Turkey today is concentrated in its one chamber.

The West has not only failed to give diplomatic recognition to the government of the Grand National Assembly, but has ignored its very existence. The Occident has looked upon Mustafa Kemal Paşa as a 'dictator,' who considers himself to be the government of Turkey. It calls the Nationalists 'Kemalists.' It refers to a member of the Nationalist cabinet as 'Mustafa Kemal's minister.' But the truth is that if Mustafa Kemal Paşa can be called a dictator it is because he dictated - or rather, used his tremendous personal influence to establish- democratic government in Turkey. Many of the Nationalist leaders thought that he should be a dictator temporarily, while war was going on and while chaos reigned throughout Anatolia. As it is, he is simply a deputy chosen by the voters of Erzurum (a city in Eastern Anatolia) who has been elected by his fellow Deputies as President of their assembly. He has not our President's power to veto; he must sign the laws it passes. How this came about is of more than passing interest.

When the Allies occupied İstanbul, Mustafa Kemal Paşa immediately called for the election of a Grand National Assembly. Turkey was divided into fifty-four electoral districts, each of which was entitled to send five Deputies to the Assembly, making a total of 270. Men above the age of thirty, regardless of their race or religion, were free to vote for electors who in turn met and selected the Deputies from their district. The great majority of the Ottoman Christians refrained from voting, following the advice of their leaders who were hoping to establish independent government. Nor did some of the 'Old Turks,' who were not in sympathy with the Nationalist movement and had no confidence in its success, exercise their suffrage. The Deputies, as in England, did not have to reside in the districts they represented, though they actually do in the majority of cases. Sixty-eight members of the Parliament at İstanbul who had escaped to Asia Minor were recognized as members of the new Assembly. So, too, were twelve others who were held prisoners in Malta by the British. Many of them represented the zones occupied by the enemy. Mustafa Kemal Paşa had been elected to the İstanbul Parliament but voluntarily resigned and was reelected to the Assembly.

How President Mustafa Kemal 'dictated' democracy in 1920

The new government was inaugurated on April 23, 1920, when these 338 Deputies assembled in Ankara. Mustafa Kemal Paşa opened the session with a long speech in which he gave the Deputies in detailed and documentary form the history of the Nationalist movement and of his negotiations with the Sultan's government at İstanbul. Then he addressed the question of the powers of the Assembly itself. I shall quote his own words:

> Now I shall outline the line of organization which our Assembly should follow. It will control the destinies of the nation not only through

legislation, but it will actually administer its affairs. All nations in extraordinary circumstances accept one of these alternatives: They either suspend the legislative body, and give full power to the executive branch of the government, or they act by consulting the whole nation. We are of the opinion that, with our religion of Islam, which gives full freedom for discussion, the latter course is the better, and therefore we wish to see the whole nation administer its own will.

After the acceptance of this principle, your body will provide for a division of labor by electing Commissars from your number to carry on the work of the different executive departments who will be, individually and as a unit, responsible to the whole Assembly. The gentleman who presides over your Assembly will also be president of the Commissars. He will have to accept and enforce the decisions of your body and will be responsible to it.

He then referred to the presidential form of government and continued:

Our studies show that there may be danger for us in this system. The Ottoman government, unlike others, is not merely a temporal power. The head of our government is also the head of Islam. Therefore, we cannot recognize any one man as the head of this government nor can we even replace the Sultan by a regency at Ankara. Moreover, it is disastrous to create a chief executive who is irresponsible. In Islam which holds even the Caliph responsible such a thing cannot exist.

Therefore we are obliged to recognize this power to be vested in your Assembly which represents the will of the nation and which alone has the power to act on its own responsibility in behalf of the nation. For, since you have been elected with full powers, it is evident that the nation itself accepts this principle and has entrusted its destinies to you. Your Assembly, then, is gathered not only to make laws and control the affairs of an executive body, but it has also the duty of exercising the executive functions. Therefore, no power exists today in Turkey which is superior to you.

Such are the fundamental principles which I suggest, in view of the costly experiences we have had in the past, that we adopt in organizing our government and in carrying on our national affairs and our wars in these troublous and most difficult days. Naturally, the decision rests with you.

This speech is sufficient to give Mustafa Kemal Paşa a unique distinction among the statesmen of today. The presidents and premiers of Western countries, which pride themselves on their democratic traditions, demanded absolute powers when their nations were involved in the World War. But the leader of the Turks, whose government had long been an example of despotism, not only rejected the dictatorial powers which were within his grasp, but also used the very gravity of the crisis which confronted Turkey to establish its government on a basis more democratic than that of any Occidental power, even in times of peace.

The Constitution of the National Government

The principles advocated by Mustafa Kemal Paşa were adopted by the Assembly. The first words in the constitution which it drew up are: "*Sovereignty is vested unconditionally in the nation.*" It goes on to state that executive and legislative power is centralized in the Grand National Assembly, and that the basic principle of the government is the active and personal control by the people of the affairs of their country. Article VII reserves for the Assembly the power to conclude treaties, sign peace and make war, and turns over to it the enforcement of the Sherii [*Şeriat*] Holy Law. Both the Sultanate and the Caliphate are ignored in this fundamental law of the new Turkey, neither office being even mentioned. Among other things, the Assembly has taken over the Sultan's traditional prerogative of conferring upon military officers above the rank of brigadier general the title of Paşa.

The executive branch of the government is divided into ten departments or Commissariats; National Defense, Foreign Affairs, Interior, Public Instruction, Public Economy (including agriculture, commerce, forests and mines), Justice, Public Health, Finances, Public Works and Religious Affairs. The Assembly administers each of these departments through a Commissar which it selects from its membership. In carrying out his executive duties the Commissar is required to follow the directions drawn up by the Assembly. The Commissars elect one of their body as 'President of the Council of Commissars.' This official is little more than the presiding officer at cabinet meetings. He has not the power of a Western premier. He does not form the cabinet, nor is he responsible for it. Each Commissar is directly responsible to the Assembly. Of course, the Assembly, if it wishes, can dismiss the whole cabinet, but so far this has never been done. It has, however, frequently exercised its power of control by recalling individual Commissars.

At first the Commissars were nominated and elected by the Assembly. But it soon became evident that it was impossible to obtain in such a way a harmonious and efficient cabinet. After several Commissars had been removed from office it was decided to have Mustafa Kemal Paşa, as President of the Assembly, nominate two candidates when there was a vacancy in the cabinet, and this system has been followed since then. If neither candidate receives a sufficient majority in the Assembly, the president nominates others until one is found who has the confidence of the Deputies. The voting is by secret ballot.

The Assembly exercises additional control over the Commissars through three Deputies whom it selects as 'Inspectors' to check the expenditures of government officials.

The presiding officer of the Assembly, who is known as the 'President of the Government of the Grand National Assembly of Turkey,' is elected for a term of two years by the Deputies; a two-thirds majority is required for election. According to article IX of the constitution, "*He has the right to sign and promulgate on behalf of the Assembly all measures passed by it and to act as its official representative.*" He is also president ex officio of the Council of Commissars. The duty of presiding over the sessions of the Assembly is entrusted to the First and Second Vice-Presidents, who are selected by the Assembly in the same way as the Commissars.

Article V of the constitution says: "*The Assembly holds office for two years. Members may be reelected. The Assembly in power continues its duties until the new Assembly meets. In case it is impossible to hold an election at the regular time, the life of the Assembly in power may be extended for not more than one year. Each member of the Grand National Assembly, instead of being the representative merely of the vilâyet which elects him, is the representative of the whole nation.*"

The next article states: "*The Grand National Assembly meets without summons at the beginning of October. The presence of two thirds of the members is required.*"

The Government in operation

By a special enactment, the life of the present Assembly has been extended until a two-thirds majority of its members decides that its peace terms have been secured. The Assembly is in continuous session, but the Deputies keep in touch with their constituents by taking turns going on vacation. This is an innovation, and a very good one, in Turkish government. The İstanbul parliaments were dominated by European Turks and city-dwellers that knew next to nothing about conditions in Anatolia and paid little attention to their constituents.

The fact that the Assembly meets in Ankara is also of great benefit to Turkey, for this forces the Deputies to become acquainted to some extent at least with Asia Minor where the real strength of the nation lies. At the same time it removes them from the distractions of the cosmopolitan and luxury-tempting city of İstanbul and from the corruption influence of foreign diplomats and concession hunters. The level of official morality in Ankara is certainly far higher than it ever was in İstanbul.

The salary of a Deputy is 200 Turkish paper pounds (equivalent, in gold, to $140) a month; of a Commissar, $210; of the President, $700. As far as I could see, none of them is making money out of his connection with the government. Most of the Nationalist leaders live very plainly and many of them consistently work fourteen or more hours a day.

The Assembly is the most representative the Turks have ever had. The Deputies come from all parts of the country, from both European and Asiatic Turkey, and they include all walks of life - teachers, doctors, lawyers, poets, journalists, soldiers, businessmen, farmers, religious leaders. Among the latter are representatives of the various Muslim sects, including Tchelebi Effendi [Çelebi Efendi],[120] chief of the Mevlevi dervishes at Konya. About forty of the Deputies are hocas. They constitute the most conservative element in the Assembly. There are no Christian Deputies, although I was told that Christians were not barred.

Many of the Deputies are small proprietors or small businessmen who live in the districts they represent. They display a lively interest in everything which touches the lives of the common people. Some of the more advanced Turks told me that the general intellectual standard of the Assembly was not as high as that of İstanbul parliaments. Though this no doubt is true, it has its advantages. The weakness of previous Turkish attempts at self-government was that most of the Deputies were too far removed intellectually from the majority of their countrymen. The presence of so many representatives of the common people in the National Assembly tends to give its government stability, to keep its feet on the ground. What these Deputies lack in culture they make up for in common sense and in knowledge of local conditions. What they lack in political experience they are gaining in the school of practice. Moreover, they have served to arouse the interest of the peasantry in the government, to give them confidence in the Assembly. The response of Mustafa, the peasant mayor of the village of Ceritmüminli, where I spent a night, when I asked him what the villagers thought of the new government, will furnish a typical example of the way in which the Assembly has obtained the loyalty of the people:

> It is much better than the old government. Formerly we never knew who our representatives were. Now they come around to see us and ask us for our opinions. We know them. We trust them. It is a good government. If it were bad it would be our own fault for we chose the Deputies.

During my travels in Anatolia I met a number of Deputies who were on vacation and were visiting their constituents.

While there is a fair sprinkling of old men in the Assembly, most of the Deputies are below the age of forty. Turkish nationalism is distinctly a young men's movement. Mustafa Kemal Paşa is forty, and nearly all of the Commissars, generals and provincial governors are about that age, or younger. Only one of the Commissars ever held a ministerial position before. Some of the others, however, have occupied subordinate position in İstanbul cabinets.

AN ARMENIAN EVALUATION OF THE ANKARA LEADERS

I showed an Armenian intellectual in İstanbul, who was hostile to the Turkish Nationalists, a list of the names of the men who occupied prominent positions in the Ankara government and asked him if he knew of anything black in the pasts - war crimes, complicity in massacres, etc. He admitted that none of them had even

[120] **Note**: Abdülhalim Çelebi Efendi (1874-1925). Last *Postnişin* (Head of a religious order) of the Mevlevi Dervish Lodge in Konya. Elected as a Nationalist Parliamentarian from Konya, he held the position of First Vice President in the first Parliament in Ankara [HWL].

been accused of any such things, that their records were clear.

Nor have any of these leaders in the New Turkey played an important part in the Committee of Union and Progress after it degenerated into an instrument of tyranny. At the Erzurum Congress held by the Nationalists when they were first organizing, they all took an oath not to attempt to revive the notorious Unionist Party. As far as I could observe, they have loyally kept that oath. Certainly the Nationalist government has had nothing whatever to do with Enver Paşa, the Unionist leader, despite all his overtures.

Some rascals, no doubt, have attached themselves to the Nationalist movement - as they do to every movement everywhere. This is harder to prevent in Turkey where the ruling class has grown up under the corrupting influence of Abdülhamid with his army of spies and of the temptations of foreign intriguers. The effects of such an environment cannot be dispelled in a day.

Democratic army officers and civilian leaders

While some of the Nationalists I encountered made a disagreeable impression on me, the most influential leaders, especially Mustafa Kemal Paşa, the rank-and-file of the Deputies and the people inspired me with confidence in their sincerity.

Strange as it may seem, this was particularly true of the military leaders, such as İsmet Paşa, generalissimo on the Greek front, his chief of staff, Colonel Nadji [Naci] Bey, and many of the subordinate officers with whom I became acquainted. The liberal sentiments with which these men are imbued augurs well for the future of the Nationalist cause because control of the army is bound to be of exceptional importance to it for some time to come.

The spirit of the democracy and equality which reigns in the Assembly is, indeed, the most striking thing about it.

From Grand Vezirs and Şeyhs to Presidents and Commissars

The exaggerated Oriental reverence for authority is neither asked for nor given in the Nationalist government. When Mustafa Kemal Paşa enters the Assembly hall or walks or drives through the streets of Ankara, he causes no such stir as does even the Grand Vezir in İstanbul; nor is his office surrounded by a crowd of attendants and flunkeys as is that of the Grand Vezir in the Sublime Porte. The Commissars and Deputies are, in general, simple and informal in their manners. No special benches in the Assembly are reserved for the Commissars; they take whatever vacant seats among the Deputies they can find. Contrary to some reports, the head of the Commissars, Fevzi Paşa,[121] is not called the 'Grand Vezir' by the Nationalists, but simply, 'President of the Council.' Not only has the ancient title of 'Grand Vezir' been abandoned, but that of 'Sheik ul Islam' [*Şeyhülislâm*], equally time-honored, has been transformed into the prosaic 'Commissar of Religious Affairs.'

The Deputies are no respecters of persons. When a Commissar addresses the Assembly he is heckled in the most approved Western fashion. I have seen the Deputies give some of them a most uncomfortable half-hour. "*What a noisy assembly*!" was the comment one of the Russian Bolsheviks at Ankara made to me. Certainly among these Deputies there is not that air of boredom which one sees in most legislatures. The attendance each day is surprisingly large, and the members take a close

[121] **Note**: Fevzi [Çakmak] Paşa (1876-1950). At the time of Streit's visit, Fevzi Paşa, was the head of the Council of Commissars from January 24, 1921-July 9, 1922. In 1924 he resigned from Parliament and gave up politics. In the years 1924-1944 he served as Chief of the General Staff of the Turkish Armed Forces [HWL].

and critical interest in all that goes on in the chamber. A remarkably great number take an active part in the debates, but as their speeches are usually short and to the point they get a great deal of work done.

In the first nine months of its existence, the Assembly discussed 380 laws, 104 of which were passed, 149 rejected and the remainder were referred for examination to the cabinet or to special committees. Some of the more important of the measures passed were: against treason, for the organization of revolutionary tribunals (necessary at first for the establishment of order but abolished during my stay in Anatolia, except in the vilâyet of Ankara), for the repeal of all laws passed at İstanbul since the Allied occupation, for the betterment and relief of the peasants, for the prevention of venereal diseases, for the establishment of a budgetary system, and finally, prohibition.

I HEAR A TYPICAL ASSEMBLY DEBATE

One of the sessions of the Assembly which I attended will show how the Deputies are fulfilling the trust which their constituents have in them [**Plate 62**]. The budgetary estimate for the gendarmerie was being discussed and hocas and the farmer Deputies in particular used the occasion to criticize the gendarmes for oppressing the peasants. One white-bearded hoca demanded: "*Why don't these gendarmes when they come to village eat the pilav of the peasants instead of asking for their chickens?*" Another deputy accused some of the gendarmes of being in league with the bandits. Several urged local control of the gendarmes. Said one: "*The government doesn't want the gendarmes to live in the district where they are on duty. That is wrong. If they come from the locality they will be held in check better.*" And, pounding upon the desk, he added, "*Those who are interested in a district and who have*

Plate 62: The Turkish Nationalist Grand National Assembly in Session[122]

[122] LC Catalogue #: DLC/PP 1994: 064.200. **Note**: On the back of this photo Streit wrote: "*The Great National Assembly in session* [discussing the Budget] *February 21, 1921*" [HWL].

its welfare at heart are the ones who live in it, not men who come from the other end of the country."

"*If you want to have peace in the land,*" shouted a heated voice in the Assembly, "*you must first pass a law giving the villagers the right of control in their territory.*"

"*Then the villagers will cut your throat,*" someone replied.

"*Better the villagers should do it than the gendarmes,*" the voice answered.

One deputy, however, attacked the government in the interests of the gendarmes. "*Remember that these gendarmes are Turks - they are our children. There are good as well as bad gendarmes,*" he said. Turning to the Commissar for the Interior, he asked, "*Where are the schools for the gendarmes? What have you done to better their living conditions? Why, the habitations of most of them are worse than stables.*"

The Assembly is very jealous of its rights. It knows that all power has been accorded to it, and it never forgets it - or allows the executive branch to forget it. The administration, for instance, wished to send several experts, who were not Deputies, as delegates to the London Conference held in the spring of 1921. The Assembly, however, refused to send any delegates who were not members of its body, although it allowed experts to accompany the delegation. The same was true of the delegation sent to Moscow. Turkey has so often been betrayed by corrupt officials that the Assembly has adopted the plan of allowing only its own members to speak for it. Even then is does not hesitate to reject the agreements they sign. Thus, it refused to ratify the conventions with Italy and France which Bekir Sami Bey,[123] when he was Commissar for Foreign Affairs, negotiated. The Assembly pursues the same policy with regard to important officials in its own territory. These are not only selected by it but many of them, including all the members of the special revolutionary tribunals and some of the provincial governors, are Deputies.

Open diplomacy in Ankara

An example of how the Assembly controls the administration occurred during my stay in Ankara. The Russian attack on the Republic of Georgia had brought to a crisis the negotiations between Turkey and Georgia over the provinces of Ardahan and Artwin [Artvin], which the Czar took from the Sultan in 1878 in lieu of a cash indemnity, and which the Nationalists wanted returned. For two days the cabinet in secret meetings discussed the matter far into the night. Then the council placed its program of action before the Assembly which went into executive session and for another two days and nights debated the question. They ended by deciding to send an ultimatum to Georgia demanding the evacuation of the district. No sooner was it decided that it was done. The Georgian ambassador complained to me the next day that the Commissar for Foreign Affairs had routed him out of bed at four o'clock that morning and delivered the ultimatum to him!

The absolute control which the Assembly has over treaties and war and peace has made for open diplomacy. The Deputies are bound to know the diplomatic negotiations of the government - and the secrets of an executive session cannot be kept very long from the public. The Assembly is in a better position than our Senate, as far as treaty making goes, since it, and not Mustafa Kemal Paşa nor the cabinet, has the right not only to ratify treaties but also to select the men to negotiate them and to represent it abroad.

[123] **Note**: Bekir Sami [Kunduh] (1867-1933). Of Circassian origin, he joined Mustafa Kemal in Ankara in 1920, and served as the first 'Commissar for Foreign Affairs' of the Nationalist Government from May 1, 1920 - May 16, 1921. During his term in office he negotiated a series of agreements with Moscow and London. When the Parliament refused to ratify these agreements he resigned. Tried and acquitted on charges of plotting to assassinate Mustafa Kemal in 1926 [HWL].

Mustafa Kemal Paşa began the Nationalist government's commendable record of open diplomacy by publishing, when the Assembly first met, all of the notes he had exchanged with İstanbul government. While I was in Ankara the diplomatic negotiations of the government were published with little delay both in the Turkish press and in the bulletin in French which the government publishes each day. The notes exchanged with İstanbul concerning the London Conference were printed in full. So, too, were Chicherin's[124] note to Ankara concerning the Anglo-Russian trade agreement, the notes exchanged with Georgia at the time of that crisis, and also the negotiations with Armenia in the autumn of 1920 and the resulting Treaty of Alexandropol [Tr. *Gümrü Antlaşması*].[125] The official views of Armenia, Georgia, İstanbul and of the Allies were thus fully given to the Turks.

WARTIME RESTRICTIONS ON THE PRESS AND POLITICAL PARTIES

I asked Mouhiddin [Muhittin] Bey,[126] the Director of the Press, why the government gave its enemies this opportunity for propaganda. The question was apropos of his remark that the Allies at the London Conference were trying to undermine the morale of the Turkish population. His answer was:

> Under our system, secrecy is impossible. The people will get the news in the end, anyway. It is better that they should get it from us at once. That will increase their confidence in us and show them that we are so strong that we are not afraid of what our enemies say.

I was able to check some of these published notes with the originals. In no case did I find that the text had been altered for home consumption.

It cannot be said, however, that the press is free in Nationalist Turkey. But that, it seems, is hardly to be expected anywhere in time of war and least of all in time of revolution. Though there is no censorship of the Turkish press, as there is of news going out of the country, the editors are held strictly responsible for everything which appears in their papers. No attack on the Grand National Assembly is permitted, but its debates are freely reported and discussed in the press. The government, now that it has become more firmly established, allows more latitude to the press. This will undoubtedly increase when the Assembly divides, as it is already tending to do, into parties.

Until there is peace, however, there can be no real party division, nor a real opposition press, because the war imposes upon everyone the necessity of remaining united. Many, if not all, of the newspapers, I believe, are now subsidized by the government. There are two daily papers in Ankara, the semi-official ***Hakimiet Millieh*** [*Hâkimiyet-i Milliye*][127] (National Sovereignty) and ***Yeni Gun*** [*Yeni Gün*][128] (New Day), both representing what might be called the left center or majority of the Assembly, though the latter is the more extreme of the

[124] **Note**: Georgy Vasilyevich Chicherin (1872-1936) was a Marxist revolutionary and a Soviet politician. He served as People's Commissar of Foreign Affairs in the Soviet government from March 1918 to 1930. His name was subsequently erased from Soviet history [HWL].

[125] **Note**: Treaty signed on December 2, 1920 between the Grand National Assembly of Turkey and the Democratic Republic of Armenia. It brought an end to the war between Turkey and Armenia. Its terms were negotiated by Kâzim Karabekir Paşa and the Armenian Foreign Minister, Alexander Khatisyan [HWL].

[126] **Note**: Muhittin [Birgen] Bey (1885-1951) was the nationalists' press director (*Matbuat Müdürü*) in Ankara. At the time of Streit's visit to Ankara, Muhittin Bey was hosting the young poet Nazim Hikmet, who had arrived in the city a few days earlier. There is nothing in Streit's manuscript or notes suggesting that he met Nazim while in Ankara [See: pp. 63-64, fn. 98] [HWL].

[127] **Note**: Founded as the first newspaper in Ankara on January 10, 1920 (by Mustafa Kemal Paşa), it was the semi-official voice of the Nationalist government. Later its name was changed to '***Ulus***' [HWL].

[128] **Note**: Published by Yunus Nadi [Abalıoğlu] it originally appeared in İstanbul in 1918. After Nadi joined the Nationalists in Ankara (1920), it continued under the same name there. In 1924, Nadi formed a partnership and thereafter the newspaper was published under the name: '***Cumhuriyet***' [HWL].

two in its views. The small groups of conservatives, reactionaries and communists have no organs.

The government does considerable propaganda work for the Nationalist cause, but not nearly as much as the Bolsheviks in Russia. The newspapers, of course, are used for Nationalist propaganda. The Turkish press service - the Anatolia Agency [*Anadolu Ajans*], is directly operated by the government and it supplies telegraphic news to all papers of the country and to all towns with telegraph stations, as well. Where there is no local paper, a news bulletin is posted. The daily bulletin in French which the agency also published in Ankara is intended for foreign circulation.

Deputies are also selected to tour the country and lecture on the aims of the Nationalists. Special attention is paid to imbuing the troops with patriotism. Contests are held to encourage the composition of Nationalist military marches and songs. Propaganda reading rooms are maintained in the larger cities, where local newspapers, those from Ankara and other places, and Nationalist tracts are at the disposal of the public. The walls of these room are embellished with photographs and drawings, some of the Nationalist army, others of the poets and writers who in the last generation started the Nationalist movement, and still others of Greek and English atrocities. Pictures of the present Nationalist leaders were conspicuous by their absence - another proof of how the Nationalists are emphasizing the fact that theirs is a government of the people and not of one man. These propaganda rooms are much used by the public.

I observed no attempt to arouse religious fanaticism in the Nationalist war propaganda. The only use made of religious sentiment is the argument made to the peasants that the Caliph is a prisoner in the hands of the Allies and must be liberated. The atrocities committed by Greeks and Armenians are not held up as the acts of Christians against Muslims, but as the crimes perpetrated by people of these two nationalities against the Turks - a vast difference. The Nationalists make comparatively little use of propaganda on atrocities, much less, indeed, than do the Greeks and Armenians. The policy of the government is to make the issue not one of conflicting religions, but of conflicting national claims, and especially of Turkish independence.

Self-determination within Nationalist Turkey

The faith which the Nationalists have in self-determination extends to their internal policy. The 'Constitution' or 'Fundamental Law' which they have adopted remedies the over-centralization, which has been one of the evils to Turkish administration by providing for a large measure of local self-government not only in the vilâyets [provinces], but in the smaller districts into which they are divided. The vilâyets have been made into entities which are independent in many respects. They are to be governed by district councils, elected by the people for two-year terms. The councils are to administer public works, health and instruction, agriculture, social aid, finances and the pious foundations within their territory. The council elects a board which is in permanent session and in which executive power is vested. The central government is represented by the vali (governor), who is appointed by and responsible to the Grand National Assembly. The valis are shorn of much of their former power. The vali is to interfere in vilâyet affairs only when national and local interests come in conflict.

The vilâyets are joined together, according to their economic and social relationships, into zones which are supervised by general inspectors elected by the Grand National Assembly. The duty of these officials is to inspect the work of the local administrative bureaus and to promote harmonious relations among the vilâyets in their zone in carrying out policies in which they have a common interest.

Each vilâyet, in turn, is divided into *kaza*s (districts) and nahiehs [*nahiye*s] (sub-districts). The kaza is simply an area for the purposes of administration and policing. It is under a *kaymakam* (official charged with governing a provincial district) appointed by the Grand National Assembly and subject to the orders of the vali. The nahiye, as far as its local affairs are concerned is an independent unit. It is governed by a council elected directly by the people. The council elects a president mudir [*nahiye müdürü*] and a permanent executive board. The council and board have an authority, defined by special laws passed by the Grand National Assembly, over judicial, economic and financial affairs of the nahiye. A nahiye consists of a small town or of one or more villages.

Such, in general are the foundations upon which the government, national and local, of the New Turkey will be permanently based. When peace is established, however, the republican character of the present regime will probably disappear for the Nationalists declare that they have no intention of abolishing the Sultanate, at least, not immediately. That could constitute too great a break with the past, especially since the Sultan as Caliph has jurisdiction outside of Turkey and Islam requires that its Caliph be vested with temporal power. While Turkey will thus remain a constitutional monarchy, the Sultan will be a mere figure-head, the Caliph, a temporal ruler in name only. He will be deprived of nearly all the power which was left to him after the Revolution of 1908.

"*The present and the future regime in Turkey will be based upon the absolute sovereignty of the people,*" declared Mustafa Kemal Paşa in a written statement he gave me. "*The existence and the power of the Turkish people are the true sources of strength of the caliphate and the sultanate.*"

"*Your fundamental law gives both executive and legislative power exclusively to the Assembly. How is that going to affect the future position of the present Sultan*?" I asked Mustafa Kemal Paşa later. He smiled and replied: "*He will have to accept our fundamental law - or get out. It will be easy for us to find a Sultan who will be amenable to our wishes.*"

The weakness of the present Sultan, Mehmed VI,[129] has greatly diminished his prestige throughout orthodox Islam, and his reactionary tendency and his hostility toward the Nationalists have brought him their enmity. At first the Nationalists, in order to strengthen their plea that the Caliph must be liberated and to show that they were not too extreme in their revolutionary aims, had to be careful in their references to Mehmed VI. But when I was in Ankara they had come to feel more certain of their strength and open criticisms of the Sultan were becoming frequent in the press. In talking to me privately Nationalist leaders were severe in their condemnation of him. Some of them did not hide their leaning toward a republic, their desire to dispense entirely with the Sultan and to relegate the Caliph to a position in Islam similar to that of the Pope in the Catholic world. These men overlook no opportunity for emphasizing the fact that democratic government has saved Turkey from the abyss into which despotism had all but thrown it; that the provisional republic has succeeded where the monarchy failed. The contrast is so evident and the conclusion so plain that republican sentiment has greatly increased among the Turks since the establishment of the government of the Grand National Assembly. A victorious conclusion of the present war with the King of the Hellenes and a strong manifestation of sympathy for the Ankara government on the part of Western republics would so augment the prestige of republicanism in Turkey that it might lead to the immediate abolition of the monarchy.[130]

In any event, democratic government has now secured so firm a foothold in Turkey, thanks to the wisdom and remarkably self-abnegation of the 'dictator,' Mustafa Kemal Paşa, and to the ability of the Turkish people, that it is no longer threatened by serious opposition from within the country. The only menaces to its continued existence are external - the present war, the imperialistic greed of Western powers and the fanatical prejudices of their citizens against the Turks. If the latter angers are overcome, it makes little real difference whether the new Turkish state is a republic or a constitutional monarchy. If the latter is true, it is probable that Mehmed VI will abdicate, voluntarily or involuntarily, and will be succeeded by the Crown Prince who has openly manifested his sympathy for the Nationalist cause.

[129] **Note**: Mehmed VI [Vahdettin] (1861-1926). Ottoman sultan and caliph, brother of sultan Abdülhamid II, ruled from July 4, 1918 - November 1, 1922. On the night of 16/17 October, 1922 he fled İstanbul on a British warship for Malta [HWL].

[130] The Sultanate was abolished on November, 1, 1922, and the Caliphate on March 3, 1924 [CKS].

Chapter VI

Mustafa Kemal Paşa

THE TURKISH GEORGE WASHINGTON

In Mustafa Kemal Paşa, President of the Government of the Grand National Assembly at Ankara, Turkey has produced one of the most noteworthy men of the present day - a man who would make his mark in any country. The Turks who call him "*our George Washington*" realize what he has done for them, for he too, is 'the Father of his Country.'

That in two short years the darkest hour in the history of the Turks has changed into the brightest and most promising for the future; that out of the ruins of the Ottoman Empire has sprung into existence -despite both foreign and internal resistance- the new, democratic and progressive Turkish State, which holds so strong a position in the Orient today, is nothing short of a miracle. And the miracle-maker is Mustafa Kemal Paşa. By his patriotism, courage, idealism and statesmanship in the face of almost overwhelming difficulties, he has ushered in a new day for the Turks and perhaps for the entire Islamic world.

Every newspaper reader knows the name of the Nationalist leader, but few, even among the well-informed, know much more about him than his name. Although he was one of the greatest, if not the greatest, of Turkish generals during the World War, the man himself has remained in obscurity. While the war lasted his name was purposely kept in the background even in Turkey through the jealousy of Enver Paşa,[131] then practically dictator, who was fearful of any other Turk rising to fame and who was a personal enemy of Mustafa Kemal Paşa; and also through the hostility of the German generals in command in Turkey with whom he could not agree. He has since become the most powerful man in Turkey and one of the most influential men in the Muslim world. I was told that I was the only foreign correspondent to have talked with him since he became President of the Great National Assembly in Ankara.

Note: Certainly, the highlight of Streit's stay in Turkey from today's perspective, were the close to 200 hitherto unpublished photographs he took, together with the hours he spent interviewing Mustafa Kemal Paşa on March 3, 1921 in the small residence he then occupied across from the Ankara train station. While Streit referred to this meeting in the dispatches he filed with the Philadelphia ***Public Ledger***, and indeed used them extensively in his unpublished manuscript entitled: ***The Unknown Turks***, the present publication represents the first time these unique materials have been published.

Streit's unpublished manuscript gives us a unique glimpse into the thinking of Mustafa Kemal Paşa at a point in time when the Ankara government was still in its infancy and when the outcome of the Greco-Turkish war was far from certain. About their two-hour long talk on March 3, 1921, which occurred in the pleasant surroundings of Mustafa Kemal Paşa's residence next to the Ankara train station [**Plate 63**] [HWL]. Streit writes:

> I had been told that he did not like to be interviewed and took the precaution of submitting to him a list of 19 questions. His answers, written in French, filled nine typewritten pages.[132] He received me informally later and with true Turkish hospitality offered me cigarettes and coffee. I was surprised, in view of what I had heard, to find him to be very easy to interview. He talked freely with me for two hours, answering all my questions with engaging frankness.

131 **Note**: Enver Paşa (1881-1922): Soldier, Statesman. Youngest, but best known of the Young Turk Triumvirate. Unionist Minister of War during the World War. Fled abroad (with other Unionist leaders in 1918). Killed fighting the Bolsheviks in Turkestan in 1922 [HWL].

132 A copy of the questions Streit submitted to Mustafa Kemal Paşa (in Ottoman Turkish), are given in facsimile with a modern Turkish transcription; together with Mustafa Kemal's answers (in French) in: T.C. Kültür Bakanlığı (Ministry of Culture): *Atatürk'ün Milli Dış Politikası*. 2 Volumes (Ankara, 1992). See: Volume I., Document #45: pp. 261-276 [See: **Appendix IV.**, pp. 193-210].

Streit wrote: "*when I interviewed Mustafa Kemal Paşa I noted that his hands were soon playing unconsciously with a string of amber beads.*"

Plate 63: Mustafa Kemal Paşa at Home on March 3, 1921[133]

Few men have impressed me as favorably as did this Turkish Washington. He would make his mark in any country. It is a rare man who has the gift he has of quickly inspiring confidence in himself. He is the kind of man, men will die for. Physically he is a handsome, well-built man, forty years in age. His forehead is the high one of the intellectual; his mouth and chin are those of the man of action - the fighter. There is something of the idealist -the dreamer- in his face, especially in his eyes, but of the dreamer who makes his dreams come true. A thorough gentleman, courteous, cultured, refined, and always well dressed, he would be at home in any Western drawing room. I talked with him in French, which he speaks fluently.

I INTERVIEW KEMAL PAŞA ON RELIGIOUS AND OTHER ISSUES

When I interviewed Mustafa Kemal Paşa [**Plate 64**] I asked him what the official attitude of the Nationalist government toward religious affairs and Holy War was. He laughed, and said:

> I am not very well acquainted with religious matters, but from what I have heard the Caliph has the right, when Islam is in danger, to call upon all Muslims to wage a holy war of defense. The Sultan, during the Balkan War and the World War, made such an appeal, but as you know it met with no response. Here, we do not believe in mixing religion with political affairs. We make war with only the material forces at our command, without calling religious sentiment to our aid. The Turks are not fanatics. Of course, there are hocas among us, as in every nation, who try to stir up the people, but we must and we will keep them in hand.

A confident smile accompanies his last words.

"*Would you say that there is a tendency here to separate the Church from the State*?" I inquired.

Mustafa Kemal Paşa nodded his assent. He said:

> At İstanbul the Sultan as Caliph names the *Şeyhülislâm*, who acts for him as head of the Church, controls religious affairs and is a member of the cabinet, ranking next to the Grand Vezir. Here we have no such şeyh. It is true that we have a Commissar for Religious Affairs in place of him, but he is concerned simply with spiritual questions and is a deputy elected by and subject to the Grand National Assembly, just like any other Commissar.

The written answers the Turkish President gave to some other questions I put to him will help make clear the general policy of the Nationalists [See: **Appendix IV**; pp. 193-209].

> **Q. What is your attitude toward Pan-Islamism and Pan-Turanianism?**
>
> A. Pan-Islamism, insofar as it means the union of all Muslims under Turkish domination, and Pan-Turanianism, insofar as it means the union of all countries of the Turkish race under Turkish domination, are bugaboos which the English imperialists use to lead their people in a perpetual crusade against us. We have no intention, nor desire, to conquer half the globe, as has already been done by those who from the banks of the Thames launch these ridiculous accusations against us, while continuing each day their efforts to add to their own conquests. Our National Pact, moreover, is explicit on this point. Our policy is the exact opposite of that of the British, for we are convinced that only a sincere application to all peoples, including Muslims, of the principle of self-determination can save humanity from the catastrophe to which the perpetuation of wars is leading it.

[133] LC Catalogue #: DLC/PP 1994: 064 – Folder 2.

Streit wrote: *"On the wall back of his glass topped desk hung a sword presented to him by the Muslim people of Georgia, and beside it a sword cane which the Nationalist soldiers after the victory of İnönü had made from a captured Greek sword and given to him."*

Plate 64: Mustafa Kemal Paşa at Home in the Ankara Stationmaster's House on March 3, 1921[134]

Q. What is your policy in religious affairs?

A. I think each individual as each people, ought to enjoy absolute liberty of conscience. This principle, unfortunately is trampled upon by our enemies, who believe our people, because it is Muslim has not the right to independence. What is going on now in Syria, Mesopotamia and Anatolia is the best proof of my statement. Our religion is Islam, which, considered in its undogmatic part, is at bottom only a politico-social system based on the greatest tolerance and forming a mean between individualism and communism.

Q. What are your relations with and policy toward other Muslim countries?

A. Naturally we are maintaining extremely cordial relations with all Muslim states. An important Turkish military mission requested by the Emir of Afghanistan should soon go to join at Kabul, the Turkish officers already working there, to make the Afghan army an instrument of modern war. As I have said above, my most ardent desire is to see the right of self-determination granted to all Muslim peoples.

He is unmarried and lives with his aides-de-camp in the small house near the Ankara station which was formerly occupied by the railway division superintendent. [**Plate 65**]

His study in which he received me is furnished in good taste with paintings, photographs, books, objects of art, and upholstered furniture – a room such as one would expect to find in any Western home of the upper class. [**Plate 66**]

Plate 65: Mustafa Kemal Paşa's Residence[135]

Plate 66: Mustafa Kemal Paşa in His Sitting Room (March 3, 1921)[136]

[134] LC Catalogue #: DLC/PP 1994: 064.37. **Note**: On the back of this photo Streit wrote: "*Atatürk in office arm-chair in Angora (Feb. 7, 1921). Return to C. K. Streit. 2853 Ontario Road, D.C. 20009.*" This is clearly a note Streit wrote many years after the fact; presumably when he lent this photograph to someone. This is clear from his referring to Mustafa Kemal as 'Atatürk' (a name he only acquired in 1934), and from the fact that he has mistakenly given the date of his meeting as February 7, 1921 rather than March 3, 1921, as well as from the fact that the address he gives is in Washington, D.C. [HWL].

[135] LC Catalogue #: DLC/PP 1994: 064 [Red Album: Turkey, 1920-1921 by C. K. Streit].

[136] LC Catalogue #: DLC/PP 1994: 064 - Folder 2.

Streit wrote: *"A born gentleman, courteous, cultured, refined and always well-dressed. Mustafa Kemal Paşa would be at home in any Western drawing room."*

Streit wrote: *"See him with his glasses on and without his kalpak and he has the appearance of a professor. In his face, especially in his eyes there is something of the idealist, the dreamer and the realist – a realist who does not forget his ideals, who makes his dreams come true."*

Plate 68: A Rare Photo of Mustafa Kemal Paşa With Eye Glasses[138]

Streit wrote: *"Yet Mustafa Kemal Paşa is no common man. Even without knowing of his accomplishments one could not be with him long without sensing this. While simple and informal in his manner, there is a natural dignity, a poise, a calm self assurance in him which at once distinguishes him from other men. He impressed me as being a man of tremendous force of character who, while not being conceited, is sure of his own strength. After meeting him and talking with him I could easily understand why his countrymen have so much faith in him, why his word enjoys such prestige. There are few men who have the gift he has of quickly inspiring confidence in himself. He is the man for an emergency, the born leader, the man of character whom men will die for."*

Plate 69: Mustafa Kemal Paşa[139]

Streit wrote: *"Physically, Mustafa Kemal Paşa is a handsome, well-built man, nearly six feet in height. He is forty years old, although he appears to be somewhat younger. His forehead is high, his mouth and chin are those of the man of action – the fighter."*

Plate 70: Mustafa Kemal Paşa[140]

Plate 71: Mustafa Kemal Paşa in His 'War Room'[141]

Streit wrote: *"He is, however, the official head of the Nationalist armies and because of his recognized military ability is consulted when important strategic questions are under consideration. But he does not directly command the army."*

Plate 72: Mustafa Kemal Paşa in His 'War Room'[142]

Plate 73: Mustafa Kemal Paşa[143]

Plate 74: A Soldier Saluting Mustafa Kemal Paşa as he Rides by in his Chevrolet[144]

[**Note**: Streit reported that the photograph of Mustafa Kemal "*in the costume of an Arabian sheikh.*" [**Plate** 73] was presented to him by Mustafa Kemal Paşa when he interviewed him on March 3, 1921.

One of the features which most endured Mustafa Kemal Paşa to Streit was what he saw as the complete lack of pretension on the part of the Nationalist leader and his lifestyle. In this regard he wrote [HWL]:

> Other than that a Chevrolet car, one of the two automobiles in Ankara, is at the disposition of the Turkish president, [**Plate** 74] and that guards are stationed at the gates of his modest house, there is none of the pomp and circumstance for Mustafa Kemal Paşa which other heads of state consider necessary [**Plate** 75].

Plate 75: Topal Osman [Kayıkçi]: Nationalist Guerilla Leader Who Guarded the Residence of Mustafa Kemal Paşa in Ankara[145]

---

[137] LC Catalogue #: DLC/PP 1994: 064. **Note**: On the back of this photo Streit wrote: "*Moustapha Kemal Pasha*" [HWL].

[138] LC Catalogue #: DLC/PP 1994: 064. **Note**: Just three months after Streit met with Mustafa Kemal Paşa, the U. S. High Commissioner in İstanbul, Admiral Mark Bristow's intelligence officer, Robert Steed Dunn, also sat down for a long talk with the Nationalist leader. On July 1, 1921, Mustafa Kemal received Dunn (as he had Streit) at his house at the railway station (he had as yet not moved to Çankaya).

Dunn, who was accompanied by Miss. Annie T. Allen, a remarkable American missionary born and raised in Anatolia, describes his impressions of the Nationalist leader in his book: *World Alive: A Personal Story.* New York (Crown Publishers),

'Rebel,' 'dictator,' and 'demagogue?'

The professional soldier and the sincere democrat, the man of action and quick decision, the dreamer, the organizer, the practical statesman and the idealist: it is indeed a rare combination of qualities which characterize Mustafa Kemal Paşa. 'Rebel,' 'dictator,' 'demagogue,' he had been frequently called in the Western press. A rebel no doubt he was. He revolted against both the cruel fate which the Allied Imperialists had so confidently expected to mete out to the Turks and the reactionary Turkish government which they were supporting in İstanbul and which even condemned him to death for rebellion. But, as for the other two epithets, to meet the man, to see him in his daily life at Ankara, is to realize their absurdity.

A dictator? I know of no other head of a government, who, while his country was at war, has more loyally followed democratic principles than Mustafa Kemal Paşa. He has surely done more than any other man to establish democracy in the Near East.

A personally ambitious demagogue? In Greece I saw pictures of King Constantine everywhere. In Smyrna [İzmir] and İstanbul I saw an equal abundance of pictures of Venizelos.[146] In Nationalist Turkey not once did I see in public places a picture of Mustafa Kemal Paşa. It was not that the Turks had no photographers or were opposed to the display of pictures. In various public places in Anatolia I saw portraits of the late sultan and a few of the present sultan. I was about to call Mustafa Kemal Paşa 'ruler' but that he emphatically is not. There were photographs of Turkish nationalist poets and authors, but there was none, not even in the propaganda rooms, of the present head of the Turkish government. Yet if one half of the popular admiration and respect which Mustafa Kemal Paşa enjoys Constantine had, his crown would cut fewer lines in his brow. The Turkish leader has simply chosen to subordinate himself to the movement

---

1956. pp. 412-415, in the following passage: "*Upstairs Mustapha Kemal stood alone, nervously dangling conversation beads of pink coral with a blue tassel. The office was bare except for a large table and lots of chairs. 'The well-trained superior waiter,' was my first thought. But even as we sat down, face to face across green baize, I changed it to, 'tough customer!' He wore a slate-blue lounge suit, quite natty, with soft-collar white shirt and a black bow tie. His age was forty-one but he looked younger, with a college boy's slicked- back sandy hair. Chin small, but doughty, cheekbones high, trim reddish mustache over a mouth that was but a line. His eyes lay in narrow slits, their straight brown brows close over the steel-blue pupils... The whole face was sensitive rather than cerebral, subtle and mercuric rather than domineering. I felt his power of concentration, a ruthlessness with an instant grasp, but wondered—was he adolescent still, or man? Yet, three years younger than me, he'd cleaned up Churchill's Gallipoli.*"

Dunn, who was a cynic through and through, concluded his observations on the meeting, with the following analysis: "*Nor had I believed in Kemal's stirring vision. Yet I thought him sincere, unselfish, able, adamant and clever, to win the world of that day by 'democracy,' a revolutionary doctrine for a Turk.*" Compare Dunn's official report on his interview [See: **Appendix VII.**, pp. 221-227], with the above description taken from his memoir. See also: Heath W. Lowry: "Richard G. Hovannisian on Lieutenant Robert Steed Dunn," in *Osmanlı Araştırmaları* [*Journal of Ottoman Studies*], Volume 5 (İstanbul, 1986), pp. 209-252 [HWL].

139 LC Catalogue #: DLC/PP 1994: 064.214. **Note**: On the back of this photo Streit wrote: *'Mustafa Kemal Pasha.'* There is no indication as to the source of the picture [HWL].

140 LC Catalogue #: DLC/PP 1994: 064.141. **Note**: There is no indication as to who took this photograph [HWL].

141 LC Catalogue #: DLC/PP 1994: 064 [Red Album: Turkey, 1920-1921 by C. K. Streit].

142 LC Catalogue #: DLC/PP 1994: 064 [Red Album: Turkey, 1920-1921 by C. K. Streit].

143 LC Catalogue #: DLC/PP 1994: 064 [Red Album: Turkey, 1920-1921 by C. K. Streit].

144 LC Catalogue #: DLC/PP 1994: 064 [Red Album: Turkey, 1920-1921 by C. K. Streit].

145 LC Catalogue #: DLC/PP 1994: 064.146. **Note**: Topal Osman Ağa (1883-1923), was born in Giresun on the Black Sea coast. He fought in the Second Balkan War (where he was lamed). Following the establishment of the Ankara government, he became Commander of Mustafa Kemal Paşa's bodyguard. After assassinating a Deputy from Trabzon, Ali Şükrü Bey, on March 27, 1923 (over the deputy's having insulted Mustafa Kemal), he was shot and killed by regular troops (while resisting arrest) in Ankara on April 1, 1923 [HWL].

he has organized. His renunciation of dictatorial powers is evidence enough of that.

Note: By the time Streit returned to İstanbul in 1923, the cult of the personality (which had been so noticeably absent two years earlier) had begun to emerge.[147] One of the more interesting and unique mementos he picked up during his second visit, was a poster/postcard [**Plate 76**] depicting now *El-Müşir* (Field Marshal) *El-Gazi Mustafa Kemal Paşa*, flanked on the left by the Libyan leader *Es-Sayyid Es-Şerif, al-Şeyh Ahmad Sennusi*, and on the right by *Es-Sultan Selâhaddîn-i Eyyûbî el-Kebir*, the 12th century Muslim hero who reconquered Jerusalem from the crusaders in 1187 [148] [HWL].

Plate 76: Great Heroes of Islam[149]

[146] **Note**: Eleftherios Kyriakou Venizelos (1864-1936): Greek revolutionary and statesman. Defeated in the national elections held in 1920, he later played a key role in negotiations that led to the signing of the Treaty of Lausanne and the subsequent population exchange between Greece and Turkey [HWL].

[147] **Note**: The extent of the change in this regard is readily apparent when one reads Grace Ellison: *An Englishwoman in Angora*. London (Hutchinson & Co.), 1923. Ellison, who was an unabashed Turcophile, visited Ankara in November-December 1922, and enjoyed unparalleled access to Mustafa Kemal, even being his luncheon guest at his new home in Çankaya. Her visit, which occurred some twenty months after that of Streit, came at a time when the Nationalists had successfully defeated the invading Greek forces, and were preparing for the Peace Conference at Lausanne. Among the changes which had occurred in the intervening months, none is more striking than the emergence of a full blown personality cult, surrounding the personage

The fairness with which Mustafa Kemal Paşa exercises his powers as President may be seen in the manner he selects candidates for executive positions. He has the right to nominate these men. The Commissar for Public Instruction was recalled shortly before I arrived in Ankara. There is a fairly strong conservative element in the Assembly, centering around the hoca Deputies who do not look with favor upon the modern educational program which Mustafa Kemal Paşa, an advanced liberal, desires. Yet, he nominated for this a hoca and Hamdoullah Soubhi Bey [Hamdullah Suphi],[150] one of the most radical of Turkish intellectuals. The latter man was elected by a large majority.

While I was in Ankara, the term of office of the first Vice President of the Assembly, Djelal Eddin Arif Bey [Celaleddin Arif],[151] expired. This is a most important post in the government, for in practice the Vice President acts as a liaison officer between the President and the Assembly. Unless he is fully in accord with the President, the government cannot proceed smoothly. The relations between Mustafa Kemal Paşa and the incumbent, while not exactly strained, were not as good as they should have been. The Vice President recently had been accused of having tried to use his position for his personal profit in connection with a coal concession. It is a point of honor among the executive officials of the government to keep out of all business affairs. Celaleddin Arif Bey had cleared himself apparently to the satisfaction of the Assembly but there was a strong feeling among the liberals that a new man should be placed in his position. The conservative element, however, sought a leader in Celaleddin Arif Bey.

Mustafa Kemal Paşa nominated for this office the incumbent and Dr. Adnan Bey [**Plate** 77], Commissar for Public Health and Acting Commissar for the Interior (Dr. Adnan Bey's wife was the Turkish author Halide Edib Hanım) [**Plate 78**]. It was evident that the President preferred the latter nominee who was his close friend and physician and one of the strong men of the liberal group, although he never had any official candidate. The vote the first day gave 82 to Celal and 80 to Dr. Adnan, with 86 required to elect. The liberals rallied their missing members and the next day on the first ballot Dr. Adnan was elected by 111 votes to 76. The strength of the opposition shows how free from dictatorship the Deputies are.

It would be wrong, however, to interpret this vote as evidence of a lack of confidence in Mustafa Kemal Paşa. Had it been cast on that issue it is safe to say that it would have been unanimously in favor of him, for the Deputies have all faith in him personally. Nor does the vote indicate that the liberal policy of the government is in danger. About one half of the Deputies were absent from Ankara at that time. Some were on vacation; others were away on diplomatic missions or on official business within the country. The majority of them may

of Mustafa Kemal Paşa. While two years earlier Streit had been struck by the complete absence of any pictorial representations of the Nationalist leader, Grace Ellison writes: "*There are pictures of Ghazi Pasha all over the town, and in one or two bookshops you can also buy his principal colleagues, patriotic postcards, and other 'Nationalist' pictures in gaudy colours*" [pp. 135-136] [HWL].

148 **Note**: The iconography of this picture is somewhat strange and calls for explanation. The portrayal of Field Marshall Mustafa Kemal (who stopped the Greek Christian attempt to conquer Anatolia), with the 12th century Muslim hero (who drove the Crusaders out of Jerusalem) on one side and the Libyan (credited with the defeat of Italy) on the other, appears to be nothing less than an attempt to place Mustafa Kemal into the pantheon of Islamic heroes [HWL].

149 LC Catalogue #: DLC/PP 1994: 064.173. **Note**: On the back of this photo Streit wrote: '*Saladin Eyub el-Kebir*' & '*Essayid Essherif Sheikh es-Senussi*' [HWL].

150 **Note**: Hamdullah Suphi [Tanrıöver] (1885-1966). A Circassian by origin, at the time of Streit's visit he was a Deputy from Antalya and Commissar for Public Education. See: **Appendix I.**, pp. 170-171 [HWL].

151 **Note**: Celaleddin Arif Bey (1875-1928/1930?). When Streit was in Ankara, he was the Commissar for Public Justice (May 3, 1920 – May 19, 1921); after a falling out with Mustafa Kemal in early 1921 he was appointed Ambassador to Italy and his post as Commissar was temporarily filled by Zekai Apaydın [HWL].

Plates 77 & 78: Adnan Bey & Halide Edib Hanım[152]

be counted as liberals. What the vote does indicate is the tendency to split into political parties which is manifesting itself in the Assembly.

Aside from the fact that a Chevrolet car, one of the two automobiles in Ankara, is at the disposition of the Turkish president, and that guards are stationed at the gates of his modest house, there is none of the pomp and circumstance for Mustafa Kemal Paşa which other heads of states consider necessary. I happened to be in the Assembly one day while a new Commissar for Public Economy was being elected.[153] Mustafa Kemal Paşa entered alone, took a vacant seat among the Deputies and chatted with those around him as the clerk called out the names of the Deputies according to the constituencies. Near the end of the long list came 'Mustafa Kemal Paşa' -pronounced in exactly the same monotonous tone as the names of the other Deputies- and the 'dictator' walked up to the ballot box, dropped in his ballot, and returned to his seat. That was the first time I saw Mustafa Kemal Paşa. Had I not known him from a photograph I would never have recognized in this simple deputy the man whom the world considers so autocratic that it dismisses the Turkish Nationalists as 'Kemalists.'

The incident is a typical one. Mustafa Kemal Paşa may be seen walking unattended in the streets of Ankara, talking and joking with those whom he meets, or, as

[152] LC Catalogue #: DLC/PP 1994: 064 [Red Album: Turkey, 1920-1921 by C. K. Streit].

[153] **Note**: This was at the February 28, 1921 session of Parliament, when Mahmud Celal(eddin) [Bayar] was elected as People's Commissar for the Public Economy [HWL].

on the Friday -the Muslim Sunday- before I left, sitting at a table with Ahmed Mouhtar [Muhtar] Bey,[154] the Acting Commissar for Foreign Affairs, amid the crowd in front of a dairy lunch. And his democracy is not that of a king shaking hands with a working man as the cameras click; it is in the natural democracy of the man who moves among the folks as one of them. His intimate acquaintance with the Turkish common people is, indeed, one of the sources of his strength.

Yet, Mustafa Kemal Paşa is no common man. Even without knowing of his accomplishments one could not be with him long without sensing this. While simple and informal in his manner, there is a natural dignity, poise, a calm self-assurance in him which at once distinguishes him at once from other men. He impressed me as being a man of tremendous force of character who, while not being conceited, is sure of his own strength. After meeting him and talking with him I could easily understand why his countrymen have so much faith in him, why his word enjoys such prestige. There are few men who have the gift he has of quickly inspiring confidence in himself. He is the man for an emergency, the born leader, the man of character whom men will die for.

Plate 79: Mustafa Kemal Paşa Addresses the Grand National Assembly (March 1, 1921)[155]

[154] **Note**: Ahmed Muhtar Bey (1870-1934). Served as the Acting Commissar for Foreign Affairs from February 9 - May 17, 1921. See: **Appendix I.**, p. 170 [HWL].

[155] LC Catalogue #: DLC/PP 1994: 064.219. **Note**: On the back of this photo Streit wrote: "*Mustapha Kemal Pasha addressing the Great National Assembly of Turkey, March 1, 1921. Photo by Essad Nedim, Photographer for Mustapha Kemal Pasha*" [HWL].

Frankness and courage in reminding his people of their faults and in pointing out the dangers that lie ahead are characteristic of him. Mustafa Kemal Paşa is not the man to seek popular favor by flattering the people. In the speech I heard him give before the Assembly March 1, 1921 [**Plate 79**], after having reviewed the work accomplished by the government, he added these words of advice:

> Gentlemen, our people have exceptional qualities, the development of which will undoubtedly be productive of great results. But I must remind you of the hard facts of history. Comrades, degeneration and utter ruin are the inevitable fate of any nation whose people place self-interest and bigotry above the supreme duties of patriotism. I do not doubt that our Assembly will always be free from these evils.

He is not a great orator, although I was told that when occasion requires he can be very eloquent. When it is known that he intends to address the Assembly, the hall at once fills with Deputies, and the galleries for the public become packed. On the day when I heard him speak he made his way alone through the crowded aisles to the chair. When the applause had subsided -there is generally very little applauding in the Assembly- he read the long speech he had prepared. His sonorous voice and his very personality made his delivery effective. The Assembly listened with close attention. He speaks, both in public and in private in a slow measured tone which gives a peculiar force to what he says.

I talked with him in French, of which he has a fluent command. I had been told that he did not like to be interviewed and took the precaution of submitting to him a list of nineteen questions. His answers, written in French, filled nine typewritten pages. He received me informally later and with true Turkish hospitality offered me cigarettes and coffee. I was surprised, in view of what I had heard, to find him to be very easy to interview. He talked freely with me for two hours, answering all my questions with engaging frankness.

A born gentleman, courteous, cultured, refined and always well-dressed - when I talked with him he wore a light brown English-cut sports suit with a soft collar [See: **Plates 63-64**, pp. 94 & 96]. Mustafa Kemal Paşa would be at home in any Western drawing room. Contrary to numerous reports, he no longer wears his military uniform having resigned from the army when he became President. He is, however, the official head of the Nationalist armies and because of his recognized military ability is consulted when important strategic questions are under consideration. But he does not directly command the army.

He is unmarried and lives with his *aides-de-camp* in the small house near the Ankara [train] station which was formerly occupied by the railway division superintendent. His study, in which he received me, is furnished in good taste with paintings [**Plate 80**], photographs, books, objects of art, and upholstered furniture - a room such as one would expect to find in any Western home of the upper class. On the wall back of his glass-topped desk hung a sword presented to him by the Muslim people of Georgia, and beside it a sword cane which the Nationalist soldiers after the victory of In Eunu [İnönü] had made from a captured Greek sword and given to him.

Plate 80: Painting on the Wall of Mustafa Kemal's Sitting Room[156]

[156] LC Catalogue #: DLC/PP 1994: 064.162. [Photo: C.K. Streit] **Note**: On the back of this photo Streit wrote: "'*Threshing Scene ' by Namık İsmail Bey - Bought by Mustafa Kemal Paşa*" [HWL].

Physically, Mustafa Kemal Paşa is a handsome, well-built man, nearly six feet in height. He is forty years old, although he appears to be somewhat younger. His forehead is high, his mouth and chin are those of the man of action - the fighter. See him with his glasses on and without his kalpak (the soft sheepskin cap shaped much like a fez which he usually wears) and he has the appearance of a professor. There is something of the idealist -the dreamer- in his face, especially in his eyes, but of the dreamer who makes his dreams come true.

THE RISE FROM OBSCURE BIRTH TO A POSITION OF GOD-GIVEN OPPORTUNITY.

Mustafa Kemal Paşa is of Osmanli [*Osmanlı*] origin - I know of no foundation for the stories that he and the men around him are Jews. The Osmanlı is the result of such a mixture of races that one can only guess the blood in his veins from his physical characteristics. Turks in whose words I have complete confidence and who know Mustafa Kemal Paşa told me that he is of Turkish origin with perhaps a trace of Slavic blood in him. His light complexion, which is unusual among Turks, and his features, would seem to confirm this theory.

Born in an obscure family in Salonika [Selânik] where his father was a customs official, Mustafa Kemal Paşa is a man of the people who has made his own way to the foremost place in Turkey. That, however, is no stranger phenomenon in Turkey than in America. Tallat Pasha [Talât Paşa],[157] for instance, who was recently killed in Berlin, began life as a telegraph operator and rose to the position of Grand Vezir.

The Nationalist President received a purely Turkish common school and military education, making the army his career. His preference for the army was, in a peculiar sense fortunate for Turkey. Abdülhamid,[158] who when he reigned, made but one exception to the otherwise absolute ban he placed upon Western Education for his Muslim subjects. That exception included simply the army officers. He was afraid to neglect the army and, in his efforts to bring it up to the Western standards, he permitted the officers to study in the Occident. That concession led to the downfall of the sultan himself in 1909, for the army became saturated with revolutionary doctrines.

Mustafa Kemal -he was not a 'Paşa' then- early became interested in the movement for political reform. In 1903, when he held the rank of captain, he was imprisoned by Abdülhamid because of his opinions and exiled to Damascus. There, his friends say, he began the dreams of a democratic and purely Turkish state which he has now realized. Six years later he had the pleasure of being Chief of Staff of the Reserve Division in Selânik which dethroned Abdülhamid.

He remained in the army under the 'Young Turk' regime and became director of the first section of the General Staff at İstanbul. Shortly before the war with Italy he went to France as the delegate of the Turkish Minister of War at the French military maneuver. On his return he became one of the officers on the staff of Mahmud Chevket [Şevket] Paşa[159] in the military operations in Albania. During the Turko-Italian war over Tripoli he was in command at Derna. He was also in command at the Dardanelles and was later Chief of Staff of the Ninth Army Corps in the Balkan wars. When peace was signed he was sent as military attaché to Sofia [Sofya], Belgrade [Belgrad] and Cettinge [Çetince].

When Turkey entered the World War, Mustafa Kemal held the rank of Lieutenant-Colonel. He was placed in

[157] **Note**: Mehmed Talât Bey, awarded the rank of Paşa in 1917 (1874-1921). Unionist deputy, minister and Grand Vezir (in 1917). Throughout the war years he was the dominant figure on the CUP's Central Committee. At the end of the war he fled abroad with other Unionist leaders. Assassinated by an Armenian in Berlin on March 16, 1921 [HWL].

[158] **Note**: Sultân Abdülhamid II. (1842-1918), ruled from 1876-1909 [HWL].

[159] **Note**: Mahmud Şevket Paşa (1856-1913). Of Chechen ancestry, he was a soldier, minister and Grand Vezir. Played a key role in crushing the April 1909 insurrection against the Unionists. Assassinated on June 11, 1913 while serving as Grand Vezir in the CUP government [HWL].

command of the Nineteenth Division which at that time was not completely organized. When by his personal efforts he had succeeded in bringing his division up to standard, he was sent with it to Maidose [Madytos = Eceabat] on the Gallipoli peninsula.

It was Mustafa Kemal, acting on his own initiative -General Liman von Sanders[160] had ordered him to retire with his troops- who stopped the British offensive in Gallipoli after the landing at Ari Bournou [Arıburnu]. In the bloody combats which followed, the troops under his command reached the total of five divisions. Despite this he was promoted only to the rank of Colonel, for his very success had aroused the jealousy of Enver Paşa, the Minister of War, and of the German command. But when the British landed at Anafarta he was placed in command of this front and remained there until the end of the Gallipoli operations. He had now become a general, and the sultan bestowed upon him the title of 'Paşa.'

Placed in command of the Sixteenth Army Corps he was ordered to the Caucasian front where he recaptured the cities of Bitlis and Mush [Muş] from the Russians. But, after a sharp interchange of views with Enver Paşa, he was sent in disgrace to command the army of the Hedjaz [Hicaz]. Later he was named Commander in Chief of the Second and then of the Seventh Army, both of which were concentrated in Syria. Here he again disagreed with the German command, this time with Marshal von Falkenhayn;[161] he resigned his post to return to İstanbul. He then accompanied the present sultan, at that time the Crown Prince, on his visit to Germany. After his return he fell ill and went to Austria for treatment by specialists in Vienna. He has also had the opportunity of studying conditions in Europe at close hand.

When the death of Muhammed V [Mehmed V] brought the Crown Prince to the throne, Mustafa Kemal Paşa enjoyed more favor in the capital and returned to İstanbul by the special invitation of the government. In September 1918, he was again given command of the Seventh Army which was then endangered by the English offensive in Syria. He succeeded in saving his army and defeated the Anglo-Arab troops near Ryak. Shortly afterwards he replaced Marshal Liman von Sanders as commander in chief of the armies in Syria. It was then that Sultan Mehmed VI gave him the title of honorary *aide-de-camp*. He was in command in Syria until the Armistice was signed and then went to İstanbul.

He remained in the capital for six months, smarting at the affronts which his country early began receiving at the hands of the Allies and anxious for its security, which he clearly saw was menaced by imperialism from without, and despair from within. As a soldier he knew only too well the terrible tribute in blood which his people had paid for the maintenance of the Ottoman Empire. He was willing to see the Empire go, but he was determined to save the national existence of Turkey.

His chance came when he was sent in May, 1919, to the Eastern provinces of Anatolia as inspector of the Third Army.

"*I considered this appointment as a God-given opportunity for helping my nation*", he declared in his speech at the opening of the Grand National Assembly a year later, "*and I left İstanbul pledging myself to labor until the independence of my country was safely secured.*"

And so well has he labored that history will recognize in Mustafa Kemal Paşa the founder of the new Turkish State.

[160] **Note**: Otto Liman von Sanders (1855-1929), a German general who served as a military commander with the Ottoman army during the World War [HWL].

[161] **Note**: Marshall Erich von Falkenhayn (1861-1922), Chief of the German General Staff during the World War and after being replaced in that position by Hindenburg, he commanded the Ottoman forces (unsuccessfully) against Allenby in Palestine [HWL].

A CENTRAL ANATOLIAN CITY TO REPLACE İSTANBUL AS CAPITAL

Just as the Nationalists plan to make the sultan a figurehead, so they intend to deprive İstanbul of the dominating position it has occupied in the Ottoman Empire. İstanbul as a capital is too exposed to attack, too far removed from Anatolia where the strength of Turkey lies. Yet it must remain the seat of the caliphate. The tradition of centuries and the sacred character of the city itself combine to give İstanbul the same position in the eyes of orthodox Muslims as Rome has for Catholics. The fact that for five centuries it has been the seat of Turkish temporal government makes it difficult for the Turks, despite the disadvantages of İstanbul, to establish their capital elsewhere. The abandonment of the time honored capital would deprive the Nationalists of the prestige of following in the steps of the conquering sultans. Moreover, such a move would seem to the many Turks who are accustomed to associate authority with İstanbul to be an admission of weakness on the part of the Nationalists. It should not be forgotten that much of the strength of the Ankara government at the outset came from its declared aim being the recovery of İstanbul, enshrined in both the religion and history of the Turks. The project of the Nationalists is a compromise: to keep İstanbul as the nominal capital but to have the real seat of government established in Anatolia. In answer to my question as to their policy in this regard, Mustafa Kemal Paşa said:

> İstanbul is, of course, our traditional capital, and as such it must continue to be. But we have had an experience in the World War which has taught us a lesson. The sultanate and the caliphate will remain in İstanbul, but the seat of the real government, that of the National Assembly and the cabinet, should be situated here in Anatolia, in the center of the country, where it will be better protected than at İstanbul. The Assembly, of course, can go from time to time to İstanbul, but the permanent seat of the government should not be there. The question has not been decided definitely, but it is being discussed. We are considering Kaisarieh [Kayseri], Sivas and Yozgat as possible sites. We will have a commission investigate this central area with a view to establishing our capital there. The site should have groves of trees, a stream, in a word, natural beauty.[162]

On April 23, 1920, the Turkish people, through their Grand National Assembly, took upon their own shoulders the double task of governing themselves and of liberating their country. Confronted, as their President has said, "*With a broken-down administrative machine based upon the traditional principle of despotism,*" they have created the remarkable democratic government which I have described. They have maintained by the force of their arms the independence of all but a small portion of their territory. The achievement of the Turks, as Mustafa Kemal Paşa in his speech in the Grand National Assembly on March 1, 1921, has justly summarized it, is one of which any people might well be proud. He said:

> The Entente Powers believed that we were incapable of maintaining our existence as an independent state. They thought that they could partition our country among themselves and enslave our nation. Where they made their mistake was in thinking that we lacked the capacity of governing ourselves. For, during the past year, our nation, cut off from the rest of the world, deprived of all aid and guidance and suffering from the greatest calamity which could befall a country, has governed itself in a most civilized and tolerant way, respecting all the principles of liberty.

[162] **Note**: Clearly, as late as March 3, 1921, Mustafa Kemal Paşa was still not overly enamored with Ankara. He was committed to removing the capital from İstanbul, but seemingly desirous of finding a secure location which also had the advantage of a "*natural beauty*," something he found Ankara lacking in [HWL].

Chapter VII

A Pay-As-You-Go War

FROM INSOLVENCY TO A BALANCED BUDGET IN TWO YEARS

The Turkish Nationalists have not only tried the experiment of giving a democratic government control in wartime, they have also been paying for that war almost entirely by taxation. There are only two exceptions so far as I know. One is the gold bullion, which amounted to at least 800 pounds, given them outright by the Bolsheviks. The other is the fact that the Nationalists have suspended the payment of the interest on the Ottoman Public Debt. Because they intend to pay the accumulated interest when peace is established, this might be called a loan. They have made no internal loan, however, and have contracted no additional foreign debts. Nor have they issued any paper money. The money of the Ottoman Empire is still the medium of exchange in Asiatic Turkey as it is in İstanbul. There seems to be plenty of this money in circulation all through Anatolia. Many of the small notes, however, are becoming tattered and will soon have to be replaced. The same postage stamps are also used in Nationalist territory as in İstanbul.

I had bought Turkish gold at İstanbul for 608 paper piastres to the pound; in Asiatic Turkey this gold was worth only 500 piastres.[163] I had no occasion to use the gold; the paper money I had was accepted everywhere, and none of the merchants showed the slightest desire to be paid in gold. The chief reason for the lower value of gold in Anatolia is probably the prohibition of its export. It also indicates popular confidence in the new government, for if this were lacking it would seem that the people would pay more of a premium than they do for hard money. This belief is strengthened by the fact that the Armenian, Greek and Jewish traders, who certainly are not lacking in business acumen, were no more willing than the Turks, who, in general, have not had so much commercial experience, to give me as much paper money for a gold pound as I had to pay in the İstanbul banks.

The Ankara government carries on its banking business through the Imperial Ottoman Bank, an institution controlled by French and British capital, which is the state bank of the Ottoman Empire. Its branches in Nationalist territory are still governed by Italian and French directors. At Ankara the director is an Italian and he is assisted by two French inspectors -one arrived from İstanbul only a month before I did- and by an English inspector who, however, is practically a civil prisoner of the Turks. He is allowed the freedom of Ankara and can live as he pleases but cannot leave the city. The reason given by the Turks is that the British are holding a number of Turks as civil prisoners on the island of Malta. As a sidelight on Turkish toleration I might add that the employees of these banks are still Greeks and Armenians. This fact is also indicative of their common sense, for the Turks have not now the personnel to replace the Christians if they caused them to be discharged and such an action would disturb their finances. They are following the very practical policy of leaving the direction and employees of the banks unchanged but controlling their operations.

These banks continue to carry on business with the outside world, though to a very limited extent, as they are handicapped, Inspector Henry [Henri] Maubert[164] told me, by the slowness of communication.

The Commissariat of Finances, of course, is in the hands of the Turks. It has encouraged the establishment of agricultural banks whose capital and personnel are purely Turkish. These banks were commended by Inspector Maubert as "*sound institutions.*"

---

163 According to Webster's ***New World Dictionary Second College Edition***, a piastre is equal to 1/100 of a lira, the current Turkish monetary unit. The dictionary uses the exchange rate of one lira [CKS].

164 **Note**: Is it possible that this could have been: Henri Maubert, the violent and impetuous French colonial administrator, who during the World War had served in French West Africa, where he earned a justifiably bad reputation for his mistreatment of Muslim leaders, subjecting them to public whippings, humiliations and torture, in the course of the Volta-Bani War. I am unable to confirm or disprove this, although it seems unlikely [HWL].

One of the first acts of the Assembly was to establish a budgetary system. Turkey is one of the few countries in the world today, as Inspector Maubert remarked, which is being run without a budgetary deficit. This due in part to the fact that the government has taken over temporarily the revenues of the Ottoman Public Debt Commission. For the first nine months, from June, 1920 until March 1, 1921, the beginning of the Turkish fiscal year, the receipts and expenditures of the government balanced, each amounting to approximately 50,000,000 Turkish pounds.

The budget estimates for the present year were: revenue, 79,333,440 Turkish pounds; expenditures, 86,519,650. The latter, however, includes some projects which cannot be carried out during the year and some items, such as the 551,012 Turkish pounds, set aside for the sultan and royal family, which will not be paid unless peace is established and İstanbul and Anatolia are reunited. In the Assembly debates on the budget, several of which I attended, the Deputies trimmed some of the expenditures, so that the budget approximately balances.

To appreciate the present budget of Turkey it is useful to compare it to the one made at İstanbul the year before the Ankara government was established. The revenues of Turkey in 1919 were only 34,000,000 Turkish pounds, while its expenditures were 52,000,000 Turkish pounds. The new government, with less territory then the old one under its control, has more than doubled its revenues, not by levying new taxes, but by raising the old ones, in some instances as much as 300 percent, and by a more efficient system of collecting taxes. Except for the tax on livestock, which is now about 30 cents a head, the peasant's burden has not been increased. He still pays the same tenth of his crop to the government as he has done for years. But the total revenue from this source amounts to only 1,700,000 pounds; while the tax on city land brings in 4,000,000 pounds; the tax on business profits, including licenses, 6,500,000; the monopoly of salt, tobacco, and cigarette papers, 10,000,000; and exemptions from military duty 5,000,000. As to the latter item, a Christian Ottoman subject can secure freedom from military service by paying 300 pounds. A Muslim subject cannot escape this duty unless he is physically unfit, and then he has to pay the same amount as the Christian. In addition, the government officials and employees are taxed three percent of their salaries because they do not serve in the military. The rest of the government's revenue comes from fifty sources, none of which produces more than 2,000,000 pounds. Most of the taxes are direct.

More than half of the total expenditures of the state, 45,000,000 pounds, is devoted to carrying on the war with Greece. An additional 7,000,000 pounds is spent on the maintenance of internal order. The government does not requisition its supplies for the army but advertises its needs in the press and asks for bids. The other expenditures of the government, in Turkish pounds, are:

Assembly	982,995
Pensions and Salaries	8,056,578
Finances, including Bureau of Deeds	7,527,638
Bureau of Accounts	624,539
Office of the Presidency	120,368
Interior	446,842
Post Office and Telegraph	1,825,071
Public Health and Social Aid	1,120,836
Foreign Affairs	449,296
Justice	2,832,301
Religious Affairs	580,801
Public Instruction	1,587,618
Public Works	2,103,375
Public Economy, including commerce, agriculture, forests, & mines	1,879,325
Propaganda and Press	151,187

THE NATIONALIST LEADERS: NOT 'DREAMERS' BUT 'PRACTICAL MEN'

"*We are not dreamers,*" Ahmed Ferid Bey, the Commissar for Finances,[165] told me, "*but practical men.*" He continued:

> There are many reforms in our financial system which we know should be made. Some of them we have already carried out, but others, such as the abolishment of the tithing system, which is antiquated and thoroughly bad, must wait until we have peace. What we need above all is a durable peace. We have suffered too much from a durable war. What we are fighting for now is, above all, the recognition of our economic independence. Peace will do us little good unless we have that.
>
> If we are to develop our country we must have the power to establish a protective tariff where it is needed. This, the European Powers will not permit us to do. The free-trade doctrines of the Manchester School are suited for industrial nations, not for us. We are in the same position as America was when she adopted a protective tariff. Consider the question of sugar. We use a tremendous amount - as you know, we are very fond of coffee and tea and pastries. We can raise sugar beets. But up to the present time we have had to import our sugar because the Powers would not allow us to protect this home industry.
>
> We have no intention, however, of taxing the importation of machinery or of agricultural implements. On the contrary, we are making every effort to promote their importation. We are especially desirous of buying these things from America. We are afraid of European capitalists because they go hand in hand with their imperialists, but we trust the United States. We would make every possible sacrifice if an American company would make us an offer to build some of the railways we need.
>
> Previous Turkish governments have preferred to borrow money instead of raising it by taxation. We have no intention of making even an internal loan. Our policy is to pay as we go. We have succeeded so far in keeping our books balanced. How long we can continue, I do not know. We must have outside capital later in order to carry out our projects for the development of the country. We would like to borrow $100 million a year for three years from the United States with which to buy American railway material, farming implements and other manufactured goods. If we could get that money now we would be willing in return to give America concessions to the oil fields of Turkey, including those in the vilâyet of Mosul which is Turkish territory and which we expect to regain from the British who now occupy it.[166]
>
> We do not intend to issue any paper money. Our credit now is good, and we do not wish to weaken it by inflating our currency. We realize that it is necessary for us, if we wish to do business with your country, to show you that you can have confidence in us. Up to the present time the exchange rate on the Turkish paper pound has been higher in our territory than in İstanbul. It has never been more than 525 piastres to the English pound here, while in İstanbul the exchange for months has been about 575. The reason is that we have goods which we are exporting while İstanbul has nothing. We do not intend to lose our advantageous position by giving the outside world reason to say that we are issuing new money which has nothing behind it.

[165] **Note**: Ahmed Ferid [Tek] (1878-1971), was serving as Commissar for Finances during the period Streit was in Ankara. He was replaced on October 26, 1921, at which time he was sent to Paris [HWL].

[166] **Note**: Clearly as late as February 1921, the Ankara government was still planning on the British ultimately returning the Province of Mosul to their control [HWL].

CONCRETE PROOF OF WOMEN'S LIBERATION

I have already pointed out the attention which the Nationalists are paying to the education of girls, and that veils, except in the provinces, have already become a rarity. In Ankara I was received in some Turkish families exactly as if there had never been a tradition of female seclusion. In company with three Turks and three Russian Bolsheviks I had tea with a Nationalist official, his wife and her sister. The two women were clad in European costume; they not only wore no veils, but, what is much more, their hair was uncovered. Another Turk proudly showed me the photograph of his wife, and she, too, had the appearance of a European. I have already mentioned the Turkish doctor and his wife who dined with me at the home of the American director of the Near East Relief Commission in Samsun. In Ankara I found women contributing articles to the daily newspapers [**Plate 81**]; in İstanbul I bought Turkish magazines, such as the weekly '***Kadınlar Dünyası***,' ['Women's World'] devoted to the interests of women and edited entirely by Turkish women. In literary magazines, such as '***Ümid***,' ['Hope'] edited by Turkish men, pictures of Turkish women were even more freely displayed than in the feminine publications.

While all these things bear witness to the profound revolution in the attitude toward women which has taken place in Turkey, one additional fact will serve still better to demonstrate how far the Turks of today have progressed from the conception held only ten or fifteen years ago of women as a secluded being.

Plate 81: Müfide Ferid [Tek] One of the 'Liberated' Turkish Women Streit Met in Ankara[167]

MUSTAFA KEMAL PAŞA FAVORED NAMING A WOMAN AMBASSADOR TO THE UNITED STATES

The Nationalists are contemplating nothing less than sending a woman, Halide Edib Hanım[168] [**Plate 82**], as Turkish ambassador to the United States when relations are resumed between the two countries. When I heard

[167] LC Catalogue #: DLC/PP 1994: 064.247c. **Note**: On the back of this photo Streit wrote: "*Muffide Hanoum.*" Müfide Ferid Tek (1892 – 1971). Later to become a novelist, she was the wife of Ahmet Ferid [Tek], the Public Commissar for Finances in the Ankara government. She was an accomplished French translator who worked with Mustafa Kemal, at the time of Streit's visit [HWL].

[168] **Note**: Halide Edib [Adıvar] (1882-1964): Politically active author, successful journalist. Sentenced to death, together with Mustafa Kemal by the Sultan's government for her support of the Nationalists, fled İstanbul (together with her husband: Adnan Bey) and joined Mustafa Kemal in Ankara (1920). Played a variety of roles throughout the War of Independence, including serving as the official guide/hostess for visiting foreign journalists and delegations and translator for Mustafa Kemal's English correspondence [HWL].

of this at Ankara I made a point of asking various Turks whom I met what they thought of such an appointment. None of them made any objection, and a number were outspoken in their approval of it. When I interviewed Mustafa Kemal Paşa I asked him if it were true that such a nomination might be made. His reply was:

> We have women in Turkey who are as capable as men of occupying such high posts as that of ambassador. Halide Hanım is one of these women, and it is certain that she could fill the office perfectly. The occasion to nominate an ambassador to the United States, however, has not yet presented itself to us.

Aside from the evident value such an appointment would have in proving to skeptical Westerners the social revolution which has taken place among the Turks, there is, indeed, much to be said in favor of her being sent to Washington to represent the new Turkish state. Although she has never been to the United States, there are strong bonds which connect Halide Hanım to America. She is a graduate of Constantinople College [for Girls], the American institution on the Bosporus for women. She was the first Muslim girl to study at that school. That was in the days when Abdülhamid ruled Turkey with an iron scepter, and her enrollment caused a great stir in the capital. The Sultan ordered her to leave the college immediately, and she was forced to comply temporarily. But her father, Edib Bey, the private secretary of the sultan, who was bent upon his children having the benefits of Anglo-Saxon culture which he greatly admired, persisted, and she was allowed to return. If may be added that now there are a number of Muslim women attending this institution. To indicate the attitude of Halide Hanım toward America it need only be mentioned that her two sons, Ali and Hassan, are now studying at the University of Illinois.

She has already had some experience in diplomacy and public life. After the Armistice she acted as unofficial intermediary between the Turkish Government and the American High Commission at İstanbul. Before that she had occupied such posts as Inspector of Schools in İstanbul and Professor of English Literature in the University of İstanbul. She was one of the first Turkish women to travel in foreign countries, having made a tour before the war in England and France [**Plates 83 & 84**].

Known throughout Turkey before the war as a novelist, intellectual and feminist leader, Halide Hanım has, since the Armistice, become an even more prominent figure because of her courageous patriotism. As Hamdullah

Plate 82: Halide Edib Hanım in her office at the General Staff Headquarters[169]

[169] LC Catalogue #: DLC/PP 1994: 064.

Plate 83: Halide Edib Hanım in Front of Her Village Home[170]

[170] Photo by Clarence Streit. **Note**: On the back of this phograph Streit wrote: "*Halideh Edip Hanoum* (*taken at Angora*), *autographed by her in Turkish and in French.*" This photo was given to Heath Lowry by Clarence Streit in Washington, D.C. in 1983 [HWL].

Plate 84: Halide Edib Hanım in Front of Her Village Home[171]

[171] LC Catalogue #: DLC/PP 1994: 064 Presented to Clarence Streit by Halide Edip (Photographer: C.K.Streit). **Note**: Interestingly, in 1928, when Halide Edib sat down to write her memoirs of the early days in Ankara, she did not mention Streit's visit, but described at length her meeting with another American journalist who visited the Nationalist capital. This was Paul Williams, a journalist with the ***Chicago Tribune***, who met with Mustafa Kemal on April 26, 1920. In her work *The Turkish Ordeal* [Halide Edib, 1928: p. 142] she writes: *"An American journalist representing the '**Chicago Tribune**,' a young and pleasant man named Williams, arrived in Angora and had an interview with Mustafa Kemal Pasha. I naturally interpreted for them. Before he left the room he took Mustafa Kemal's photograph. Next day he took mine at the farm. When the film was developed the pictures were superimposed so that I appeared behind Mustafa Kemal Pasha against a background of a single cypress. Williams showed it to me and said laughingly, 'The woman behind Kemal.' Strangely enough, although he promised not to publish the funny thing, it appeared in several American papers under the title 'The Woman Behind Kemal.'* ' See: **Appendix III.**, pp.189-192 for Paul William's dispatch based on his April 26, 1920 interview with Mustafa Kemal Paşa.

Suphi [Tanrıöver], Nationalist Commissar for Public Instruction, said to me:

> We cannot help suspecting the schools established in Turkey by most foreign countries as being instruments of propaganda against us, but the fact that an American college has given us Halide Hanım is enough to justify the continued existence of the institutions your countrymen have established here.

Halide Hanım was the first Turkish woman to address a public mass meeting of men. That was at the time of the Greek occupation of İzmir. Later, just after the Allies occupied İstanbul, she left the capital to join the Nationalists at Ankara. Her departure was none too soon - a week later her name appeared on the same list with that of Mustafa Kemal Paşa as condemned by the sultan's court martial to be hanged as a rebel. At that time British troops occupied much of Anatolia. But she succeeded in slipping through their lines after hardships and dangers worthy of a movie serial and reaching Ankara after having been en route more than a month.

MADAM THE GENERAL: HALİDE HANIM

The only woman to occupy a high post in the Nationalist government -few of the Turkish women intellectuals, it should be said, have succeeded in reaching Ankara- Halide Hanım is in charge of a bureau in the military intelligence section, with offices in the General Staff Headquarters.[172] There she is treated with the greatest admiration and respect by the Turks, both officers and soldiers saluting in military style when the passes or when they enter her office.

In the villages, where she is beloved as a social worker and friend; the peasants, who consider her as a phenomenon neither male nor female, have invented a special title for her. 'Paşa Hanım,' they call her, which might be translated as 'Madam the General.' Titles, however, are not to her liking. "*I would abolish them all if I had my way,*" she told me. She is a thorough democrat and lives very plainly near a village [Kalaba] a few miles from Ankara in a little house of sun-dried bricks where several times I had the pleasure of having tea or dinner with her. In her salon I met several Nationalist leaders.

Although she is doing what is considered even in the West to be man's work, there is nothing mannish about Halide Hanım. Dressed as she was when first I met her in her office in a simple black costume, Turkish in its cape and headdress but Parisian in its cut and in the audacious golden curls which peeked out from under her tightly wound scarf, she was altogether feminine in charm. Her conversation increases her attractiveness for intellectually she would hold a high rank among Western women. She is one of the leading Turkish novelists of today. A number of her works have been translated into German and French although none, as yet, has appeared in English. 'The George Eliot of the Near East,'[173] she is sometimes called. In addition to her other attainments, she is a crack shot with a rifle or revolver and an expert horsewoman [**Plate 83 & 84**]. Her husband, Dr. Adnan Bey, one of the most prominent Nationalists, is the First Vice-President of the Government of the Grand National Assembly.

In one of my talks with Halide Hanım, she declared, "*If Turkey has ten years of peace, you will see Turkish women voting.*" In reply I asked her to help prepare the West for such a development by writing a brief review of the rise of Turkish feminism. The history of the movement, which she found time to sketch in English for me, follows:

---

[172] **Note**: Streit is the only source I have encountered who clearly states that in early 1921 Halide Edib Hanım was actually running a section in the Bureau of Military Intelligence, with her office in the General Staff Headquarters [HWL].

[173] **Note**: George Eliot was the pen name of the English novelist and leading Victorian writer Mary Anne Evans (1819-1880) [HWL].

The Rise of Women in the New Turkey

by

Halide Hanım

The development of the Turkish woman as an idea dates far back to our renaissance in literature when the Turkish artist began to liberate himself from the Persian yoke in language and in ideas, when the subjects of Turkish literature ceased to be the conventional themes of old, - the nightingale, the rose and the spring. With the entry of the human element into Turkish literature, influenced by the French classics, woman also entered, and she began to be considered as a part of the Turkish nation which constitutes its life in the realm of everyday and in the realm of society.

From an object of love she gradually began to be considered as a factor for the regeneration and in the new life of the nation. Abdülhaki Hamid [Abdülhak Hâmid (Tarhan)], the great Turkish poet, made woman a living figure and a center of high thought and capacity. In '*Taribi*' [sic. '*Tarık*'],[174] the great Turkish drama, he began to set forth the Muslim Arab women of old as patriotic, military and intellectual figures. This new ideal and idea continued to be a decorative theme for over thirty years. The women who received education and culture were those of the highest class and of the higher middle class. Their education was obtained mostly from English and French governesses. For the people there was one unique normal school for girls, with a more or less rigid and old-fashioned system of training for the preparation of women teachers. There were also some secondary schools, very poorly distributed through the country - most of them, in fact, being in İstanbul.

The education and development of women continued to be an intellectual fantasy and mere literary talk until the revolution of 1908 invaded Turkey with an extraordinary enthusiasm and capacity for life. The revolution in Turkey was not the consequence of a clear, decided program and preparation. The terrible suppression of Abdülhamid, for a quarter of a century, created a natural desire for breath and for a freer and newer life. And when that new life burst out in a wonderfully natural and almost wild enthusiasm, the difference of sex and the traditions and dogmas of centuries gave way. For a short time everybody, men as well as women, were drunk with new life and freedom, and in that moment women took their first steps in their social and human progress spontaneously and naturally.

When the Committee of Union and Progress took up the extremely difficult task of creating a new country and a new regime after the short honeymoon of the revolution, they were convinced of the necessity of giving women an equal chance for development. Whatever the political errors, even sins, of the Unionist Party may be, there was one thing in which they were constant, brave, and persevering to the last, and that was their attitude toward the development of women.

There sprang up a very large number of secondary schools for women and seven normal schools and lycées. The apparently simple matter of opening such a number of schools meant a gigantic struggle against constant reaction and deep rooted prejudice. The schools and the new institutions for work for women were far from perfect, and there was a great deal of criticism of their principles and methods among the intellectuals. But the Unionists did what was within their capacity to change the mental attitude towards the

[174] **Note**: This appears to be a misprint for: ***Tarık Yahut Endülüs'ün Fethi*** [Tarık or The Conquest of Spain], a well known play of Abdülhak Hâmid's, written in 1879. Among other themes this work portrays the military role of women in the original Arab conquest of Spain [HWL].

status of women, always maintaining that a new Turkey meant a new people, including women as a part of the whole national scheme. Reaction and bitter opposition to women's education and emancipation continued to manifest itself in the form of revolts but the Unionists held on.

With the Great War economic necessity created easily a working class among women with much less opposition than one would suppose. Turkey sent to the fronts a much larger mass of the intellectual, official, working and industrial elements than she could afford. Yet the government as well as the social machinery with its thousand and one needs had to go on. So by pure necessity women stepped forward and began to fill the gap.

During the Balkan War public opinion was on the verge of revolt at seeing Turkish women nursing men in the hospitals. But in the Great War the inundation of women in the government departments where they worked side by side with men did not cause a very great shock. The shops in the cities, the public institutions, the industrial departments were obliged to take women employees. The city women were forced by the threat of starvation to work and to enter business in order to support their families. The agriculture of the whole country had to go on, with greater responsibility placed in the hands of women. Although the peasant women had always worked in fields, they had never been left so entirely to their own resources in the management of village life. This activity and responsibility welded the souls of the women with a new sense of ownership in their land.

In the great national calamities that followed the war, men found it natural to see women at their sides crying, working or even fighting. The cooperation of men and women in ordinary life began in Turkey in the imperious necessity born of the tragedies of war. And the gap, intellectual and otherwise, between men and women will be filled much more naturally in Turkey than in Europe, I believe, for women and men here struggle together not as rivals but as comrades in misfortune and in misery to create a new atmosphere and a new life.

Ankara trusts United States more than European Allies

The Turks not only want an open door maintained, but they want to trade with us especially. From experience they have become intensely suspicious of the European powers. They have found that the schools they allowed them to establish in their territory and the concessions they gave them were too often used to promote political ends. But the Turks realize that to carry out their plans of progress, to develop their natural resources, to build railways, to teach the peasants to farm scientifically, to spread Western culture through their country, they must have the aid of Western experts and capital. For that aid both officials and people look to America alone, for they have faith in the United States as a disinterested and humanitarian Power.

Mustafa Kemal Paşa but expressed the sentiment I heard on every hand in Anatolia when he told me:

> We greatly desire to enjoy the friendship of America. We have never considered ourselves at war with the American people and we are astonished that they have not yet resumed the usual diplomatic relations with us. We are ready to resume diplomatic relations with the United States on the basis of our National Pact, independently of our political situation vis-à-vis other powers. We already have presented this matter to your government.
>
> Naturally, we will need a great deal of help in building up our country, and we are especially desirous of obtaining both material and technical aid from America in preference to any other country, for we know that the United States has no political ambitions in the Near East and no desire for any part of our territory.

The Turks believe not only that they have nothing to fear from close relations with us, but also that they will get a square deal. American businessmen, such as our tobacco buyers at Samsun, with whom the Turks have already come in contact, have made an enviable reputation in Turkey for American business methods.

"*Traders from other countries come here simply with the idea of exploiting us, of getting as much from us as they can while giving us as little as possible in return,*" Turks told me. "*We believe that trade ought to benefit both parties and so, apparently, do the Americans with whom we have done business. They do not try to take advantage of us. We can depend upon their honesty,*" they said.

Plate 85: Fevzi [Çakmak] Paşa (directly under the sign) with Mustafa Kemal Paşa to his right, Attending the First Graduation Ceremony at the Ankara Military School[175]

[175] LC Catalogue #: DLC/PP 1994: 064.2476 or 21/76 [?]: **Note**: On the back of this photo Streit wrote: "*Fevzi Pasha, President of Cabinet and Mandataire for National Defense; Mustafa Kemal Pasha, President of Great National Assembly; First commencement exercises, new Turk military school established at Angora. Cadets at left.*" Mustafa Fevzi [Çakmak] *Paşa* (1876-1950). Turkish military officer, promoted to the rank of Field Marshall in 1922 (only Mustafa Kemal and he were awarded this title). In 1919 he played a key role in gaining military support for Mustafa Kemal. In April of 1920 he was made a member of parliament, and Commissar for National Defense, Deputy Prime Minister, and Deputy Chief of the General Staff. From August of 1922 until his retirement in 1944 he served as Chief of the General Staff [HWL].

ANKARA: A CITY AT WAR

Note: During his stay in Ankara, Streit also attended the commencement ceremony for the first graduating class of cadets at the city's newly formed Military Academy [**Plate 85** previous page]. Mustafa Kemal Paşa, and Fevzi [Çakmak] Paşa were also in attendance.

In one part of the ceremony, Streit observed as Mustafa Kemal Paşa reviewed a regiment of Nationalist troops, and even managed to take a photograph of the President returning the salutes of the troops [**Plate 86** below & **Plate 87** opposite page [HWL].

Plate 86: Mustafa Kemal (red arrow) Reviewing Troops in Ankara[176]

176 LC Catalogue #: DLC/PP 1994: 064.247d [Album]. **Note**: On the back of this photo Streit wrote: "*Angora review of troops, Mustapha Kemal Pasha – saluting*" [HWL].

Plate 87: Mustafa Kemal Paşa Reviewing Troops[177]

[177] LC Catalogue #: DLC/PP 1994: 064 [Album].

CHAPTER VIII

RUSSO - TURKISH RELATIONS: NEW STYLE

Moscow - Ankara alliance: Russia cooperates with but does not dominate Ankara

The Russo-Turkish alliance means neither that Turkey is going Bolshevik nor that the Bolsheviks dominate the country. The Turks are opposed to Communism. For one thing, their social system is based on their religion which, while it provides that every man shall have the fruit of his labor, insists upon a large measure of cooperation. The competitive struggle for existence in Turkey has never been as harsh as in the West. The country is largely agricultural; the peasants own their own land. Their fields -except orchards and vineyards- are not fenced in. They live together in villages and work the outlying land more or less together. Each family cultivates its own soil, but those who finish first help the weaker. There is no caste system in Turkey, no hereditary nobility, no plutocracy. There are, it is true, some rich Turks and some large proprietors, but not enough to be a major factor in the country's economy. The Turkish peasants have, indeed, been oppressed in the past. They still bear the greatest burden of taxation.

But this oppression has been due partly to the continual wars in which Turkey has been involved, and more to the arbitrary acts of local officials of the central government, and to the exploitation of the peasants by Greek and Armenian traders, and most importantly, to the past faults of the Turkish administrative system. Political more than economic and social reforms are needed in Turkey.

The Grand National Assembly, in which a large number of small proprietors are represented, has set to work to accomplish these reforms. It is endeavoring to give the country a durable peace by establishing it on an ethnographic basis. It has provided a large measure of local self-government. District councils, elected by the people for two-year terms, are to administer public works, health, instruction, agriculture, finances and the pious foundations within their territory. The central government is represented by the governor, appointed by the National Assembly. He is thus held in check by the local and notional representatives of the people. The government also plans to reform its antiquated system of taxation when the war ends. The reforms, as well as the Agricultural Bank the Assembly is organizing with the aid it is giving the peasants for the purchase of agricultural machinery on long-term installments, will remove many sources of agrarian discontent.

The aim of Bolshevik policy in the Near and Middle East is to gain the friendship of the Muslim peoples by aiding them in their attempts to escape from Western domination and thus to protect their Southern frontiers from attack. Chicherin, a highly influential Russian career diplomat, is the great exponent of 'self-determination' in the Orient. He has succeeded marvelously in changing Islam from being a possible source of danger to Russia into becoming not only a protective barrier but also a positive danger to the Allies. Russia is now free to concentrate her army on her Western fronts.

The key to Bolshevik success in the Near East is their frank recognition that the dominating forces in Islam today are nationalism and, to a lesser degree, religion. By attempting to foist Communism upon the Muslim people, the Bolshevik realize that they would be running into opposition with the teachings of the ***Qur'an*** and that they would weaken the nationalist movements which are of such precious aid to them now. Consequently, they are now willing to let Communism in the Orient wait.

In the first flush of revolutionary zeal, they did try to propagate Communism in Islam. But, as Ahmed Muhtar Bey, the acting Turkish Commissar for Foreign Affairs, said to me: "*The Bolsheviks have had a sad experience in attempting to communize the Muslim population of Azerbaijan, and they've modified their policy in that regard. They have never asked us to become Communists. If they had, we would have refused.*"

The mistakes the Bolsheviks made in the Caucasus in dealing with the Muslims were nearly fatal to them in the Near East. When they gained control of Azerbaijan, they put Armenian Communists in charge. These Armenians were Communists only so far as the Muslims were concerned, it seems. The Armenians confiscated

Muslim property and massacred those who resisted -as well as many who did not resist- but they spared the lives and property of Armenian capitalists. The tales of those massacres spread like wildfire through Islam. I met several Azerbaijani Turks in Ankara who were seeking Turkish aid against the Bolsheviks.

Members of the Bolshevik Embassy at Ankara with whom I talked admitted these mistakes. As a result they ousted the Armenians. They had given the Muslims primary schools in their own language, which the Czar had never allowed. This educational policy, Turks told me, had done much to help the Bolsheviks regain Muslim favor. In Turkey itself they have tried to allay the suspicions aroused among the Nationalists. Oupmal, the first secretary of the Bolshevik legation at Ankara, being too fervent a Communist, was recalled by Moscow at the request of the Nationalist government. The Bolsheviks apparently are no longer trying ambitiously to spread communist propaganda in Turkey.

"*It is evident that it is impossible to communize Turkey now,*" Boudou Mdivani, the Bolshevik envoy at Ankara, explained to me. He went on:

> The Muslim peoples must first have their independence and establish political democracy. Our policy, as was settled upon at the Baku Congress of Oriental Peoples[178] last September, is to encourage the nationalist movements among them and help them free themselves from the domination of foreign imperialists and capitalists. But they cannot remain free unless they improve their system of administration and government, and we are trying to advise them along those lines.

As a result of this change of policy the Bolsheviks have been able to keep their relations with Turkey "*most cordial,*" to cite Mustafa Kemal Paşa. Indeed, the Turks keep Moscow informed of their negotiations with the Allies, and Moscow returns the favor. But, as far as internal policies are concerned, the Turks will permit no Russian interference. They will allow no Communist propaganda in their army; they suppressed a communistic newspaper in Ankara. They refused to allow the Bolsheviks to install a wireless station at their embassy in Ankara. The Russians, contrary to many reports, did not organize the Turkish army, and they have nothing to do with it now. The Bolsheviks, however, have given the Turks material aid. According to Polakov, interpreter for the Bolshevik legation, they have made the Turks a gift of at least 800 pounds of gold bullion. The Turks have also received munitions and other supplies from Russia, though not to a great extent. Now that communication between the two countries is better this material aid will no doubt increase.

Bolsheviks accept Ankara's policy on Straits

The traditional fear of Russia still persists among some of the Turkish leaders, but most of the influential ones believe the Bolsheviks are sincere and have no imperialist aims in Turkey. And, if the Bolsheviks are overturned, the Turks feel that they are safe anyway, for they think it will take years for the old Russia to regain its former power.

As to İstanbul, Mdivani laughed at the suggestion that the Bolsheviks hoped to control the city and said: "*That was the policy of the old regime, it is not ours. Of course, we must have a free outlet from the Black Sea, but we can arrange that to our satisfaction with the Turks.*" The Bolsheviks have accepted the Turkish project to internationalize the Straits at a conference in which the Black Sea states shall be represented. The Turks intend to keep İstanbul as their traditional capital, but they are resolved to fight no more wars over the Straits if they can help it. And their hostility to the British is such that, as several Nationalists expressed it, "*If we can't have İstanbul*

[178] **Note**: Meeting organized by the Communist International, which was held in Baku, Azerbaijan on September 1, 1920. Attended by close to 2,000 delegates from twenty-five Near and Far Eastern countries [HWL].

ourselves, we would much prefer to see the Bolsheviks get it then anyone else."

The Turks realize that they must get foreign capital if they are to develop their country as they wish. They do not wish to give the impression abroad that because of their alliance with Russia they are imbued with Bolshevik principles. All the leaders with whom I talked emphasized the fact that the alliance was simply of a political nature. Celal [Bayar] Bey, the Commissar for Public Economy,[179] wanted it made plain that "*the commercial interests of foreigners in Turkey would enjoy the same protection as before the war.*" Ahmet Ferid Bey, Commissar for Finances, said to me: "*We are not dreamers like the Bolsheviks. They canceled their foreign debt, and now they're willing to pay it; we say from the start that we are entirely willing to pay our debts to other nations.*"

Some of the Turks, in their anxiety to remove any trace of Bolshevism from the Nationalist government, even object to the members of the Cabinet being called 'People's Commissar.' They prefer that the Turkish word be translated, 'People's Mandataire' or 'Steward' or 'Minister.' But because the government, in its diplomatic correspondence, which is written in French, still uses the term '*Commissaire du Peuple*' I have followed this usage.

Concerning public utilities and natural resources, the Turks will probably follow, as far as possible, a policy of public ownership and control.

The Bolsheviks are also endeavoring to promote trade relations with Turkey. They have a consulate at Trebizond [Trabzon], an agent at Samsun and a Consul General at Ankara. The latter is Prince Chatopski who for 25 years was in the Czar's consular service in Asiatic Turkey. He is not a Bolshevik - he is the only member of the legation at Ankara who is not called 'comrade.' Naturally, he isn't called 'prince.' Plain 'Chatopski' suffices for him in the minds of the Bolsheviks, with whom he seems to get along well. The Bolsheviks employ him as an expert. His children are being brought up in Communist schools.

Several members of the embassy are either Azerbaijani or Ottoman Turks who are Communists. The Ambassador, Mdivani, was in Ankara only provisionally and was to leave for Persia as soon as Iliave, the permanent ambassador, arrived in the Turkish capital. Mdivani speaks Persian, and the Bolsheviks, as far as possible, seek in their diplomatic agents men who know the language of the country to which they are assigned.

---

[179] **Note**: Mahmud Celal(eddin) [Bayar] (1883-1986), served as People's Commissar for the Public Economy from February 28, 1921-January 14, 1922. A one-time member of the 'Special Organization' (*Teşkilât-ı Mahsûsa*), the secret security service of the Committee of Union & Progress, whose activities (under the *nom de plume*, Gâlip Hoca) he directed first in Bursa and later in İzmir, he was one of the Young Turk activists who successfully made the transfer to the Nationalists. He eventually was to become the 3rd President of the Turkish Republic, before being overthrown by a military coup in 1960. He died on August 22, 1986, at the age of one-hundred-three. See: **Appendix I.**, p.169 [HWL].

Chapter IX

Outward Bound

I MEET İSMET PAŞA, CHIEF OF THE NATIONALIST GENERAL STAFF; HE HAS JUST WON THE IMPORTANT BATTLE OF İNÖNÜ

Plate 88: İsmet Bey/Paşa[182]

I had no difficulty in obtaining a vesika, or permit to leave Ankara and Nationalist territory. The Turkish authorities were willing to let me take any route I desired and I elected to go to the port of Antalya as that would give me an opportunity to cross Asia Minor and see better the military strength of the government.

The day before I left I met İsmet Paşa, Chief of the Nationalist General Staff[180] [**Plate 88**]. İsmet Paşa, who happened to be in Ankara, was in command at Eskişehir through which city I was to pass. He said that he would telegraph to his officers to show me their troops.

İsmet Paşa was one of the most charming Turkish officers I met.[181] Modest, affable and absolutely informal, there is nothing of the militarist in him. He is all energy - he seems to walk on springs. He bounded in the reception room at the staff head-quarters where I was awaiting him, introduced himself, shook my hand cordially, and was apologizing for being late, almost before I knew it. French officers who knew him told me later that İsmet Bey -he was made a Paşa by the Grand National Assembly after he defeated the Greeks at İnönü- was a very capable commander. The disaster which the Greeks later encountered when they attempted to take Eskişehir is evidence of his ability.

The story of my stay in Ankara would not be complete without mention of a phenomenon I witnessed one night which would have been full of significance for the astrologers of the old East. Over the National Assembly building the crescent moon hung low with a brilliant planet near its two ends. Thus emblazoned in the sky was an exact replica of the star and crescent flag of Turkey which floats over the Assembly day and night. Tradition says that Sultan Murad saw this same phenomenon the night before the Battle of Kosova in which he conquered the Serbs in 1389. He hailed the combination as a sign from Heaven and adopted it as the emblem of his Empire.

I left Ankara on the express train which runs once a week to Konya, making the trip in thirty hours [**Plate 89**]. The cars were clean, and my first-class compartment was comfortable. The train was much better than those I saw later in the Balkan States,[183] and, despite the fact that wood was used for fuel, made faster time than does the much-advertised Orient Express in the Balkans. The roadbed was in good condition, and we averaged a little less than thirty miles per hour to Eskişehir, where we arrived on schedule time. The train crew was entirely Turkish - I mention this detail because of the absurd but common belief that the Turks are incapable of doing technical work.

---

[180] **Note**: On the day prior to his departure from Ankara, Streit has the opportunity to meet and talk with the individual credited with the organization which just a few weeks earlier (January 9-11, 1921), had led to the first Nationalist victory against the invading Greek armies, the First Battle of the İnönü. He refers to him variously as Colonel İsmet Bey and İsmet Paşa, in all likelihood a reflection of the fact that it was in return for his victory on January 10th that then 'Colonel' İsmet was promoted to the rank of 'General' (Paşa), quite likely on or about the time Streit met him [HWL].

[181] **Note**: This footnote is taken from Streit's revised 1982 manuscript [HWL]. I again met İsmet Paşa as chief delegate for Turkey at the Lausanne Peace Conference (1922-23), which I covered for the ***Public Ledger***. At Lausanne he proved to be as successful a diplomat as a general [CKS].

[182] LC Catalogue #: DLC/PP 1994: 064 [Album]. **Note**: At the bottom of this photo a typed note has been added which reads: "*Col. Ismet Bey as C.K.S. saw him soon after he won the battle of Inonu*" [HWL].

Plate 89: The Ankara – Konya Express Train[184]

While I was waiting for the train to start, the locomotive engineer, Sabri Sefi [Seyfi], came up and introduced himself, speaking in French. He had studied mechanical engineering in Germany during the war and was anxious go to the United States to continue his studies. He invited me to tea later at Eskişehir and introduced to me another young Turk, Mehmed Selâmi, an electrical engineer, who also had studied in Germany and also wished to go to the United States. Mehmed Selâmi was working on a project for the development of hydroelectric power so as to electrify the railroad the Turks plan to build from Samsun to Sivas. He wanted to get the advantage of the experience America has had in this work. The eagerness of these two Turks to train themselves so to better serve their country was touching.

Plate 90: Nationalist Troops in Eskişehir[185]

[183] The Balkan States include those countries in the Balkan Peninsula: Yugoslavia, Rumania, Bulgaria, Albania, Greece and the European part of Turkey [CKS].

[184] LC Catalogue #: DLC/PP 1994: 064.50. **Note**: On the back of this photo Streit wrote: "*Turkish Express Train on which I rode from Angora to Eski-Shehr*" [HWL].

[185] LC Catalogue #: DLC/PP 1994: 064.156. **Note**: On the back of this photo Streit wrote: "*Turkish Nationalist infantry*" [HWL].

At one station along the route I got an insight into the reason why the Turkish army is so good a fighting organization. A Turkish officer in the town was leaving on our train for another post. The private soldiers were crowded around him to bid him goodbye. Each of them saluted the officer in Turkish style, touching first their chin and then their forehead with his hand, then shook his hand and kissed it. There were tears in the eyes of some of them when the train left. I had seen other examples of the good feeling between Turkish officers and soldiers, but none which equaled this for affection [**Plate 90**].

ESKİŞEHİR GREETS ME WITH A 'COMMITTEE OF 3' –OFFICERS AND LOCAL EDITOR– TO BE MY GUIDE.

At Eskişehir I was astonished to hear a voice ask in English "*Is this the American correspondent?*" The speaker, a Turk, Ali Kemal Bey,[186] told me that he was a member of the committee which had been named to receive me. He introduced the other two members, who spoke French, Lieutenant Ferid [Ferit] Bey of the Intelligence Section of the Army, and Basri Bey,[187] editor of the local newspaper, '***Istiklal***,' [***İstiklâl***] or 'Independent.'[188]

They conducted me to the 'Osmanlı Hotel' where a comfortable room furnished in European style had been reserved for me. It was the hour for the afternoon prayer, and when we opened the door to my room we found a policeman in it, praying. I could not help but respect the man's simple faith in the one God whom the Prophet had revealed to him and we stood aside until he had finished. The members of my reception committee smiled tolerantly at the policeman. It was easy to see that their religion had lost its hold on them. Islam occupies no more place in the lives of the young educated Turks that does Christianity in the youth of the West.

While tea and French pastries -I had not tasted the latter for over a month- were being served, Ali Kemal told me that I was to consider myself as the guest of the city. He said he and his friends were there to show me whatever I wished to see, and that I was to regard them as my personal attachés. And attachés they were - one of them at least was with me nearly every hour of the three days I spent in Eskişehir. My visit to the city was indeed personally conducted, but this was true of no other part of my trip. Two carriages and a policeman were also placed at my beck and call.

The three members of the committee were all young men. Kemal had studied in Robert College and in the Royal College in London. He was one of the few Turks I met who had a good word to say for the English. He had been in Paris, Vienna, Berlin and Hamburg and had studied in Germany during the war. In addition to English, he spoke French, German, Hungarian and Greek. He was technical inspector of the government telegraph and telephone system and was devoted to his work. His dream was to go to the United States so as to inspect our telephone system. He was amazingly well-informed as to technical improvements of the telephone and telegraph in America. With great pride he showed me later the fourteen cables he had installed in a new office in the city and told me of the telephone service maintained with the front. If any line to the front remained out of order for more than two hours, he said, the heavy hand of the General Staff would fall upon him.

"*Our wire system,*" he told me, "*would astonish an expert from the West. We have lacked much essential equipment and have had to improvise it ourselves. We long ago ran out of the regular material for insulation, but we have*

[186] My efforts at identifying individuals Streit met in Eskişehir have been greatly assisted by Yilmaz Büyükerşen, Mayor of Eskişehir and founder of the city's Anadolu University. He put me in touch with Dr. Şaduman Halıcı, a young historian on the faculty of the Anadolu University, who was able to identify and provide family names for a number of Streit's contacts. I am most grateful to both for their kindnesses.

[187] **Note**: [Hasan] Basri [Aytöre] Bey was later to serve as Mayor of Eskişehir (1922-1923). He played a key role in the rebuilding of the city following the retreat and burning of the city by the Greek army in 1922 [HWL].

[188] **Note**: Actually *istiklâl* means independence [HWL].

invented a substitute that does just as well. The system doesn't work according to Hoyle, but it works, and that is the main thing."

Ali Kemal was homesick for the music and society of İstanbul and the Occident. He wanted to know what the latest American songs were and sang some he knew - 'The River Shannon,' 'Dreamland,' 'You Made Me Love You,' and 'Swanee River.'

Lieutenant Ferit was of a quieter type. He spoke French exceedingly well, though he had never been in France, and had learned the language by the self-help system. He had even written some books in French. He also spoke German, Bulgarian and Russian and had a limited reading knowledge of English. He had been a prisoner of war in Egypt and declared that much of the present hostility of the Turks toward the British was due to the treatment they had received in the English prison camps.

"*When a soldier no longer has his gun, he is merely a man and is entitled to be treated as such,*" was the point of view Ferit expressed.

He laughed at the English craving for souvenirs.

"*They used to strip us prisoners of our watches, cigarette cases, of all our personal effects which were of any value,*" he said. "*The word 'souvenir' will now always be associated in my mind with the phrase our brigands employ when they hold up a man,*" he continued, "*They say to their victim, 'Sou-ouni-vir!*" [sic.: *şunu ver*] *which sounds much like 'souvenir' and means 'Give me everything you've got!*'" [sic.: give me that].

Basri Bey, in addition to being editor, was also a member of the City Council, and while I was in Eskişehir, he lost in an election for Mayor by only a few votes.

My meals were served in my room; they were the best I had while in Turkey. Some dishes were European -there was beefsteak which I had given up hope of tasting in Anatolia!- and some were Turkish, but they were all well-cooked.

After tea, my guides took me to the Staff Headquarters, where I met Lieutenant Baki Bey, head of the Intelligence Section, and Colonel Nadji [Naci] Bey, Chief of the Staff,[189] both charming men. The latter said that he was at my disposal and said that he had heard that I wanted to see their troops, he had ordered a review of the HQ's companies of infantry and cavalry to be held immediately. My talk with İsmet Paşa, it was easy to see, had been productive.

Hailed by 'Hello!' in unison from Turkish troops; Turkey Red Wheat in native home; meerschaum galore; fine faience

I went to the parade ground with the colonel. When we approached the Company of Infantry he gave an order and with one voice the soldiers shouted "Maraba!" [*merhaba*] the common word of greeting in Turkey which may be translated as 'Hello!' The colonel then asked me to walk down the line with him and inspect the company.

When we had finished, he asked me, "*Have you any orders you wish to give?*" I told him I had none. The colonel then put the company through maneuvers which ended with the men marching by us to the music of the band. When he asked me if I found his men well-trained and well-disciplined, I could not but answer in the affirmative. The men were sturdy and determined-looking. They were well-clad in British and

[189] **Note**: [Ahmet] Naci [Tınaz] (1882-1964). Regular army officer. He appears to be the individual who hosted Streit in Eskişehir. He is listed in Aydemir, 1967: Vol. II: p. 603 as having been a *Kurmay Albay* (General Staff Colonel), and the Commander of the 15th Division in September of 1922 during the final National offensive against the Greek army. He later rose to the rank of *Korgeneral* (Lieutenant General). Following his retirement from the military he served three terms in Parliament [HWL].

American uniforms and overcoats and had most of the usual equipment of the modern soldier. The company included a couple of squads armed with light machine guns and an ambulance section.

Then we turned to the cavalry and went through the same ceremony. The cavalrymen carried sabers as well as rifles and rode small but robust native ponies, many of which appeared to have Arab blood in them. Four mounted machine-gun sections were attached to the company.

The next morning Colonel Naci held a review of several batteries of artillery for me. The guns were 120-caliber, German made. They had been used by the Turks during the war, but after the Armistice the British dismantled them, removing the breech locks, rangefinders and other parts. Under the direction of a Turkish officer, Captain Djevdad [Cevdet] Bey, the Turks made the missing parts in the railway machine shops at Eskişehir - work which was far beyond the Turks, according to foreigners in İstanbul. But the Turks have learned a great deal of engineering from the Germans during the war. They showed me, at my request, about twenty artillery parts which they manufactured [**Plate 91**]; the tool work was very good, and I was astonished more than once by the technical ability the Turks displayed.

After watching raw recruits being drilled and machine-gun and bayonet practice by the regulars, Colonel Naci told me that he wanted me to see their schools. A kind, fatherly man, I was not surprised at his interest in children. Two of the seven passenger Benz touring cars of the General Staff had been provided for the trip through the city. We first had coffee with the mutasarrıf (governor) Sami Bey, who then accompanied us. Next we visited three of the military and Red Crescent hospitals in the city. (The Turkish branch of the international Red Cross Society is called the Red Crescent having as its insignia a red crescent). Their beds were Turkish made. But the hospitals were clean, bright and sunny and the patients seemed to be well cared for. Many of the nurses

Plate 91: Artillery Parts Manufactured by the Nationalists in Eskişehir[190]

[190] LC Catalogue #: DLC/PP 1994: 064.187. **Note**: On the back of this photo Streit wrote: "*Some of the artillery parts made by the Turks – Eski-Shehr*" [HWL].

were Turkish women, an innovation of the Balkan war which at that time caused great outcry.

The excursion ended with a call on the director of the Turkish Agricultural Bank and an inspection of the town library and museum. The library was none too large but it was a good beginning. The museum was more interesting, for here the many products of the rich agricultural district of which Eskişehir is the center are gathered. Every farmer and miller knows of Turkey Red Wheat; few probably know that it originated in Eskişehir. We speak of Missouri Meerschaum but most of the world's supply of the best quality of this mineral comes from Eskişehir. In the train approaching Eskişehir I saw hills of meerschaum. Two beautiful strings of meerschaum beads, one black, the other white were hanging in the museum. When I admired them, the Turks took them out of the case and insisted that I had to accept them. A factory at Eskişehir for the making of meerschaum buttons and beads as well as pipes and cigarette holders should do a profitable business.

That evening Lieutenant Baki Bey invited me to the local moving-picture show. A military band furnished good music, but the films were old and flickered so much that they hurt the eyes. The titles and sub-titles were in French, not Turkish, though the films were Italian and German, the latter being relics of the war. The program consisted of a color travel film depicting scenes in Switzerland and the Chicago stockyards, a German spy drama and a German comedy. The travel film was stupid and preposterous and the German films vulgar and disgusting. The house was well-filled and among the spectators were some women and girls. This co-mingling was a distinct innovation in Turkey, for Muslim conventions demand that the sexes be kept rigidly separate and matinees are usually given exclusively for the women and evening performances for the men. But the old social order is now rapidly changing in Turkey. Venders moved about the theater selling lemonade and simits. I noted with surprise that the room was equipped with electric fans. Once a week the movies are free to the soldiers.

The next day we visited the bazaars and shops. In one store I found a remarkable collection of the renowned faience (a fine grade of pottery) made in the neighboring city of Kutahia [Kütahya]. The faience was on sale at a tenth and even as low as a twentieth of the price it commands in the West. This is another product of the region which could be developed. No one, after seeing this 'Kütahya ware.' is likely to say that the Turks are lacking in artistic sense. The pitchers, vases, plates and other pieces, which I brought back to Paris, where the standard of taste in ceramics is exceptionally high, were greatly admired. But I bought them not without difficulty, for my hosts insisted upon paying the bill. I was the guest of the city, they urged, and it was the custom of the country that anything a guest wanted he should have. I told them that under such conditions I would not feel like selecting anything in the stores, and thus I succeeded in buying what I wanted. But I had to let the city pay my hotel bill.

Among the things I got were some pretty meerschaum chaplets. Nearly every Turk –and many a Greek as well - carries a small string of beads of some sort with him and toys with it in his hands as he talks. They are not rosaries as one is likely to think. They have no connection with religion though, no doubt they once had. The chaplet is simply a plaything, an outlet for nervous energy - something to keep the hands occupied. It has the additional advantage of helping to keep one from smoking too much. Every chaplet has exactly 33 beads, except those which the hodjas [hocas] or priests carry, which have 99.[191] When I interviewed Mustafa Kemal Paşa I noted that his hands were soon playing unconsciously with a string of amber beads.

[191] **Note**: Streit was misinformed as to the significance of the *tespih/tesbih* (prayer beads). While true that not all those who carry them do so out of religious sentiment, in point of fact, the ninety-nine beads correspond to the names of God given in the ***Qur'an***. For religious Muslims, then and now, who recite these names, they are in fact a kind of rosary. Likewise, the significance of the string of thirty-three beads is religious, i.e., the user simply goes through the beads three times while repeating the ninety-nine names of Allah [HWL].

SACRED TOMBS; JEWISH, RUSSIAN, GREEK, ARMENIAN AND TURKISH PROSTITUTES; RUGS MADE BY YOUNG GIRLS

In the afternoon I visited the tomb of Ede Bali [Şeyh Edebâlî], the father-in-law of Sultan Osman [sic. Osman Gâzi],[192] who founded and gave his name to the Ottoman Empire (the Turks call themselves 'Osmanlı'). The sacred tombs of the Turks are all much alike. They are covered by a dome-shaped building which contains a sarcophagus in heroic size for the great man, and others in ordinary size for his wives and children. These sarcophagi are all alike in design, they differ only in size. Those of men, have a turban stuck at their head. The tomb of the great man is usually eight or ten feet long, about four feet wide and four feet high at the head and three feet wide and high at the foot. It is built something like a house with a gabled roof and is invariably covered with a green cloth. It is sometimes decorated with silk handkerchiefs of various colors. The framework is usually of wood, the bodies being buried in the earth below. The building is often decorated with framed verses from the ***Qur'an***: '*There is no God but God, and Muhammed is his Prophet,*' '*Allah Akbar*' – *God is Great*. As in the mosque, one takes off his shoes before entering one of these tombs.

The caretaker is usually a hoca, and we found the one in the tomb of Edebâlî sitting cross-legged on the floor, reading the ***Qur'an*** which was placed before him on one of the small stands made for that purpose. "*The **Qur'an**, the **Old** and **New Testament** they are all good,*" the hoca told me. "*Our religion contains much of both Judaism and Christianity - a combination of the two which we think is better than either of them. But that is a matter which can be settled only by the conscience of each of us.*"

Most of the young Turks whom I was with didn't want to go to the bother of taking off their shoes, they remained outside. To the very portico of the tomb one of them, an electrical engineer, talked to me incessantly of his scheme for developing hydro-electric power in Turkey, a subject which we resumed as soon as I had my shoes on again. It was a typical instance of the trend of mind in the rising generation.

Next we went to the mosque of Sherif Roumi [Eşrefoğlu Rûmî],[193] built by the Turks 450 years ago (Eskişehir, by the way, means old city). This mosque was the most beautiful I saw in my travels in Asiatic Turkey, though there are others, which I did not see, such as those in Bursa, which surpass it in fame. A balcony shielded by a lattice work was reserved for women in the mosque. The reason for the lattice is the same as that for the veil and the shape-concealing clothing which Muslim women are supposed to wear - to minimize sensual desires among the men (it is also urged on behalf of the veil and the practice of keeping the hair covered, that the beauty of a woman should be kept for her husband).

The dervish, who seemed to be in charge of the mosque, invited our party to have coffee. Chairs were placed on the portico of the mosque and we were given not one but three cups of coffee. Turkish coffee is served in a small

---

[192] **Note**: Streit must have visited the pilgrimage site, described in the first half of the 17th century in Kâtib Çelebi's ***Cihannüma*** as the *Şeyh Edebâli Türbesi* (Mausoleum of Şeyh Edebâli). Eskişehir is home to one of several mausoleums (*türbe*s) linked to Şeyh Edebâlî. The best known of these is the tomb in the town of Bilecik, which lies some sixty miles to the West of Eskişehir. The Greek occupation of Eskişehir (which occurred a few months after Streit had been there and lasted over a year), is known to have caused great destruction to the city. As the Greek forces withdrew from the city in 1922 they attempted to burn it to the ground and this site was largely destroyed. It was later rebuilt [HWL].

[193] **Note**: I am at a loss to identify which mosque Streit actually visited. There is no *Eşrefoğlu Rûmî Câmii* or *Eşref-i Rûmî Câmii* in Eskişehir, nor can I find any reference to there ever having been one. Indeed, the only significant Ottoman mosque in the city of Eskişehir is the *Mustafa Paşa Câmii* aka *Kurşunlu Câmii* (Leaded Mosque), which dates to the first half of the 16th century and is part of the large complex (*külliye*) which was built by Çoban Mustafa Paşa (d. 1529), the son-in-law of Yavuz Sultan Selim. While this must be the site visited by Streit, I am unable to find anything linking it to Eşref-i Rûmî [HWL].

cup which contains about as much as a liquor glass. Their other favorite drink, tea, I might add, is always served in a glass, without milk.

From the mosque we went to inspect the restricted district, which consisted of three houses. The prostitutes were mostly Jewesses, although there were a few Russians, Greeks, Armenians and Turks. The Turks follow the German and French policy of recognition but rigid control and inspection of prostitutes. Officers and soldiers in uniform are not allowed to enter the district. Turkish physicians told me that the percentage of venereal disease in the army and in the civilian population was low. The government hopes to make it even lower. Mustafa Kemal Paşa in summing up, in a speech I heard him give March 1, the work done by the Assembly mentioned the law for the prevention of venereal disease as one of the best acts passed. By another law passed during the war, men must submit to a physical examination before marriage. From my observations I should say that the sexual life of the Turk is at least fully as clean as that of the Christian in the West. In all my conversations with Turks not once did I hear a smutty story told. I doubt whether this could be said by any traveler who spent six weeks living with the people of any Christian country.

The Turks seldom talked about women at all, though, queerly enough, three dishes which I found in the provincial towns bore these exotic names: 'Lady's Thigh' [*Kadın Budu Köftesi*], 'Lady's Navel' [*Kadın Göbeği*], and the 'Beauty's Lips' [*Dilber Dudağı*]. Ask for the first, and you get hamburger steak; for the other two and you are served pastries whose shape is supposed to resemble the things they are named after.

The third day I visited one of the local rug-making factories. The workers were young girls, Greeks, Armenians and Turks, many of them small children who should have been in school. The Turks told me that because of the war and poverty of most of the people, they were forced at present to wink at failures to enforce the law for compulsory education. The looms were primitive and every knot was tied by hand. The children come and go as they please. The hours of work are not fixed for the workers are paid piece rates, so much for every hundred knots they tie. By working ten hours a child can make 50 or 60 piastres - about 35 or 40 cents according to the rate of exchange at that time, although the purchasing value of the money in Eskişehir was three or four times what it would be in America.

PREPARING THE TURKS OF TOMORROW; A SOUND BASIC PRINCIPLE FOR EDUCATION

"*You see, we are paying even more attention to the schools for girls than to those for boys. The girls are going to be the mothers of the next generation, and if they are well-educated their children will be. The future is for the children*".

It was Lieutenant Baki Bey, chief of the Intelligence section of the army staff at Eskişehir, who was speaking. We had just finished visiting the boys' and girls' [high] schools and the kindergartens [primary schools] in the city. Colonel Naci Bey, Chief of Staff, had been very anxious that I see them and had taken most of the day to show them to me. The civil governor of the district, Sami Bey, had also accompanied us. The interest which these men, especially the soldiers, took in education, and their viewpoint toward it, are indicative of the new spirit which is working a social revolution in Turkey.

The Western world has dismissed the Turks as 'barbarians' and has ignored the efforts to educate the people which they have made in the past decade during which time they have had a constitutional government. That they have made any progress at all in public instruction is remarkable, for the Young Turks were continually involved in war. Nothing attests the devotion of the Turks to the cause of education better than the new school buildings which the traveler finds in many Anatolian towns. Even during the World War the Turks continued to build schools. Some of them, like the huge building in Ankara intended for a school of arts and crafts, have not yet been completed. But despite the wars which the Turks are now carrying on they are still building them. At Eskişehir the present government has nearly finished the construction of a model primary school which it began last year. During the war the Turks also passed a compulsory education law. Because of the present difficulties, they are unable, however, to enforce it, though this is being done in some cities.

It was during the war, too, in 1917, that a Turkish woman, Nakie [Nakiye] Hanım, then director of preparatory schools in İstanbul, established Faizie [*Feyziye*] School, the first co-educational high school in Turkey.[194] It is a private institution - in the public schools, except the primary schools, classes are segregated by sex. It is run on American principles, though Nakiye Hanım does not know English. Stranger still, she does not know French. The members of the faculty are Turks of both sexes. The school has 200 students between the ages of fourteen and nineteen, about an equal number of boys and girls. The two sexes mingle freely together - there is no restriction of social intercourse as one finds, for instance, at Oxford University. And, of course, neither the women teachers nor the girl students wear veils. Europe has never adopted the co-educational system in secondary schools. In Turkey, the establishment of such an institution as the Feyziye School constitutes a far more violent break with the past than it would in Europe. Yet Nakiye Hanım told me that her experiment had met with little opposition and was succeeding beyond her expectations.[195]

While Cambridge University was denying to women the right of obtaining degrees -a right which Oxford granted only last year- the Turkish University of İstanbul was opening its doors to women on a basis of equality with the men. And Western feminists have no long- standing tradition of female seclusion to contend with as those in Turkey have.

The devotion of the Turkish intellectuals to the cause of education is touching; since the Allied occupation of İstanbul, the Turkish government there has been cut off from Anatolia, thus İstanbul has been almost without funds. An Allied board now controls Turkish finances at İstanbul. It pays the salaries of the gendarmes and police, but if the university professors and school teachers today are getting ten percent of the salary they should have received three months ago they are luckier than when I was in İstanbul. And yet these professors and teachers are continuing their work.

The government of the Grand National Assembly is able to pay its officials and its teachers, but is handicapped in carrying out its educational program by the fact that it has to devote more than half of its income to defending itself from the Greeks and the Allies. It is also handicapped by a lack of teachers, as many of the educated Turks have been called to the army or to other branches of government service. When I left Ankara the Commissar for Public Instruction, Hamdullah Suphi [Tanrıöver] Bey, was seeking to remedy this by a law which he termed "*for the defense of the internal front*" and which would give him the power to mobilize young men able to teach and send them on duty to schools in all parts of the country. The government has also established at Ankara what is called a 'People's University' where lectures free to the public are given by Turkish intellectuals on such subjects as sociology, economics, history, literature, natural science, health and hygiene. The lectures are well-attended, chiefly by mature men, government employees and soldiers. The government is also maintaining normal schools in the larger cities.

In education as in politics the government is emphasizing the liberal elements in the Muslim religion. Many Turks repeated to me Muhammed's admonition to his converts to go to the ends of the earth in their search for knowledge. In the boys' high school at Eskişehir mottoes such as the following were posted on the walls:

---

[194] **Note**: Nakiye Elgün (1882- ?). Turkish educator, parliamentarian. One of the group of 17 female parliamentarians who were the first women deputies elected to parliament in 1935 [HWL].

[195] **Note**: This is the only instance in the text of ***The Unknown Turks*** where Streit describes life in İstanbul. While it is clear from his work that he visited the city before departing for Ankara, this is his only reference to interviews he may have held while there [HWL].

'Knowledge is worth more than prayer'

'A Muslim never lies'

'System is half of human life'

'The search of knowledge is obligatory for every Muslim man and woman'

'A good man is one who is of use to his fellow-beings'

'The fear of God is the beginning of wisdom'

'The school is the educator of humanity'

'Respect your flag'

'The future of your country depends upon your work today'

'Islam consists in living straight, clean lives'

'The best religion is Islam'

'Progress comes from doing things and not surrendering them to God'

'One hour spent in the search of knowledge is worth more than a night spent in prayer'

To appreciate fully the change which is being brought about in Turkish schools, it is necessary to remember that formerly they were in the hands of the religious leaders and instruction was based largely on a study of the ***Qur'an***. The chief goal of education was to commit the ***Qur'an*** to memory - the boys who achieved this distinction could call themselves 'hafouz' [*hafiz*], the title for a Muslim who has memorized the ***Qur'an***. Pictures of living beings were forbidden.

The schools today are in the hands of laymen. The boys are taught by men, the girls by women, who also are in charge of the primary schools. The study of the ***Qur'an*** occupies a subordinate place. The schools still have a special room in which the students may say their prayers, but this seems to be more out of deference to tradition than for daily use. In one school I visited, science had crowded religion out of every room, the only space left for those who wished to respond to the muezzin's [*müezzin*'s] call being a corner of the hall screened by a couple of rugs. Pictures, far from being forbidden, line the walls and much use is made of them in instruction. Most of them are German lithographs and charts. I saw pictures of Washington, London, Paris, Berlin, and of old ruins in Rome or Athens, of the different races of people, of all kinds of animals and plants - pictures of all sorts in all the schools. One of the teachers in the boys' school which I have mentioned, Hafız Kerun, is a painter of no mean ability. Several of his mural paintings, one of them portraying a woman without a veil, hang in one of the coffee houses in Eskişehir. I was shown sketches and water-colors made by the boys; some of them, also, pictured women without veils.

'Where is my cavalier?' 'Here I am my lady,' is heard in Turkish kindergarten

By far the most interesting schools I visited were the primary schools. There I found little Turkish boys and girls sitting side by side in sunny rooms well supplied with pictures and sand-piles. In one of them, the teacher had a boy and a girl give declamations for us, all their comrades applauding them when they finished. In another five boys and five girls gave a rather complicated dance, singing all the while. Both the steps and the music were European, and the dance ended with the boys and girls coupling off and waltzing! And waltzing very well, I may add [**Plate 92**].

I was as much amazed as delighted at the charming sight and asked that they resume the waltz so that I could take a picture of them. They reassembled, but one little girl could not find her partner at first and asked in a plaintive voice, "*But where is my cavalier?*"

At that a little boy stepped up and gallantly offering his arm said in the most natural way, "*Here I am, my lady.*"

Plate 92: Turkish Primary School Boys & Girls Waltzing in Eskişehir[196]

And Colonel Naci Bey, whose kind, fatherly face was beaming with pride, turned to me and said smilingly: "*And they call us 'barbarians!' Ah, if the Powers would only leave us in peace! But we will save our country for these little ones. They shall have the chance we have never had.*"

In the boys' school I found one class studying the Reformation and the Renaissance; another, German; another French. The study of French is obligatory in the Turkish public schools. I heard one Turk, a boy of eleven years who was the son of poor parents, give an explanation in French of a colored picture representing a village scene in Western Europe. Both his accent, which was almost perfect, and his vocabulary and knowledge of the rules of grammar would have put to shame most American college students of French. Yet his instructor, a Turk, had never been in France.

One room in this school was arranged so that theatrical productions could be given. I also noted that the secondary schools were surprisingly well-equipped with good apparatus for the study of physics and natural sciences. Some of them had small zoological, botanical and geological Museums.

In the class in home economics in a girls' school I heard one of the students tell how to prevent tuberculosis. She was questioned by Dr. Salih Bey, in charge of the military hospitals in Eskişehir, who was also with me, and she showed a thorough grasp of the subject. Other girls whom he examined at random displayed a commendable

196 LC Catalogue #: DLC/PP 1994: 064.43.

Plate 93: Women Primary School Teachers in Eskişehir[197]

knowledge of sanitary principles. A Turkish violinist, a man, was giving singing lessons to some girls in another room.

At noon the girls assembled in the hall before leaving the school. One of them held up the Star and Crescent flag of Turkey, which all the students saluted. Another girl then declaimed a poem by a Turkish poet in honor of the flag. In another girls' school they also gave a flag ceremony for me, but here they sang in chorus a Nationalist song, 'Osmanlı,' standing at military attention while they sang.

Tell America "We are doing all we can"

It is evident that the Nationalists are losing no time in instilling patriotism into the minds of the rising generation. This effort to make the children think of themselves as Turks first of all and as Muslims only secondarily, is one of the many innovations of the Nationalists, for the reverse was formerly true. The music to which the song was sung was European in style, though it was written by a Turkish composer. In the same school I heard more declamations and dramatic readings. All the girls spoke with good expression and used gestures to advantage - they showed not only that they had received considerable training, but also that they had much native ability.

The teachers, both men and women, impressed me as being very much in earnest and anxious to improve the schools [**Plate 93**]. They were modest, and apologized for their schools not being all they should be. Judged by Western standards, their schools, of course, are backward, although not nearly so much as is generally supposed. But judged by the past in Turkey, and with allowance made for the religious prejudices and the never-ending wars with which public instruction has had to contend -and this, it seems to me, is the only fair standard- they represent a remarkable and praiseworthy advance. The fact that the teachers are not satisfied with the schools speaks well for the future.

[197] LC Catalogue #: DLC/PP 1994: 064.44. **Note**: On the back of this photo Streit wrote: "*Teachers Girl's School Eski-Shehr*" [HWL].

In no better way can I give my personal opinion of the work which I saw the Turks doing for the education of the people, than to deliver the message given me by the gentle-mannered and devoted woman who was Principal of the Girls' High School in Eskişehir:

> Please tell our sisters in America that we are doing all we can to bring civilization and progress to our country.

A DAY ON THE 16,000 ACRES FARM OF HASAN BEY, A PROGRESSIVE ENTREPRENEUR; HIS 19-YEAR-OLD SON IS AMONG THE WAITERS SERVING US AT BANQUET WHERE I AM GIVEN AN ENTIRE LEG OF LAMB

Then I went with Osman Ferid Bey, Director of Scientific Agriculture in the district and caretaker of the museum, to visit the estate of Hassan [Hasan] Bey a few miles from the city. Osman Ferid had the devotion to his work which I found to be typical of the young Turks. He had studied agriculture several years in France and kept informed of developments in the Western world through the International Institute of Agriculture in Rome. He was in charge of the model farm which the district maintained.

Hasan Bey is one of the comparatively few large proprietors among the Turks. He owns a block of 16,000 acres [60,000 *dönüm*] stretching across the rich plain of Eskişehir which, I was told, had been the property of his family for 250 years. His domain was not fenced in; a ditch marked its boundary. When we alighted from our carriage at the house [**Plate 94**], a man came forward to meet me. Clad in a turban, with a worn, fur-lined cape over his shoulders, and rough riding boots on his feet, he looked much like some of the peasants, and I should not have imagined that this was the Turkish 'millionaire' had

Plate 94: Hasan Bey's Çiftlik Outside Eskişehir[198]

[198] LC Catalogue #: DLC/PP 1994: 064 [Red Album: Turkey, 1920-1921 by C. K. Streit].

not my guide nudged me. Osman Ferid had told me that he was one of the most progressive farmers. I had noticed modern agricultural implements, including a gasoline tractor, scattered about the place, and was expecting to find Hasan Bey clothed more like a European than a Turk. There was something of the feudal lord, of the man born to rule in his bearing, though he was modest and not at all domineering. His fierce mustache and the horrible disfigurement caused by the loss of his nose, belied his kind nature.[199]

He welcomed me cordially and led the way into his house, the cleanest and most modern I saw outside of the towns in Turkey. It was three stories high but it was not so imposing as one would expect on such an estate. We were late and our host had already had lunch. A table was spread in European style for the five men of our party - Lieutenant Ferid, Osman Ferid, Mehmed Ali, the policeman who had been attached to me, and I. The fact that the Turks evidently considered it but natural for one in a subordinate position, as was the policeman, to eat with us is a typical instance of the spirit of equality which reigns among them. Djevad [Cevat], the unique son and heir of Hasan Bey, an attractive young man of 19 [**Plate 95**], joined the two men-servants in waiting on us, while his father stood in the room and chatted with his guests.

The meal, which was purely Turkish, began with a thick soup made of yaourt [*yoğurt*], a sort of cottage cheese for which the Turks are famous. Yoğurt and pilav form the principal items of the peasant's diet.

"*It is not the custom of the country to serve lamb at this season,*" Hasan Bey explained, "*but as it is one of our specialties, I have had one baked for you.*"

A whole lamb was then brought in on a huge platter, and my host proceeded to put a full quarter of the animal on my plate. Out of politeness I had to eat the tremendous helping, and fortunately it was tender and delicious - the best, I believe, that I have ever tasted. A glass of another variety of yoğurt [= *ayran*] was served as a drink with this *pièce de resistance*. The beverage, Hasan Bey told me, was another specialty of the country.

Then came the pilav - served with a bowl of thick *yoğurt*. I began to eat the rice alone, but my host informed me that it was customary to eat it with *yoğurt*, and so I tried the combination, which was rather good. The others at the table, who had evidently been waiting for me to take some yoğurt then helped themselves to it. The meal ended with a Turkish sweet, bakaloff [*baklava*], which might be described as a thick, light pie crust soaked in syrup.

Hasan Bey was proud of the hospitality of his countrymen.

"*If one of our peasants has only a bit of bread, he will give half of it to any hungry stranger who comes to him,*" he said. "*It is nothing for me to give you a lamb. The peasants give you far more than I have offered you, for they give you half of the little they've got.*"

He wanted to know my impressions of the Turks and was glad to hear that I had not found them, as he said most Europeans seemed to think they were, "*lazy, barbarous, fanatical.*" He showed a broad and patriotic interest in the affairs of his country. He was all in favor of modernizing the agricultural methods in Turkey and was anxious for American aid toward this end. He dwelt on the friendly attitude of the Turks toward Americans, the esteem in which they were held, the benefits both countries would

[199] **Note**: Hasan Bey's family took the surname Ünügür in 1934, by which time he was deceased. His granddaughter, Professor Asuman Müftüoğlu (a retired professor of medicine at İstanbul University), most generously shared a number of family photos with me. Among these is one showing Hasan Bey and his son Cevat, which was taken some five years prior to Streit's visit. In this photo, Hasan Bey still has his nose, although there appears to be a blemish next to it (cancer?), which may have later led to its removal. Hasan Bey's farm still exists and is currently run by his granddaughter [HWL].

Plate 95: Cevat, son of Hasan Bey, a Large Landowner in Eskişehir[200]

[200] LC Catalogue #: DLC/PP 1994: 064.188. **Note**: On the back of this photo Streit wrote: "*Djevad, son of Hassan Bey*" [HWL].

derive from closer commercial relations. He complained of the profits which the 'middlemen' drew from the sale of farming implements and declared that an American factory could do a good business in his neighborhood by dealing directly with the farmers. One of the purposes of the local Agricultural Bank, of which he was one of the backers, was to cut down the middleman's profit in the purchase of agricultural machinery. He suggested that it would pay an American implement concern to establish a factory in Turkey and make or at least assemble machinery there.

We then went out and saw his racing horses and his cattle. One of his horses was of Arabian stock, another

Plate 96: Oil Burning Locomotives Held in Reserve for the Evacuation of Eskişehir[201]

had some English racing blood in him. The cattle belonged to a breed which Hasan Bey had created by crossing native and Crimean stocks. The animals, while they were a distinct improvement on the native cattle, still left much to be desired. Turkey is sadly in need of blooded bulls.

Another of Hasan Bey's experiments had been the introduction of rice-growing in Eskişehir. People had said that the altitude was too high, the climate too dry. For seven years Hasan Bey experimented before he found a 'dry' rice which would thrive in the Eskişehir district. Then the war interrupted his labors.

"*I've lost all the money I put into the experiment,*" he said, "*and now I'll have to begin all over again. But I've shown that a rice can be developed which is suited to this climate. Rice is one of our chief foods; if we can grow more of it ourselves it will be an immense savings.*"

Hasan Bey had not been out of Turkey and could speak only his native tongue, but my interpreter commented on the excellence of his Turkish. His son, who was a good looking, well built lad, dressed in European clothes, had studied in the local schools and could speak a little German. My suggestion that Cevat should study in some American agricultural college met with favor in his father's eyes.

Note: While in Eskişehir Clarence Streit saw a group of six oil-burning locomotives sitting on a siding in the town's railway station [**Plate 96**]. On the back of the photo he took of one of them, he wrote: "*Oil burning locomotives held in reserve [in Eskişehir] for troop movements in case of Greek advance (stock of crude oil held over from the World War).*" Little did he know at the time that when the Greek armies took Eskişehir a few months later on July 19, 1921, those six oil-burning locomotives would be pivotal in facilitating the Nationalist retreat [HWL].

[201] LC Catalogue #: DLC/PP 1994: 064.153.

Chapter X

From Eskişehir to Mediterranean Coast

On troop train to the Black Tower of the opium region;

Eskişehir has a population of 25,000 - it is about the same size as Ankara.[202] But it impressed me as a much more progressive, go-ahead city than the capital. Here, better than in Ankara or in any other place I visited in Turkey, one can feel the tremendous vitality of the Turks, the strength and energy behind the Nationalist movement.

The tide of Turkish reform can be measured fairly well by the position of women - for as Halide Edib Hanım told me, "*reaction in Turkey always begins by attacking the freedom won by the women.*" And in Eskişehir, far more than in any other city in the interior of Turkey which I visited, the Turkish women go about in public without veils. Eskişehir in every respect, is in the vanguard of the New Turkey.

Mehmed Ali and I left Eskişehir March 9th on a troop train. Colonel Naci Bey and Lieutenant Baki Bey came down to the station to see us off. This was a slow train - it made barely fifteen miles an hour. Night came and we were still six hours from Afiun Karahisar [Afyonkarahisar]. It was no sleeping car, but I managed to make one of it by putting up my folding cot in the aisle of the compartment.

At Afyonkarahisar where we arrived at midnight a pleasant young Turkish officer met me. Evidently they had telegraphed ahead about my coming - and took me to a hotel where I had a good room. Afioun [*afyon*] means 'opium' -this is the center of the poppy district in Asia Minor- and 'Karahissar' [Karahisar] means 'Black Tower.' The tower is a picturesque ruin dominating the town on a precipitous hill in front of the hotel. I wanted to leave for Antalya the next morning, and the officer volunteered to find a good yaylı for me. He did much better than I had at Yozgat. The yaylı he got belonged to the man who had the contract for carrying the mail and was the kind used on Turkish wedding journeys - the interior decorated with tapestry and with little mirrors and tassels. Mustapha [Mustafa], the arabadji [*arabacı*], looked remarkably like one of our Indians, but he was a good, experienced driver; and his horses were sturdy and fast.

We left Afyon in a blinding snowstorm and travelled through deep snow most of the day. We had no gendarmes - I had been in Turkey long enough to know that I did not need them. Otherwise, the trip was much the same as the earlier yaylı ride, only far more comfortable. We had plenty of good *kaymak* - pure cream fat solidified. This, with hard boiled eggs and bread and fruit, made our lunches while en route.

We spent the first night in Sandykly [Sandıklı], the next in Dinar, a well-watered town on the English built railroad from Aidin [Aydın]. At that time it was not being operated by the Turks. Before reaching Dinar we stopped at a little peasant village where preparations were being made for a wedding. When we arrived a group of peasants with a flag and a fife and drum corps -the instruments were home-made- were escorting to the village an oxcart loaded with brushwood which was to provide the nuptial bonfire [**Plate 97**]. The load was dumped at the gate of a house decorated with a flag where the wedding was to be held and the women of the village carried the wood inside. The women did not wear veils; they rarely do in many of the villages, reserving them for the occasions when they go to town.

Meanwhile, the musicians stood near and played some shrill tunes to which some of the men danced [**Plate 98**]. There were only a score of men left in the village; the wars had so depleted its population. But they were a genial and carefree lot. After I had taken pictures of their dances they crowded about me to see my camera and joked of their own distress.

[202] **Note**: Today, according to the Turkish Republic's 2008 census figures, its population is: 599,798; by contrast, Ankara's 2008 population stood at: 4,751,360 [HWL].

Plate 97: A Village Wedding[203]

"*We work and work, but we get nothing out of it,*" said one peasant. "*Always war, always war. These are the only two young men in the village, and I suppose they'll be taken soon. Look at this man.*" Laughing, he plucked at the clothing of a man beside him and said, "*he is all in rags. Pretty soon he won't be able to hold his clothes together.*" And they all laughed.

They explained to me that the wedding wouldn't take place for several days. These were only the opening festivities. The bridegroom was absent, distributing presents to -not receiving them from- the different families in the village. The bride lived in a neighboring village and would not come to her future home until two days later.

The third night we arrived in Bourdour [Burdur], a town of perhaps 15,000 inhabitants situated on the shores of a large salt lake. Here I found an Italian Catholic Mission, an Italian Doctor and an Italian manager of the local factory of the Oriental Carpet Company. Luckily for me, Signor Tuozzi, the Delegate for Asia Minor of the Italian High Commissioner in İstanbul, and the Italian Consul at Antalya, were in the town and were returning to Antalya in a light Fiat truck the next day. The gods were with me for the Italian officials had intended to return the previous day, but their car had broken down. Through their courtesy Mehmed Ali and I were able to avoid another day and a half in a yaylı for the automobile made the seventy-five miles in six hours.

My second truck ride leads to disappearing and reappearing river;

Most of the road from Afyon to Antalya is very good. The highway, I was told, was made during the war under the direction of German engineers. The stretch through the mountains from Burdur to Antalya was not without beauty and interest. At one place where the road

[203] LC Catalogue #: DLC/PP 1994: 064 [Red Album: Turkey, 1920-1921 by C. K. Streit].

Plate 98: Musicians Performing at a Village Wedding[204]

descends into a vast plain, a wilderness of rocks and shrubs, it crosses an old stone bridge, probably the most crooked example of the bridge builder's art. For two hundred yards it winds and twists along. It was only a few inches wider than the truck, and there was no balustrade or railing along the sides of much of it. This bridge, which was built centuries ago, is over the outlet of an enormous spring, the source of a most mysterious river, which, before it reaches the sea, twice suddenly disappears completely in the earth only to reappear just as abruptly a few miles distant.

DELIGHTFUL ANTALYA WHERE STREAMS CASCADE INTO HARBOR; AND WE EMBARK FOR İSTANBUL

Antalya is a city delightful to the eye, standing in a wide plain between the ranges of high mountains which run down to the coast. The blue Mediterranean stretches in front of it. A high rock wall, wrought into curious shapes by the action of the sea, forms the coast. Over it numerous streams cascade into the sea. With its olive trees and palms, its flowers and verdure, Antalya presented a pleasing contrast to the dreary wintry landscape of the interior.

In the old days the Venetian traders controlled Antalya, and the walls they erected still encircle the inner city. The Italians are now attempting to regain the position they once held there. It is the chief port - in the 'zone of influence' in Asia Minor which they have marked out for themselves. Some three hundred Italian soldiers are stationed in Antalya, but the Turkish Nationalists and not the Italians control the city. It is by her policy of friendship and not by force of arms that Italy has been able to remain in Antalya and carry on a thriving trade with the Turks.

[204] LC Catalogue #: DLC/PP 1994: 064 [Red Album: Turkey, 1920-1921 by C. K. Streit].

There are a large number of Ottoman Greeks in the city. The Greek men do not wear the fez here as they do in the interior, but curiously enough the fez forms a part of the costume of the women. Their traditional headdress is a small red fez which has almost the appearance of Happy Hooligan's (the name of Century comic strip character) famous hat. The Greeks were well dressed and seemed prosperous.

The Italian ships do not call regularly at Antalya, and there is often a wait of a week or two before one can sail. But our good luck continued - two ships anchored in the roadstead the day after we arrived and were scheduled to leave for İstanbul in a few hours (the port is too small for them to approach the insignificant dock). My baggage, however, had not arrived. Because there was not room for it in the automobile at Burdur, I had left it in the yaylı and told Mustafa to bring it to Antalya. I had already formed a high opinion of Turkish honesty and had not the slightest anxiety in leaving my possessions seventy five miles distant in the hands of my driver. Nothing would have been easier for him than to disappear with them, or, at least, to 'lose' a few things during my absence. Instead, he made the trip in record speed and delivered all my baggage to me in plenty in time to sail on the 'S. S.Milano.'

I had had most of my notes in English censored and sealed by Halide Edib Hanım before I left Ankara, but I anticipated considerable delay because of the other notes I had made in French. The Turkish port officials, had they rigidly followed their regulations, could have made me miss my boat. But they had doubtless received special instructions, for the search they made of my person was purely a matter of form and their examination of my baggage was of the most cursory kind. The Turks at Samsun, exactly six weeks previous, had accepted me on trust. With the same implicit trust in my good faith, they now allowed me to leave.

I had come to Turkey prejudiced against the Turks; I left it, like so many others who have come to know the Turks intimately by living with them, their friend and sympathizer.

Editor's Postscript

EDITOR'S POSTSCRIPT

While the focus of this work has been Streit's 1921 visit to Anatolia, the well-known Turkish journalist, Ahmed Emin Yalman, writes at length about Clarence Streit (whom he knew in 1923-1925 in İstanbul) in his book: ***Yakın Tarihte Gördüklerim ve Geçirdiklerim*** [Things I Have Seen and Experienced in Recent History].[205] While he is somewhat confused on some of the detail he provides, i.e., he incorrectly states that Streit visited Ankara during the time of the Sivas Congress (1919) rather than in 1921, he nonetheless provides some interesting anecdotal evidence which provides insight into Streit's character. For example, he writes that Streit's interest in, and assistance to, the village of Keskin Mümünlü [sic. Ceritmüminli] continued throughout his lifetime and that from time to time he continued to send modern farm implements to the villagers. He states that Streit in fact became a kind of 'Honorary Citizen' of this central Anatolian village which hosted him while he was enroute to Ankara in 1921. Yalman describes Streit as a "*hoş ve temiz insan*" (pleasant and honorable individual), and writes at some length in regard to how Streit's dispatches contributed to the dissipation of the "*dark fog*" of misinformation surrounding Turkey in the west, thereby providing a great service to Turkey by helping to present a new face for the country to the American reading public. Yalman relates that Streit's first son, with his French-born wife, was born in İstanbul and "*is still known by the nickname*: *Küçük* [little]."

Ahmed Emin relates how, while Streit was living in İstanbul, he periodically wrote a column for ***Vatan*** called '*Bir Türk Olsaydım*' ['Had I been a Turk'] in the İstanbul daily ***Vatan*** [Fatherland], which contained many useful observations and warnings. In turn, Yalman later contributed a series of columns to a Streit publication entitled: '*Bir Amerikalı Olsaydım*' ['Had I been an American'].

Finally, from Yalman's account we also learn that Streit shared with him the manuscript which is published herein, as well as telling him that he had been unable to publish it in the United States. Ahmed Emin writes: "*I truly hope that the Turkish Historical*

Plate 99: Clarence K. Streit on the Cover of ***Time Magazine*** (May 27, 1950)

[205] Erol Şadı Erdinç (Ed.): Ahmed Emin Yalman: *Yakın Tarihte Gördüklerim ve Geçirdiklerim.* Cilt I (1888-1922). İstanbul, 1970 [2nd Edition: 1997). See: pp. 456-459. **Note**: It is clear from his account that he met Streit in 1923 when he returned to Turkey as the Near East & Balkans Correspondent for the Philadelphia ***Public Ledger*** [HWL].

Association or some other body will one day translate and publish this work, which would present the true face of Anatolia during the War of Independence, as it was seen through the eyes of an American." Forty years after Yalman wrote this, Streit's ***The Unknown Turks*** is finally seeing the light of day.

In later years Streit was to become a well known figure in Washington D.C., as the author of the best-selling book ***Union Now*** and the founder of the movement known as 'Atlantic Federalism.' In 1950 his contributions were acknowledged when he appeared on the cover of the prestigious ***Time Magazine*** [**Plate 99** previous page].

While my own contacts with Streit were limited to a handful of meeting in 1983, I too was impressed by his desire to finally see his Turkish book in print. Even, sixty years after his first visit to Turkey he spent a great deal of time and effort reediting his 1921 text for potential publication. Clearly he had not forgotten his experiences.

MAP DETAILING STREIT'S TRAVELS IN ANATOLIA

Map : Clarence Streit's Itinerary in Anatolia (January - March 1921)

TIMELINE OF CLARENCE K. STREIT'S 1921 VISIT TO ANATOLIA

1/21/1921:	Sailed from İstanbul to Samsun on the American Destroyer 'Barker;'
1/24/1921:	Arrived in Samsun after port calls at Varna, Bulgaria & Constantza (Köstence), Rumania;
1/27/1921:	After several stormy days managed to disembark at Samsun;
1/29/1921:	Received permission from Ankara to make visit;
1/30/1921:	Leaves Samsun (in a light Reo truck belonging to Near East Relief) for Merzifon and Çorum; Spends first night on the road in 'Doruk Han';
1/31/1921:	Spends second night in Merzifon at Anatolia College;
2/1/1921:	Third night in Çorum at the 'Hotel Anatolia;'
2/2//1921:	Fourth day stopped for lunch in Alaca, a market town of 5,000; Fourth night spent in Yozgat in the mayor's reception room in the city hall. But with no gasoline available, Streit hired a spring wagon (yaylı) to continue the next five days of his trip to Ankara;
2/3/1921:	Fifth and sixth days were spent traversing what Streit describes as a 'rock salt desert;' he was accompanied by two gendarmes, Edhem Çavuş and Hacı; Fifth night was spent in the poverty stricken village of Sekili;
2/4/1921:	Day six a 'shortcut' on the way to Maden, they broke the tongue of the wagon and were unable to reach their intended stopping spot. Instead, they spent the night in the village of Ceritmüminli, a fairly prosperous village with a private guest house, where they were hosted by Mustafa the reis (elected headman) of the village;
2/5/1921:	Day seven they stopped for lunch at Madan (Maden), a town of about 8,000 inhabitants, where Streit ate at a Greek restaurant. In the afternoon they descended into the valley of the Kızıl Irmak and arrived at the Alevi village of Hasan Dede, remarkable for its well built mosque and türbe (mausoleum) of the saint; Baba, the hoca who was head of the village gave Streit some wine. At nightfall they reached Yahşihan, the terminus of the narrow gauge railway designed to connect Sivas and Ankara;
2/6/1921:	Day eight they got onto a freight train which was scheduled to make the fifty mile run to Ankara. Having left Yahşihan at 7:00 am they arrived in Ankara (then a city of 25,000) ten hours later at 5:00 pm. He checked into the 'Liberty Hotel' and later transferred to the 'Constitution Hotel;'
2/6/-3/5/1921:	Streit stayed in the Nationalist capital, Ankara for a total of twenty-six days;
2/28/1921:	Streit attends meeting of the Grand National Assembly where Celal [Bayar] Bey is elected Commissar for the Public Economy;
3/1/1921:	Streit attends Mustafa Kemal's speech in the Turkish Parliament;

3/3/1921:	Streit has a two-hour conversation with Mustafa Kemal Paşa in his house near the railway station; About his three week stay in Ankara, Streit writes: "*I remained in Ankara nearly a month. During that time I attended several sessions of the National Assembly and talked with nearly all the Nationalist leaders and Cabinet members;*"
3/5/1921:	Streit met with İsmet Paşa, Chief of the Nationalist General Staff, who was in Ankara at the time. İsmet Paşa cabled Eskişehir and made arrangements for Streit to be hosted by his staff there;
3/6/1921:	Streit takes the weekly express train to Konya for the thirty hour trip to Eskişehir; where he spent three days;
3/9/1921:	Streit and Mehmed Ali leave Eskişehir for Afyonkarahisar on a troop train; Streit spends the night of the 9th in Afyonkarahisar;
3/10/1921:	Streit leaves Afyonkarahisar in a blinding snowstorm in a yaylı enroute for Antalya; spends the night of the 10th in the small town of Sandıklı;
3/11/1921:	Travels from Sandıklı to Dinar, where he spends the night;
3/12/1921:	Travels from Dinar to Burdur, where he spends the night;
3/13/1921:	Travels with Signor Tuozzi, the Delegate for Asia Minor of the Italian High Commissioner in İstanbul, and the Italian Consul at Antalya, to Antalya in a light Fiat truck;
3/15/1921:	Embarks from Antalya to İstanbul on the Italian ship the 'S.S. Milano.'

Appendices

APPENDIX I: NATIONALIST LEADERS MET BY STREIT IN ANKARA (1921-1923)

Note: During his time in Turkey, Streit also took (and/or was given) a number of other interesting photographs. While these are not specifically referred to in his unpublished manuscript, these are given here (together with the notes he scribbled on their backs) in the interest of providing as complete a coverage of his visit as possible. Of his meeting with Celal Bey, Streit wrote: "*Djelal Bey* [**Plate 100**], *the Commissar for Public Economy, wanted it made plain that the 'commercial interests of foreigners in Turkey would enjoy the same protection as before the war'*" [HWL].

Plate 100: Mahmud Celal(eddin) [Bayar] - People's Commissar[206] for the Public Economy (February 28, 1921 - January 14, 1922)[207]

---

[206] **Note**: While the use of the term 'Commissar' in place of 'Minister,' sounds strange today, it was the term which was still in use in 1921. Streit, provides the following explanation: "*Some of the Turks, in their anxiety to remove any trace of Bolshevism from the Nationalist Government, even object to the members of the Cabinet being called 'People's Commissar.' They prefer that the Turkish word be translated as: 'People's Mandataire' or 'Steward' or 'Minister.' But because the government, in its diplomatic correspondence, which is written in French, still uses the term 'Commissaire du Peuple' I have followed this usage.*" The Turkish term used in Ankara at the time of Streit's visit was: *Halk Komiseri*. That this was the case is confirmed by Halide Edib: *The Turkish Ordeal*. New York (The Century Co.), 1928. pp. 144-, where in discussing the Nationalist government in 1920-1921, she consistently refers to its Ministers as Commissars, and their ministries as: Commissary for Foreign Affairs, Commissary for the Interior, etc. [HWL].

[207] LC Catalogue #: DLC/PP 1994: 064 [Album]. **Note**: On the front of this photo Streit wrote: "*Jelal Bayar, Commisar for Public Economy*" [HWL].

Note: Streit says the following in regard to the choice of Hamdullah Suphi Bey [**Plates 101** & **102**] as Commissar of Public Instruction: "*The Commissar for Public Instruction was recalled shortly before I arrived in Ankara. There is a fairly strong conservative element in the Assembly, centering around the hodja Deputies who do not look with favor upon the modern educational program which Mustapha Kemal Pasha, an advanced liberal, desires. Yet, he nominated for this [post] a hodja and Hamdoullah Soubhi Bey, one of the most radical of Turkish intellectuals. The latter man was elected by a large majority*" [HWL].

Plate 101: Hamdullah Suphi [Tanrıöver] - People's Commissar for Public Instruction (December 14, 1920 - November 20, 1921)[208]

[208] LC Catalogue #: DLC/PP 1994: 064 [Album]. **Note**: On the front of this photo Streit wrote: "*Hamdoulah Soubhi, Commissar for Public Instruction*" Hamdullah Suphi [Tanrıöver] (1885-1966) was a Circassian origin writer and politician. He served as Commissar for Public Education from December 14, 1920-November 20, 1921 [HWL].

Plate 102: Hamdullah Suphi [Tanrıöver] - People's Commissar for Public Instruction [209] (December 14, 1920 - November 20, 1921)[210]

[209] LC Catalogue #: DLC/PP 1994: 064 [Red Album: Turkey, 1920-1921 by C. K. Streit].
[210] LC Catalogue #: DLC/PP 1994: 064 [Album]. **Note**: This photo is not identified by Streit [HWL].

Note: In a discussion with Ahmed Muhtar Bey [**Plate 103**], the Acting Commissar for Foreign Affairs, Streit asked about Bolshevik attempts to propagate communism among the Turks. His response was: "*The Bolsheviks have had a sad experience in attempting to communize the Muslim population of Azerbaijan, and they've modified their policy in that regard. They have never asked us to become Communists. If they had, we would have refused*" [HWL].

Plate 103: Ahmed Muhtar Bey - People's Commissar for Foreign Affairs (February 9, 1921 - May 17, 1921)[211]

[211] LC Catalogue #: DLC/PP 1994: 064 [Album]. **Note**: On the front of this photo Streit wrote: "*Ahmed Muhtar Bey, Commissar for Foreign Affairs - Photo: CKS (1921).*" Ahmed Muhtar Bey (1870-1934). Turkish statesman, parliamentarian. Briefly served as Commissar for Foreign Affairs (February 9, 1921- May 5, 1921). In 1927 he was sent to Washington, D.C. as the Turkish Republic's first Ambassador to the United States of America [HWL].

Note: On the back of this photo [**Plate 104**] Streit wrote: "*Refet Pasha, People's Commissar for the Interior - Angora* & *Commander, Cilicia and Ouchak* [Uşak] *fronts*" Photo: CKS (1921). İbrahim Refet [Bele] (1881-1963). Military officer and early Nationalist leader. Tried and acquitted in 1926 of plotting to assassinate Mustafa Kemal Paşa. Retired from politics until 1935, when he was elected to parliament [HWL].

Plate 104: Refet [Bele] Paşa - People's Commissar for the Interior[212] (September 16, 1920 - April 15, 1921)[213]

[212] LC Catalogue #: DLC/PP 1994: 064 [Red Album: Turkey, 1920-1921 by C. K. Streit].

[213] LC Catalogue #: DLC/PP 1994: 064.210.

Note: On the back of this photo [**Plate 105**] Streit wrote: "(*Photo: Courtesy of Essad Nedim*) *Dr. Adnan Bey recently elected First Vice-President of Great National Assembly of Turkey - also People's Commissar for Public Health and formerly acting Commissar for the Interior. Formerly, Instructor in Turkish language at Robert College, Constantinople. Husband of Halide Edib Hanoum, famous Turkish authoress*" Abdülhak Adnan [Adıvar] (1882-1955). Medical doctor. Married Halide Edib Hanım in 1917. Fled, with his wife, to Ankara in 1920. Held numerous positions, including member of parliament, health minister, deputy speaker. Acquitted in 1926 of charges that he was plotting to assassinate Mustafa Kemal Paşa. Lived abroad until 1939 [HWL].

Plate 105: Dr. Adnan [Adıvar] Bey - First Vice President of the Grand National Assembly & People's Commissar for Public Health (May 3, 1920 - May 16, 1921)[214]

[214] LC Catalogue #: DLC/PP 1994: 064.152.

Note: On the back of this photo [**Plate 106**] Streit wrote: "*Presented to Streit by Kazım Karabekir Paşa in 1923*" [Photographer: Unknown]. Musa Kâzım Karabekir (1882-1948). Turkish military commander whose support was invaluable in assisting Mustafa Kemal Paşa to assume leadership of the nationalist cause. Tried (and acquitted) of involvement in an assassination attempt against Mustafa Kemal Paşa in 1926. Following the death of Mustafa Kemal Paşa in 1938 he entered politics and became Speaker of the Parliament in 1939 [HWL].

Plate 106: Kâzım Karabekir Paşa - Commander of the Armies of the East (Doğu Cephesi Kumandanı)[215]

[215] LC Catalogue #: DLC/PP 1994: 064 [Album].

Note: On the back of this photo [**Plate 107**] Streit wrote: "*Fetiy.*" Ali Fethi [Okyar] (1880-1943). Turkish soldier and statesman. Following his return from exile on Malta, he served as Interior Minister (1921-1922) and Prime Minister (November 1924 - March 1925). From August 15, 1921 on he was a Deputy from İstanbul in the Grand National Assembly; Streit must have met him on his second visit to Turkey in 1923, at which time Fetih Bey was Prime Minister [HWL].

Plate 107: Fetih [Okyar] Bey[216]

[216] LC Catalogue #: DLC/PP 1994: 064 [Album].

Note: Tevfik Rüştü [Aras] (1883-1972) [**Plate 108**]. CUP member; medical doctor. Elected to parliament in 1923, he served as Turkey's Foreign Minister from 1925-1938 [HWL].

Plate 108: Tevfik Rüştü [Aras] - Deputy from Menteşe in Grand National Assembly (from June 17, 1920-)[217]

[217] LC Catalogue #: DLC/PP 1994: 064 [Album].

Note: On the front of this photo [**Plate 109**] Streit wrote: "*Maj. Salih Bey;*" while next to it in the album in which it is preserved, he added: "*Salih Omurtak, now Chief of Staff*" [Photo: CKS (1921)]. Salih Omurtak (1889 - 1954), joined the Nationalists in Ankara on January 22, 1920. Streit identifies him as holding the rank of major and serving as Mustafa Kemal Paşa's 'Chief of Staff' in February 1921. Later became a general and served as the fourth Chief of the General Staff of the Turkish Armed Forces (June 8, 1949 - July 6, 1950) [HWL].

Plate 109: Major Salih [Omurtak] Bey:[218] Close Associate of Mustafa Kemal Paşa (Joined him in Ankara, 1920)

[218] LC Catalogue #: DLC/PP 1994: 064 [Album].

Note: On the back of this photograph [**Plate 110**] Streit wrote: "*Mustafa Kemal Pasha (and attaches) during visit to Greek front near Eskişehir (February). Photo by Essad Nedim (official photographer) Ankara.*" Salih [Bozok] Bey (1881-1941). Distant relative and close companion of Mustafa Kemal Paşa. Joined Mustafa Kemal Paşa in Ankara in 1920 where he became a member of parliament. Attempted suicide on November 10, 1938 (the day Mustafa Kemal Paşa died), but survived and died in 1941 [HWL].

Plate 110: Mustafa Kemal Paşa Visits the Front Near Eskişehir, February, 1921 [with Major Salih (Bozok) to his left in Photo][219]

[219] LC Catalogue #: DLC/PP 1994: 064.211.

Note: On the back of this photograph [**Plate 111**] Streit wrote: "*Mustafa Kemal Pasha and attaches during trip of inspection at Eskişehir (February). Photo by Essad Nedim official photographer for Mustafa Kemal Paşa*" [HWL].

Plate 111: Mustafa Kemal Paşa Visits the Front Near Eskişehir, February, 1921 [with Major Salih (Bozok) to his right in Photo][220]

[220] LC Catalogue #: DLC/PP 1994: 064.212.

Note: On the back of this photo [**Plate 112**] Streit wrote: "*Mustapha Kemal Pasha on the Eski-Shehr front. The others are attaches and staff officers* [HWL].

Plate 112: Mustafa Kemal Paşa Visits the Front Near Eskişehir, February, 1921 [with Major Salih (Bozok) to his left in Photo][221]

[221] LC Catalogue #: DLC/PP 1994: 064.247a [Album].

APPENDIX II: THE VICTORIOUS NATIONALIST FORCES ENTER İSTANBUL (OCTOBER 6, 1923)

Note: Clarence K. Streit returned to Turkey as the 'Near East and Balkan Correspondent' for the Philadelphia ***Public Ledger*** in 1923. In this capacity he was an eyewitness to the entry of the Nationalist forces to İstanbul on October 6, 1923. He took a number of photographs of the welcoming celebrations, including this one of the Commander Şükri Naili Paşa [**Plate 113**] [HWL].

Plate 113: Nationalist Commander Şükri Naili Paşa on October 6, 1923[222]

[222] LC Catalogue #: DLC/PP 1994: 064.143. **Note**: On the back of this photo Streit wrote: "*General Shoukri Naili Pasha commanding Turkish troops which entered Constantinople* [on] *October 6, 1923.*" Şükri Naili [Gökberk] Paşa (1876-1936). Turkish military commander. Fought in the Second Balkan War, and at Gallipoli (Gelibolu) during the World War. Was the 3rd Army Commander in İstanbul on October 29, 1923, who announced and planned the celebrations on the founding of the first Turkish Republic on that date. After retiring from the army he was elected to parliament in 1935 [HWL].

Note: Hüseyin Hüsnü Emir [Erkilet] (1883-1958) [**Plate 114**], who, after retirement from the army in 1933, was to become a well known Turkish fascist apologist and pro-Nazi propagandist during World War II. While not identified by Streit on the back of this photo, the picture appeared in a November 22, 1923 Streit dispatch in the ***Public Ledger*** entitled: "Mustapha Kemal Pasha: 'Purified Perfection,'" where it is labeled: *'Repeating History of 1453, Turks Re-Enter Constantinople. Colonel Hussein Husni Emir Bey leading the 'Iron Regiment'* [Tr.: *Çelik Alay* = Steel Regiment] *across the Galata Bridge following the evacuation of the city by the allied forces'* [HWL].

Plate 114: Kurmay Albay Hüseyin Hüsnü Emir [Erkilet] Leads Troops Across the Galata Bridge on October 6, 1923[223]

[223] LC Catalogue #: DLC/PP 1994: 064.242. Photo by: C.K Streit.

Note: The October 6, 1923 welcoming for the victorious Nationalist forces, included crowds on the *Galata Köprüsü* (Galata Bridge) [**Plate 115**], where Street took this photo which he labeled: "*Ladies First! Turkish girls cheering troops crossing Galata Bridge, Oct. 6*" [HWL].

Plate 115: Istanbulites Welcome the Nationalist Forces on the Galata Bridge (October 6, 1923)[224]

[224] LC Catalogue #: DLC/PP 1994: 064.163.

Note: In Beyoğlu's '*Grand Rue de Pera*' (renamed *İstiklal Caddesi* = Independence Boulevard on October 6, 1923), a massive Victory Arch had been erected [**Plate 116**]. On the back of this photo Streit wrote: "*Turkish Arch of Triumph for entry of Turkish troops Constantinople*" [HWL].

Plate 116: The '*Grand Rue de Pera*' on October 6, 1923 [225]

[225] LC Catalogue #: DLC/PP 1994: 064.176.

Note: Welcoming crowds lined the *Grand Rue de Pera* to welcome the victorious Nationalist troops [**Plate 117**]. On the back of this photo, Streit wrote: "*How the Greeks and Armenians welcomed the Nationalist troops as they marched through the Grand Rue de Pera (many of those wearing fezzes are Christians)*" [HWL].

Plate 117: Crowds Line the '*Grand Rue de Pera*' to Welcome the Nationalist Troops (October 6, 1923)[226]

[226] LC Catalogue #: DLC/PP 1994: 064.142.

Note: Among the troops honored on October 6, 1923 was Fatma [Seher] Hanım [**Plate 118**], who was more generally known as Kara Fatma (Black Fatma), an officer in the Nationalist army. She had been born in Erzurum, and first fought with the Nationalist forces against the Allied occupation of the İzmit peninsula, and later against the Greeks in Western Thrace. She reappeared in Anatolia where she became the commander (with the rank of Lieutenant) of a unit in the new Nationalist Army. In this role she saw action against the Greeks on the Afyonkarahisar and Nazilli fronts.

On the back of this photo Streit wrote: "*Lieut. Fatma Hanoum wearing decorations she gained fighting at the front in command of a company of women during the Turko-Greek War.*" Streit incorrectly states that she commanded a "*company of women*;" rather she was in command of a unit composed of men, most likely those standing to her left in the photo [HWL].

Plate 118: Lieutenant 'Kara' Fatma Hanım (at left of photo) and her troops in İstanbul on October 6, 1923[227]

[227] LC Catalogue #: DLC/PP 1994: 064.180.

Appendix III: Paul Williams' interview with Mustafa Kemal Paşa on April 26, 1920

Note: The following story appeared in the ***Chicago Daily Tribune*** on May 4, 1920. It consists of a dispatch filed from Ankara by that newspaper's foreign correspondent, Paul Williams, which is based on an interview he held with Mustafa Kemal Paşa [Halide Edib Hanım served as translator] on April 26, 1920. It is given in its entirety here, as the first interview granted to a foreign journalist by Mustafa Kemal at the very point in time at which he assumed the Presidency of the Grand National Assembly. Direct quotations attributed to Mustafa Kemal Paşa are given in bold italics [HWL].

WILSON'S 14 POINTS OR WAR – KEMAL PASHA[228]

Tribune Interviews Turk Chief in Angora

By Floyd Gibbons

[Chicago Tribune Foreign News Service]

[By Special Cable]

[Copyright: 1920 – By the Tribune Company]

PARIS, May 3 – "*You have got my goat on this assignment, but I'm on my way,*" wirelessed Paul Williams from Constantinople three weeks ago upon receipt of orders to proceed into the interior of Turkey and to interview Mustafa Kemal Pasha, Turkish Nationalist leader, who is organizing the Moslem millions in Asia Minor to fight the allied partition of his country.

After eight days journey inland through the waterless, sandy wastes of bandit ridden mountains of a country bitterly hostile to all Christians, Mr. Williams located Kemal's secret headquarters and obtained the first interview with the militant leader of the Moslem world. Then, by horse, camel, and foot back to Constantinople native couriers carried Mr. Williams' interview for wireless transmission to Paris and cable relay to Chicago.

Mr. Williams' departing message about the goat will be understood upon reading the dateline of his dispatch.

[228] Paul Williams: "Wilson's 14 Points Or War – Kemal Pasha." ***Chicago Daily Tribune***. Chicago, Ill.: May 4, 1920. p. 3.

WILSON'S 14 POINTS OR WAR – KEMAL PASHA

By

PAUL WILLIAMS

[Chicago Tribune Foreign News Service]

[By Special Cable]

[Copyright: 1920 – By the Tribune Company]

ANGORA, April 26. – "*We still have hopes that England and the allies will realize the proposed peace terms are ridiculous and impossible of application, but if we lose this hope and there is no outside help, we will not willingly accept them.*"

This is the answer given me today by Mustafa Kemal Pasha to the question of the possibility of the Turkish nationalist movement, of which he is leader, aligning itself with the Bolsheviks of Russia. His statement carried no threats.

Turkey at Stake

Conversations with other Turkish patriots, whose careers have been politically conservative, convince me they sincerely feel the allies are thoroughly unscrupulous in their decisions on the Turkish problem, and the Nationalists are justified in resorting to any affiliations that will assist them in interfering with the allied program.

These Nationalists, who have been setting up here a government for the greater part of Anatolia, which they control, believe absolutely that Turkey as a nation faces extermination. They trace the rapid eastward recession of the Turkish borders, and now the San Remo pact encroaches upon Asia Minor. Their sultan and caliph in Constantinople they regard virtually as a prisoner. Turkey is the last Moslem country yet free of Christian control. They will try to keep it so by liberating the caliph. They expect aid in some form from each of the 350,000,000 who believe in Islam.

Faith in Allies

"*We have believed,*" continued Kemal Pasha, "*that England and the allies would realize the necessity of according to us frontiers and conditions which would permit us to live as a people, and so long as this conviction lasts the Nationalists will not knowingly accept outside help. We have persistently maintained this attitude; otherwise it would have been easy to get aid from the Bolsheviks.*"

The short, thick [sic. thin?] man, who means to resist what he considers the aggression of Europe, turned his piercing blue eyes to a map in his headquarters and placed his pencil on Salonika, where he was born, and drew a long line eastward to Angora, where he is directing the stand of the Turks.

Shows Reds' Progress

On ship map numerous red flags in the Caucasus denote the progress of the Bolsheviks. He had received delegations from the Caucasian Moslems, some of whose tribes were already claimed by bolshevism and others of which may be. The word that they brought was encouraging, he said. Baku, where oil is king, may hoist the crimson banner when Turkish peace officially is announced, and it is doubtful if Azerbaijan went red, whether Georgia and Armenia could resist. If they did not, the road to Turkey would be open to the Bolsheviks.

[Azerbaijan adopted a soviet government on April 27, the Bolsheviks recognized the new government, and their troops entered Baku the following day.]

Kemal did not expect much military aid. Gold would be the main thing.

For American Mandate

When asked how the Nationalists felt about the American mandate for all Turkey, Kemal said:

"*We asked for it some time ago. Later conditions may be such that America cannot take the mandate.*"[229]

"*The aims of the Nationalists here,*" the pasha continued, "*are to keep the Turkish lands for the Turks, maintaining the integrity of Turkey as it stood when the armistice was signed. The Nationalists act by resisting execution of the terms of the treaty where they conflict with our ideas. This is a people's movement. Without their support it will die. We are depending too, upon the aid of all Islam. The Turks are the last of the Moslem races to remain free, and Islam will strive to keep them free. We have ample assurances from the Moslems of other lands that they will do their share to hamper the enemy. Most of them live in countries conquered by the British, and now it is the British who want to crush us. We have come to the last of their crusade against Islam, and today Islam is aroused to the danger.*"

British Are Our Foes

How do the Nationalists regard the Turkish government in Constantinople?

"*It is under the domination of the British and we do not recognize it.*"

And the Sultan?

"*A prisoner of the British. Every order he has issued is looked upon here as British, and Great Britain is our enemy. He cannot exercise the powers of the caliphate unless he is a free ruler. His proclamations are regarded by Islam as coming from the British. The sultan expects this as he was informed by the leaders of Islam all over the world that they would no longer regard him as the leader of the faith, should he ever*

[229] **Note**: To my knowledge this is the only statement attributed to Mustafa Kemal Paşa in which he acknowledged having actually (prior to April 1920) requested an American Mandate, a position he was later to repudiate [HWL].

find himself in the circumstances in which he is now placed. This is no time to discuss a successor to the caliphate. We must struggle to release him from European influence."

The pasha denied reports that the British assisted the nationalist movement in its inception, but he gave an instance where arms surrendered by the Turks under the armistice were redistributed through the back door of a warehouse.

Proof of British Chicanery

"*But we have proof British gold and material was used freely to stir up the factions for the purpose of creating trouble in Anatolia. The worse they could make conditions here the easier for them to influence English public opinion against the Turk, so it will accept without protest the imperialistic peace which London was about to impose.*"

"*The allies deliberately carried on a campaign in Asia Minor to sway opinion at home. Their own commission proved the Greeks landed in Smyrna under false pretenses and started the massacres of Turks. We are more than suspicious that the deplorable events at Marash were planned in cold blood. How else explain the policy of the French to arm the local Armenians and to turn them loose on the Turkish quarters. Before the French went to Marash there was no trouble, and there has been none since they were forced to leave. Now at Aintab the French are repeating what they did at Marash.*"

Where Are Fourteen Points?

"*Have President Wilson's fourteen points survived?*" the pasha asked, and knowing what the answer would be, he went on. "*If so, why weren't they applied to making the peace in Turkey? Why was the principle of self-determination applied to the Armenians and Greeks in Turkey and not to the Turks? Where is the fair play of civilized Europe, which condemns the Turk? The peace terms were conceived by imperialists, without regard to the principles of justice.*"

Mr. Wilson's note on the Turkish terms the pasha described as a "*willful intent to deceive or a distressing display of ignorance as to the situation.*"

He denied he had received any German money or other assistance from Germany. He said there were no German officers on his forces, although there were half a dozen Hungarians who already are bolsheviki. The pasha admitted Enver Pasha, head of the army during the war, also is making trouble for the allies, but he asserted everybody in Turkey knew they could never work together.

It was an eight day's journey here from Constantinople. Two of them were spent in a seagoing hack, riding across the rough, sparsely settled country, with only the driver for a companion, but the interest displayed in a stranger whose features and complexion might be those of an Englishman kept me from being lonesome, although I was not once molested nor annoyed. Here there is perfect order, and the horrors of prohibition also.

APPENDIX IV: CLARENCE STREIT'S QUESTIONS & MUSTAFA KEMAL PAŞA'S ANSWERS [DATED: FEBRUARY 26, 1921][230]

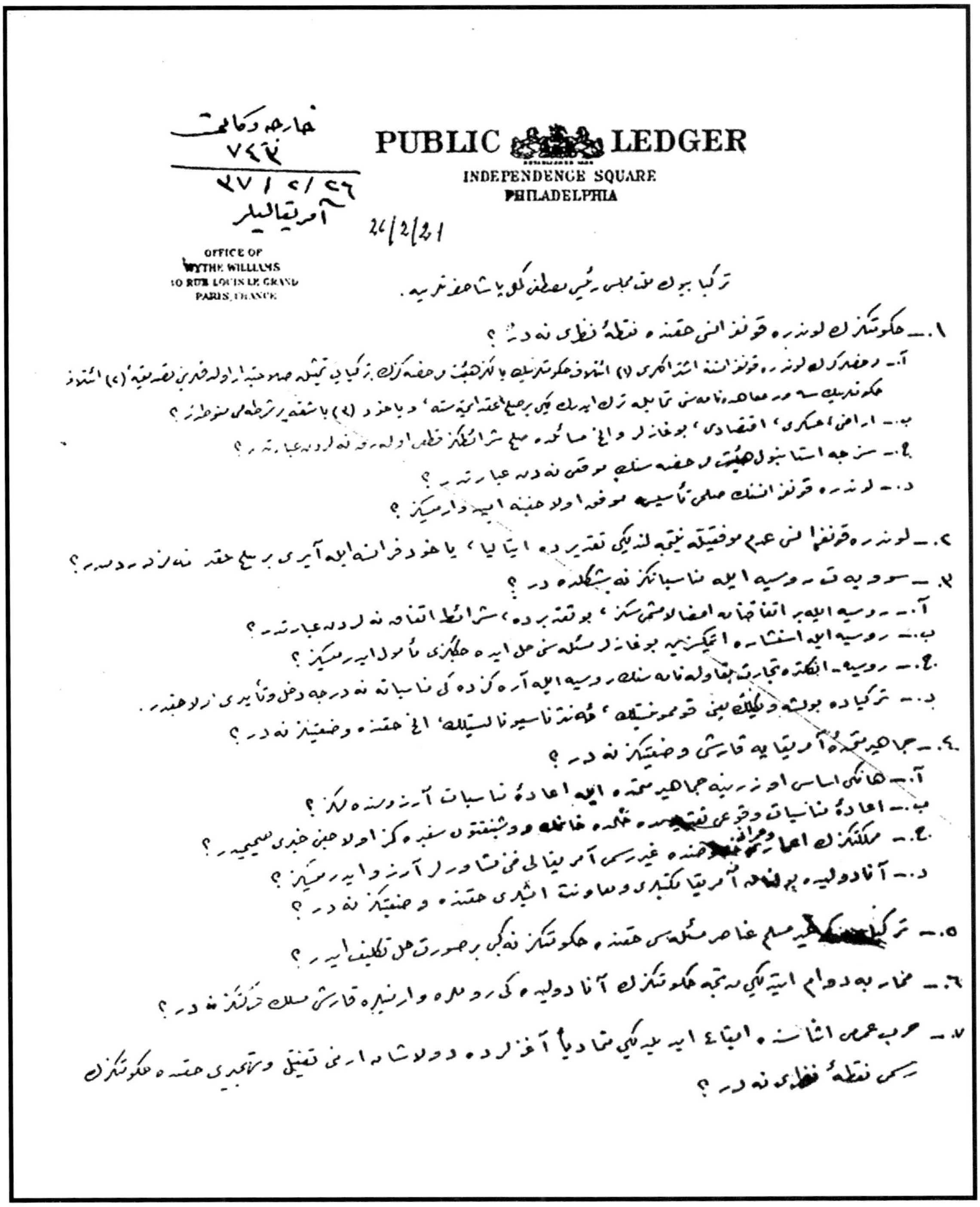
PUBLIC LEDGER
INDEPENDENCE SQUARE
PHILADELPHIA

OFFICE OF
WYTHE WILLIAMS
10 RUE LOUIS LE GRAND
PARIS, FRANCE

26/2/21

ترکیا بویوک ملت مجلسی رئیسی مصطفی کمال پاشا حضرتلرینه

---

230 T.C. Kültür Bakanlığı (Republic of Turkey – Ministry of Culture): *Atatürk'ün Milli Dış Politikası*. 2 Volumes (Ankara, 1992). See: Volume I., pp. 256-276.

٨.- ارمنیلر ورومل طرفندن ترکلره قارشی وقوعی روایت ایدیلن تقتیل حقنده نه کبی معلومات ویره بیلیرسکز ؟

٩.- اسلام وحدتی، ترکلک وحدتی، وتوران وحدتی حقنده [illegible] نه‌در ؟

١٠.- خصوصیله جهاد، شریعت، دین وحکومتک تفریقی کبی مسائل دینیه‌ده تعقیب ایده‌جککز مسلک حرکت نه‌در ؟

١١.- سائر حکومات اسلامیه ایله اولان مناسباتکز واونلره قارشی مسلک حرکتکز نه‌در ؟

١٢.- کورجستان ایله، خصوصیله باطوم مسئله‌سی حقنده، مناسباتکز نه‌در ؟

١٣.- سوویت ارمنستان ایله مناسباتکز نه‌در ؟

١٤.- ویلسون ارمنستان حدودلری حقنده‌کی فکرکز نه‌در ؟

١٤.- جمعیت اقوام حقنده فکرکز نه‌در ؟

١٥.- دیون عمومیهٔ عثمانیه‌یه قارشی مسلک حرکتکز نه‌در ؟

١٦.- محلول خاندان [illegible] قارشی سیاستکز نه اوله‌جقدر ؟

١٧.- ترکیانک استقبالی ایچون خصوصیله شکل حکومتی، موقع سلطنت وخلافتی، معارفی، وضعیت نسوانی، وسائط نقلیه ومنابع طبیعیه‌نک تکملی حقنده آتیه و تصورلرکز نه‌لردن عبارتدر ؟

١٨.- عزت پاشا حقنده بر بیاناتکز وارمیدر ؟

١٩.- آمریقا افکار عمومیه‌سنه تبلیغ آرزوسنده بولوندیغکز نقاط سائره وار ایسه تبلیغ ایدوب عرضه مع الممنونیه حاضرم.

بو سؤاللره جوابلرینی لطفاً فرانسزجه اولورسه ویررایسه‌کز ذات سامیلرینه قارشی آیریجه ممنون اولورم افندم.

Clarence K. Streit

26.2.1921 [February 26, 1921]

Türkiye Büyük Millet Meclisi Reisi Mustafa Kemal Paşa Hazretlerine,

To His Excellency Mustafa Kemal Paşa, President of the Grand National Assembly

Streit's Question: 1a

Hükümetinizin Londra Konferansı hakkında nokta-ı nazarı nedir? [What is the point of view of your Government vis-à-vis the London Conference?]

Murahhaslarınızın Londra Konferansına iştirakleri [The participation of your Delegates in the London Conference];

İtilâf Hükümetleri'nin yalnız Heyet-i Murahasanızın Türkiye'yi temsile sâlahiyeddar olduklarına tasdike [In the case of the Entente Governments only recognizing the authority of the Official Delegation as the representatives of Turkey];

İtilâf Hükümetleri'nin Sèvres Muahedenamesi'ni tamamıyle terk ederek yeni bir sulh akdetmesine, veyahut başka bir şarta mı bağlıdır? [Is it essential that the Entente Governments agree to the abrogation of the Sèvres Agreement and to the establishment of a new Peace Treaty, or is this tied to another condition?]

Mustafa Kemal Paşa's Answer

[**French**]: "***Nous avons énvoye nos délégués à la Conférence de Londres afin de montrer à tous, à notre peuple aussi bien qu'à nos ennemis, que nous ne voulons laisser échapper aucune chance de paix, si faible soit elle. Nous y exposerons encore une fois les légitimes revendications formulées aux Congrès d'Erzeroum et de Sivas et contenues dans notre pacte national dont je vous fais remettre ci joint un exemplaire.***

Si violant encore une fois les principes pour lesquels les Ententistes ont déclaré s'être battu durant plus de quatre années et ne tenant aucun compte des promesses qu'ils nous firent avant la conclusion de l'armistice nos ennemis rejettent nos conditions justes et modérées ils assumeront toute la responsabilité du sang qui continuera à couler ainsi que celle des graves crises que la continuation de la guerre en Orient provoque dans tout l'univers."

[**English**]: "**In order to show our own people as well as our enemies and everyone else that we will not overlook even the slightest possibility of peace (no matter how slight), we have sent our representatives to the London Conference. We will once again present to the Conference the legitimate conditions set forth in the National Pact (a copy of which is included for your perusal), as they were established at the Erzurum and Sivas Congresses.**

Should the Entente Powers once again chose to ignore the principles which they fought for four years to ensure, and to ignore our just and modest conditions and the promises made earlier to us, they will bear the full responsibility for the blood which will continue to flow from the ongoing wars in the East and they will likewise bear the responsibility for the terrible conditions which will result."

Streit's Question: 1b

Arazî, askerî, iktisadî, Boğazlar ve ilâhi meselelerde sulh şartlarınız kat'i olarak nelerden ibarettir? [What are your exact territorial, military and economic peace conditions, pertaining to the Straits and related issues?]

Mustafa Kemal Paşa's Answer

[French]: "***Nos conditions de paix sont contenues dans notre pacte national.***"

[English]: "**Our peace conditions are enumerated in the National Pact.**"

Streit's Question: 1c

Sizce *İstanbul Heyet-i Murahhasasının mevkii neden ibarettir?* [In your view what is the authority of the Istanbul Official Delegation based on?]

Mustafa Kemal Paşa's Answer

[French]: "***La Délégation de Constantinople est envoyée par un pseudo gouvernement à qui les généraux ententistes commandant en cette ville peuvent imposer toutes leurs volontés et qui d'autre part ne s'appuie sur aucune assemblée élue par la nation. Cette Délégation n'a donc aucune qualité pour parler au nom du peuple turc. J'espère que Tewfik Pacha chef de la Délégation envoyée par le Sultan se rendra compte de cette vérité et reconnaitra qu'en cette occurence la parole est aux seuls représentants du Gouvernement de la Grande Assemblée Nationale de Turquie.***"

[English]: "**The Istanbul Delegation, in accordance with the directives issued by the Entente Powers who are in control of the city under the guidance of their generals, has accepted all of their directives; additionally, they have been sent by a so-called government which was not chosen by elected representatives of the people. Consequently, this delegation has absolutely no authority to speak in the name of the Turkish people. I have hope that Tevfik Paşa, the head of this delegation sent by the Sultan, will recognize this reality and accept the fact that only the representatives of the Grand National Assembly's government have the right to represent [Turkey].**"

Streit's Question: 1d

Londra Konferansının sulhu tesise muvaffak olacağına ümit varmısınız? [Are you hopeful that you will be successful in laying the grounds for peace at the London Conference?]

Mustafa Kemal Paşa's Answer

[French]: "***Je souhaite vivement que la paix sorte de la Conférence de Londres. Si ceux qui ont pris l'initiative de réunir cette conférence sont sincères dans leurs intentions je considère la paix comme certaine.***"

[English]: "**It is my most sincere desire that peace will result from the London Conference. If those who strive for the prospects of the conference are sincere in their acts, then peace is certain.**"

Streit's Question: 2

Londra Konferansı adem-i muvaffakiyetle neticelendiği takdirde İtalya, yahut Fransa ile ayrı bir sulh akdetmeniz ihtimali var mıdır? [In the case that the London Conference fails to produce the desired results, is there a possibility that you would pursue separate peace negotiations with either Italy or France?]

Mustafa Kemal Paşa's Answer

[**French**]: "***Tous les pays y compris naturellement la France et l'Italie qui déclareront vouloir respecter notre droit à la vie en reconnnaissant la légitimité des revendications contenues dans notre pacte national pourront de suite conclure la paix avec nous.***"

[**English**]: "**With anyone who is willing to openly recognize our right to existence as set forth in the National Pact, and this of course would include France and Italy, we are more than willing to enter into peace negotiations.**"

Streit's Question: 3a

Sovyet Rusya ile münâsebâtınız ne şekildedir? [What is the nature of your relations with Soviet Russia?]

Mustafa Kemal Paşa's Answer

[**French**]: "***Nos relations avec la Russie des Soviets sont basées sur la compréhension mutuelle de nos aspirations, de nos droits et de nos interets. Elles sont empréintes de la plus grande cordialité.***"

[**English**]: "**Our relations with Soviet Russia; our aspirations, rights and interests all rest on mutual understanding between the two nations and are full of sincerest feelings.**"

Streit's Question: 3b

Rusya ile bir ittifakname imzalamışmısınız? Bu takdirde şerait-i ittifak nelerden ibarettir? [Did you sign a peace treaty with Russia? If so, what is the nature of that treaty?]

Mustafa Kemal Paşa's Answer

[**French**]: "***Une importante mission turque présidée par Youssouf Kemal Bey vient d'arriver à Moscou, elle est chargée d'étudier avec le Gouvernement Russe toutes les questions orientales, celles du Caucase comme celles de l'Asie entière et de régler la conduite future des deux peuples dans la solution des grands problèmes mondiaux.***"

[**English**]: "**A commission was formed under the leadership of Yusuf Kemal Bey and was sent to Moscow a short time ago. The Commission will analyze and discuss important topics regarding the Caucasus and Asia with their Russian colleagues as well as deciding on a common course of action regarding the other global problems, especially those of the East.**"

Streit's Question: 3c

Rusya ile istişare etmeksizin Boğazlar meselesini halledeceğinizi me'mul edermisiniz? [Can you explain how you intend on solving the problem regarding the Straits without first consulting Russia?]

Mustafa Kemal Paşa's Answer

[**French**]: "*La clause de notre pacte national relative à la question des Détroits a été reconnue juste par la Russie des Soviets et constitue l'article VI du traité paraphé l'été dernier par les délégués des deux Gouvernements.*"

[**English**]: "**Soviet Russia has already recognized and initialed the clause about the Straits set forth in the National Pact and likewise accepted the sixth clause of the treaty which was approved last summer by the delegations of our two governments.**"

Streit's Question: 3d

Rusya-İngiltere ticaret mukavelenamesinin Rusya ile aranızdaki munâsebâta ne derece dahl-u tesiri olacaktır? [What will be the impact of the Russo-English Trade Agreement upon your relations with Russia?]

Mustafa Kemal Paşa's Answer

[**French**]: "*La dernière note adressée à notre Gouvernement par le citoyen Tchitchérine et dont je vous fais remettre ci joint une copie constitue une réponse suffisante à cette question. Cette note a d'ailleurs été publiée le 14 courant par L'Agence d'Anatolie.*

D'autre part même si le traité russe-britannique avait revêtu la forme publiée par les anglais ce fait n'aurait pu en aucune façon porter atteinte à la force et à la puissance avec laquelle nous poursuivons la réalisation de notre idèal national."

[**English**]: "**The last communiqué sent to our government by comrade Tcitcherine, the one that you will receive a copy of, should answer your question. This communiqué was also published by the Anadolu Agency on the 14th of this month as well.**

On the other hand, even if the Anglo-Russian Agreement is drafted like the British claim, it is not going to have any impact on the strength we will show in protecting our national interests."

Streit's Question: 3e

Türkiye'de bolşeviklik yani komunistlik, enternasyonallistlik ilahır hakkında vaziyetiniz nedir? [What is your position relative to the establishment of Bolshevism, that is Communism in Turkey?]

Mustafa Kemal Paşa's Answer

[**French**]: "*Le communisme n'existe pas en Turquie.*

Tout l'univers nous considére comme des nationalistes et nous le sommes en tant que nous défendons l'indépendance, les droits, intérêts de notre nation. Si par internationalisme vous entendez le respect de l'indepéndance et des droits de tous les peuples alors oui nous sommes aussi des internationalistes.

D'autre part nous sommes attachés à notre religion. Je ne vois pas comment le communisme en tant qu'il est opposé à l'esprit national et religieux peut trouver un champ d'application chez nous. Ce n'est que dans le cas où l'attentat entrepris contre le peuple turc se réaliserait que cette éventualité pourrait se produire."

[**English**]: "Communism does not exist in Turkey.

The whole world knows us as Nationalists. As people advocating the rights of our nation and her future, we are rightly named so. But by internationalism, if you mean respect for all countries' destinies and rights, then yes, we are also internationalists.

Aside from all this, we are also attached to our religion. I don't understand how communism, which goes against our principles of nationalism and pious devotion to our religion, could ever find supporters in our country. This could only happen as a result of a vicious plan inflicted on Turkey."

Streit's Question: 4a

Cemahir-i Müttehide-i Amerika'ya [Amerika Birlesik Devletleri] *karşı vaziyetiniz nedir?* [What is your position vis-à-vis the United States of America?]

Mustafa Kemal Paşa's Answer

[**French**]: "*Nous désirons vivement jouir de l'amitié de l'Amérique. Nous ne nous sommes jamais considéré comme en guerre avec le peuple américan et nous nous étonnons qu'il n'ait pas encore rétabli avec nous les relations diplomatiques d'usage.*"

[**English**]: "We strongly wish to benefit from American friendship. We never considered ourselves in war with the American nation and we are surprised that the Americans still have not established diplomatic relations with our government."

Streit's Question: 4b

Hangi esas üzerine Cemahir-i Müttehide ile iade-i münâsebât arzusundasınız? [Under what conditions would you desire to establish relations with the United States?]

Mustafa Kemal Paşa's Answer

[**French**]: "*Quant à nous nous sommes prêts à reprendre les relations diplomatiques avec les Etats Unis sur la base de notre pacte national, indépendamment de notre situation politique vis à vis des autres Puissances.*

Nous avons déjà fait pressentir à ce sujet votre Gouvernement. J'estime que l'aide américaine nous sera précieuse pour mettre en activité nos ressources naturelles pour le plus grand profit de notre peuple et de toute l'humanité."

[**English**]: "As you can also see from our relations with other countries, we are willing to establish diplomatic relations with the United States within the framework of our National Pact. We have already expressed this wish to your government.

I am aware of the immense help the United States could give to help our nation maximize its use of national resources to increase productivity, which will be to the benefit not only to our own people but to all mankind."

Streit's Question: 4c

İade-i münâsebât vukuu takdirinde Halide Hanımın Washington sefireniz olacağı haberi samimimidir? [Were diplomatic relations to be established, is there any truth to the report that you would send Halide Hanım as Ambassador to Washington?]

Mustafa Kemal Paşa's Answer

[**French**]: "*Nous avons en Turquie des femmes qui sont aussi capables que les hommes de remplir des hautes fonctions comme celle d'Ambassadeur. Halidé Hanoum est de ce nombre et il est certain qu'elle remplirait cette fonction d'une façon parfaite. Seulement le cas de procéder à une pareille nomination ne s'est pas encore présenté à nous.*"

[**English**]: "In Turkey, we also have women who would excel in diplomatic positions, such as those in embassies, usually occupied by men. Halide Hanım is amongst those capable women and I am sure that she would succeed in this task. However, at the moment, we do not have any decision to appoint her as the ambassador to the United States."

Streit's Question: 4d

Memleketinizin imar ve ümranı hususunda gayr-ı resmî Amerikalı fen müşavirleri arzu edermisiniz? [Do you desire the presence of unofficial American technicians to assist with the development of your country?]

Mustafa Kemal Paşa's Answer

[**French**]: "*Toute aide destinée à faciliter relèvement économique sera acceptée avec reconnaissance; nous serions d'autant plus heureux du concours des techniciens américains que les Etats Unis n'ont jamais eu des visées territoriales sur aucune partie de notre pays.*"

[**English**]: "We would appreciate all support to help us maintain a high level of economic development. Given that the United States has never pursued territorial interests in Turkey, we would be gladder to see them as the ones helping us along the way."

Streit's Question: 4e

Anadolu'da bulunan Amerikan mektepleri ve muavenet isleri hakkında vaziyetiniz nedir? [What is your position relative to the American schools and relief work in Anatolia?]

Mustafa Kemal Paşa's Answer

[**French**]: "***Tous les établissements de bien faisance qui allègent les souffrances humaines sans distinction de race ni de religion sont les bien venues chez nous tant qu'ils ne poursuivent ni de près ni de loin aucune espèce de but politique.***"

[**English**]: "**We welcome any humanitarian aid as long as it is delivered on the same conditions to all religious and ethnic groups while pursuing no political gain in return.**"

Streit's Question: 5

Türkiye'deki gayr-ı müslim anasır meselesi hakkında hükümetiniz ne gibi bir süret-i hal teklif eder? [What is your government's position vis-à-vis non-Muslim minorities in Turkey?]

Mustafa Kemal Paşa's Answer

[**French**]: "***La réponse à cette question est contenue dans notre pacte national.***"

[**English**]: "**The answer to this question is set forth in our National Pact.**"

Streit's Question: 6

Muharebe devam ettiği müddetçe hükümetinizin Anadolu'daki Rumlara ve Ermenilere karşı meslek-i hareketiniz nedir? [What is your government's position regarding Armenians and Greeks who are living in Turkey in time of war?]

Mustafa Kemal Paşa's Answer

[**French**]: "***Nous ne faisons aucune distinction entre les citoyens musulmans et non musulmans de la Turquie; en conséquence les grecs et les arméniens n'ont rien à craindre tant qu'ils ne complotent pas avec l'ennemi.***"

[**English**]: "**We make absolutely no distinction between our Muslim and non-Muslim citizens. Accordingly, if the Greeks and Armenians do not seek to betray the country by siding with our enemies they have nothing to fear.**"

Streit's Question: 7

Harb-ı Umumi esnasında ika edildiği mütemadiyen ağızlarda dolaşan Ermeni takdil ve tehciri hakkında hükümetinizin resmi nokta-ı nazara nedir? [What is your government's official stance regarding the Armenian relocations and deportations during the World War, about which there has been great commotion internationally?]

Mustafa Kemal Paşa's Answer

[**French**]: *"Déduction faite des énormes exagérations auxqelles se livrent toujours ceux qui accusent leurs ennemis, l'affaire de la déportations des arméniens se réduit à ceci:*

Le Comité Arménien Dachnak alors au service du Tsarisme avait soulevé la population arménienne sur les derrières de nos troupes pendant que l'armée russe avait commencé sa grande offensive de 1915 contre nous. Obligés de reculer devant la supériorité en nombre et en matériel de l'ennemi nous nous voyions sans cesse pris entre deux feux; nos convois de ravitaillements et de blessés étaient impitoyablement massacrés, les routes et les ponts détruits derrière nous et la terreur portée dans les campagnes turques. Ies bandes qui commettaient ces crimes et qui comptaient dans leurs rangs tous les arméniens capables de porter les armes, se ravitaillaient en armes en munitions et en vivres dans les villages arméniens où grâce aux immunités accordées par les capitulations certaines puissances Etrangères [.....] *le temps de paix à constituer* [.....] *cette* [?] *intention.*

[.....] *Presque avec indifférence de quelle* [.....] *Angleterre* [.....] *traite en temps de paix et loin de tout* [.....] *Irlande ne peut en toute justice* [.....] *la résolution que nous avons été dans* [.....] *obligation de prendre relativement à la déportation de la population arménienne. Contrairement aux calomnies répondues contre nous les déportés sont en vie et beaucoup de ceux ci seraient rentrés chez* [.....] *si l'Entente ne nous avait forcé à recommencer la guerre."*

[**English**]: "Aside from the stories related with great exaggeration by our enemies, here is the reality on what happened to the Armenians:

When the Russian armies started their attack in 1915, the Dashnak Armenian Committee, which had been under the direct control of the Czar, encouraged the Armenian communities living behind the front lines to rebel against our forces. Due to our enemies' superior arms and strong army, we had to retaliate only to find ourselves stuck in between fire from the Russians on one side and the Armenian rebels on the other. Our wounded soldiers were being massacred; bridges and roads were being destroyed; and rebels were terrorizing Turkish villages. These rebels, who encouraged the participation of every Armenian capable of holding a gun, had a huge reserve of arms and ammunitions that they had acquired under the privileges offered by the capitulations, bestowed upon them by foreign powers, during peace time.

Given the international reaction to Britain's treatment of the Irish, who were far away from the frontline, other countries do not have a right to condemn us on our decision to carry out the mass deportation of our Armenian population. Contrary to what has been stated, these deportees are alive and would have even been back in their homes had the Entente Governments not forced us to engage in war once again in the region."

Streit's Question: 8

Ermeniler ve Rumlar tarafından Türklere karşı vukuu rivayet edilen katliam hakkında ne gibi malûmat verebilirsiniz? [What information can you give in regard to reports that the Armenians and Greeks have been engaged in perpetrating massacres of Turks?]

Mustafa Kemal Paşa's Answer

[**French**]: "*Il serait trop long de s'étendre sur les atrocités commises par les arméniens et les grecs contre la population musulmane tant durant la guerre mondiale qu'après la conclusion de l'armistice. Les massacres et les dévastations des bandes arméniennes alors que les russes commencèrent à évacuer nos provinces orientales après le traité de Brest-Littowsk sont suffisamment connus. Le Général Américain Harbord qui s'entretint à Sivas avec moi et qui après avoir visité ces régions et y avoir fait d'édifiantes constatations sur la conduite des bandes arméniennes, m'écrivit pour me faire savoir que tout ce que je lui avais dit était vrai est un témoin auprès dequel l'opinion américaine peut se renseigner utilement. Les Dachnaks ont d'ailleurs continué leurs forfaits dans la zone de Kars et d'Olti jusqu'à la conclusion du traité d'Alexandropol.*

Les grecs de leur côté ont commis de tels crimes lors de l'occupation de Smyrne que la Commission d'enquête Interalliée, elle même, quoique constituée par les alliés de la Grèce formula dans son rapport des critiques extrêmement sévères pour les autorités hellléniques après avoir parcouru cette province durant l'automne 1919.

Dans la zone occupée par les grecs des dizaines de milliers de turcs de tout âge et de tout sexe ont été massacrés, tout le bétail a été transporté en Grèce et plusieurs centaines de malheureux réfugiés dans notre zone s'y trouvent dans le plus complet dènûment."

[**English**]: "The suffering Muslim populations lived through, inflicted upon them by the Armenians and the Greeks, both during and after the World War would make up a long story. At this stage, everybody knows about the massacres carried out by Armenian gangs in our Eastern villages after the signing of the Brest-Litowsk Agreement which necessitated the withdrawal of the Russian forces from the region. The American General Harbord, who visited me in Sivas and then travelled through these Eastern villages that the Armenian gangs had destroyed, only to see the horrible conditions which they had left behind, could serve as an eyewitness to the American public on this events. Dashnak rebels even continued massacring Turkish populations in Kars and Olti regions well until the signing of the Alexandropol agreement.

Coming to the question of the Greeks, in the course of their occupation of İzmir, such murders were committed by their forces, that even the members of the Allied Investigating Commission (created by their allies) were forced to conclude that following the Greek occupation in the Autumn of 1919 there had been atrocities perpetrated from end to end of the province; and even their report strongly condemned the Greek authorities for these events.

In the regions occupied by the Greek forces there were tens of thousands of Turks, of every age and sex, killed. In addition, all large draft animals were rounded up and taken to Greece; and from the zone they occupied there were hundreds of unfortunate refugees pushed into our zone, thereby creating a state of poverty and helplessness."

Streit's Question: 9

İslâm Birliği [Pan İslâmizm], *Türklük Birliği* [Pan Türkizm] *ve Turan Birliği* [Pan Turanizm] *hakkında meslek-i hareketiniz nedir?* [What is your position regarding Pan-Islamism, Pan-Turkism and Pan-Turanism?]

Mustafa Kemal Paşa's Answer

[**French**]: "*Le Panislamisme en tant qu'il signifie la réunion de tous les musulmans sous la domination turque et le pantouranisme en tant qu'il signifie la réunion de tous les pays de race turque sous la domination des turcs anatoliens sont des épouvantails dont se servent les impérialistes d'Angleterre pour entraîner leur peuple à une croisade perpétuelle contre nous.*

Nous n'avons aucunement l'intention ni l'envie de conquérir la moitié ou le quart du globe comme l'ont déjà fait et le font chaque jour d'avantage ceux qui des bords de la Tamise nous lancent ces accusations ridicules. Notre pacte national est d'ailleurs assez explicite à ce sujet.

Par contre nous sommes convaincus que seul l'application sincère du principe d'auto détermination des peuples à toutes les nations y compris les musulmans peut sauver l'humanité de la catastrophe où la perpétuation des guerres la conduit."

[**English**]: "Pan-Islamism, if it means the joining of all Muslims under Turkish leadership; and Pan-Turanism, if it means the joining together of all nations in which Turkish peoples are living under a unified Anatolian Turkish leadership; are nothing but scarecrows presented by British imperialists who need them to ensure a continued support for their incessant crusades against us.

We have neither the desire nor the plan to conquer half, or at least a fourth, of the world like those along the Thames River suggest. We find these allegations only funny. Our National Pact is very explicit in laying out our position regarding our borders.

Contrary to what the British have been stating, we sincerely believe that this war will come to an end only when all nations, including the Muslim ones, are given the chance to exercise self-determination."

Streit's Question: 10

Hususi ile Cihad, şeriat, din ve hükümetin tefriki gibi mesail-i diniyede takip edeceğiniz meslek-i hareket nedir? [How will your government act regarding religious issues such as jihad, shariah and segregation of the state?]

Mustafa Kemal Paşa's Answer

[**French**]: "*Je pense que chaque individu comme chaque peuple doit jouir de la liberté absolue de conscience. Ce principe est malheureusement foulé aux pieds par nos ennemis qui estiment qu'un peuple parce qu'il est musulman n'as pas droit à l'indépendance. Ce qui se passe actuellement en Syrie, en Mésopotamie et en Anatolie est la meilleure preuve de ce que j'avance.*

Notre religion est l'Islamisme qui considérée dans sa partie non dogmatique n'est au fond qu'un système politico social basé sur la plus large tolérance et forme un moyen ferme entre l'individualisme et le communisme."

[**English**]: "I believe that like every nation, every individual should enjoy total freedom of conscience. This principle has unfortunately been violated by our enemies who have argued that 'a nation, if Muslim, has no right to freedom.' What is still going on in Syria, Iraq and Anatolia constitute the best proof of this case.

Our religious affiliation is Islam. Islam, if analyzed apart from its dogmatic principles, is nothing but a socio-political system dependent on principles of tolerance and lays out a mid way between individualism and communism."

Streit's Question: 11

Sair İslâm hükümetleriyle olan münâsebâtınız ve onlara karşı meslek-i hareketiniz nedir? [What is the nature of your government's relation with other Muslim governments?]

Mustafa Kemal Paşa's Answer

[**French**]: "*Nous entretenons naturellement des relations extrêmement cordiales avec tous les états musulmans. Une importante mission militaire turque appelée par l'Emir de l'Afganistan doit aller bientôt rejoindre à Caboul les officiers turcs qui y travaillent déjâ à faire de l'armée Afgane un instrument de guerre moderne.*

Comme je l'ai déjà dit plus haut mon voeu le plus ardent est de voir le droit d'auto détermination reconnu à tous les peuples musulmans."

[**English**]: "We are, by our nature, on very friendly terms with all Muslim nations. Soon, an important Turkish military mission will be sent to Kabul to join the Turkish army officials in Afghanistan who have been modernizing the Afghan army in keeping with the wishes of the Afghan Emir.

As I previously stated, it is my greatest wish to see all the Muslim nations practicing their right to self-determination."

Streit's Question: 12

Gürcistan ile, hususi ile Batum meselesi hakkında fikriniz nedir? [What is your stance regarding Georgia, especially regarding the problem of Batum?]

Mustafa Kemal Paşa's Answer

[**French**]: "*Nos relations avec la Géorgie sont bonnes. Je souhaite que comme la question d'Ardahan et d'Artwin, la question de Batoum reçoive elle aussi, par voie d'entente, une solution pacifique conforme aux voeux de sa population, à nos droits légitimes ainsi qu'aux intérêts des peuples caucasiens.*"

[**English**]: "I hope to see the problem of Batum resolved, like the problems of Ardahan and Artvin, in a peaceful manner which will be in accordance with the wishes of the community in Batum while respecting our legal rights and will be beneficial to all the nations of the Caucasus."

Streit's Question: 13

Soviet Ermenistanı ile münâsebâtınız nedir? Wilson Ermenistan hududları hakkında fikriniz nedir? [What is the nature of your relation with Soviet Armenia?] What do you think about the boundaries of Armenia proposed by President Wilson?

Mustafa Kemal Paşa's Answer

[**French**]: "*L'Arménie est depuis quelques jours retombée aux mains des Dachnaks. Tout gouvernement arménien qui appliquera sincérement le traité d'Alexandropol pourra compter sur notre amitié.*"

Je trouve le projet Wilson tendant à placer plusieurs millions de turcs sous la domination de plusieurs milliers d'arméniens tout simplement ridicule."

[**English**]: "For the past several of days, Armenia has once again been under the control of the Dashnaks. Any Armenian government enforcing the implementation of the conditions set forth in the Alexandrapol Agreement can depend on our friendship.

The Wilson project that aims to leave millions of Turks under the control of thousands of Armenians is simply ridiculous."

Streit's Question: 14

Cemiyet-i Akvam hakkında fikriniz nedir? [What is your opinion on the League of Nations?]

Mustafa Kemal Paşa's Answer

[**French**]: "*Je pense qu'actuellement la Société des Nations est un instrument de plus aux mains de l'Angleterre.*"

[English]: "I believe that the League of Nations is simply another of the resources used by the British."

Streit's Question: 15

Düyûnu ümumiye-i Osmaniye'ye karşı meslek-i hareketiniz nedir? [What will be your course of action against the Ottoman Public Debt Administration?]

Mustafa Kemal Paşa's Answer

[**French**]: "*Notre position vis à vis de la dette publique ottomane est définie par le pacte national.*"

[**English**]: "Our position regarding the Ottoman Government's debt has been clearly set forth in our National Pact."

Streit's Question: 16

Musul gazyağı menabiine karşı siyasetiniz ne olacaktır? [What will your policy be regarding the petroleum reserves in Mosul?]

Mustafa Kemal Paşa's Answer

[**French**]: "*Il est évident que le fait d'asservir un peuple pour s'approprier les ressources naturelles de son pays est contraire, non seulement à l'esprit du siècle mais encore aux principes les plus élémentaires d'humanité. Je pense que les richesses pétrolifére de Mossoul qui d'ailleurs se trouve à l'intérieur des frontières définies par notre pacte national doivent être exploités librement pour le bénéfice commun de la population régionale et de toute l'humanité sans qu'il y ait un accaparement d'aucune sorte.*"

[**English**]: **"It is obvious that enslaving a nation to benefit from its national resources is not only against the mentality of this century but also against basic humanitarian principles. I believe that the petroleum reserves in Mosul, which fall within the boundaries laid out in our National Pact, should be used for the well being of both local populations and all mankind. In order to do so, no monopolies or attempts at exploitation should be tolerated."**

Streit's Question: 17

Türkiye'nin istikbal için hususi ile şekl-i hükümet, mevki-i saltanat ve hilâfet, maarif, kadınların durumu, vesait-i nakliye ve tabiî kaynakların tekemmülü hakkında ümid ve tasavvurlarınız nelerden ibarettir? [What are your hopes and thoughts for Turkey's future on issues like the type of government to be established, the position of the sultanate and the caliphate, education, women's rights, means of transportation and the use of natural resources?]

Mustafa Kemal Paşa's Answer

[**French**]: "*Le régime actuel et futur de la Turquie est et sera basé sur la souveraineté absolue du peuple. L'existence et la puissance du peuple turc les véritables appuis du Khalifat et du Sultanat.*

Nous avons déjà commencé à consacrer de grands efforts à l'enseignement populaire et nous lui donnerons une nouvelle impulsion dès que nous aurons la paix. Nous attachons également une importance très grande à l'instruction des femmes.

Débarrassés que nous sommes des capitulations qui nous enchainaient nous travaillerons fiévreusement à notre relèvement économique dès que nous aurons la paix. Nous demanderons avec empressement à tous les peuples avancés le concours de leurs capitaux et de leurs spécialistes."

[**English**]: **"Turkey's prospective government rules and will continue to rule based on the principle of "sovereignty lies in the nation regardless of all circumstances." The presence and strength of the Turkish nation form the real basis of the Sultanate and the Caliphate.**

We already started putting effort into the development of our education system. We will speed up this process once we ensure peace in our lands. We also pay great attention to women's education.

We are going to work hard for economic development once we get rid of the capitulations that have been hindering our growth and once we have peace in our land. We will kindly ask for the help of experts from all developed nations as well as welcoming any help from their other resources."

Streit's Question: 18

İzzet Paşa heyeti hakkında bir beyanatınız var mıdır? [Is there any statement you wish to make in regard to the Izzet Paşa Delegation?]

Mustafa Kemal Paşa's Answer

[**French**]: "*La mission Izzet Pacha a entrepris son voyage en Anatolie avec d'excellentes intentions mais dans l'ignorance de la véritable situation tant intérieure qu'extérieure et n'a connu cette situation qu'après avoir franchi la frontière du Gouvernement de la Grande Assemblée Nationale de Turquie. Parce que les membres de cette mission étaient venus avec la résolution de servir les intérêts du pays et de la nation, ils ont accompli le devoir commandé par le bien public ainsi que par leur conscience en se joignant au peuple. Toutefois iles sont libres de leurs faits et gestes, c'est à dire qu'ils peuvent rester ici s'ils le désirent ou bien rentrer à Constantinople pour n'importe quelle affaire privée. Au fond cette mission n'a aucun rapport avec le vrai travail que nous accomplissons.*"

[**English**]: "The Izzet Paşa Delegation started their trip to Anatolia with good intentions but were unaware of the conditions in the country until they entered the boundaries of our government. Since this delegation wished to help the nation, they joined our forces as their consciences dictated. But they are free in their decisions and actions. This means that if they wish, they may stay here; or if they wish, they may return to Istanbul for their private affairs. In reality, this mission has nothing to do with our real work."

Streit's Question: 19

Amerika efkârı umumiyesine tebliği arzusunda bulunduğunuz sair noktalar var ise, tebellüğ edip arza malûmemnuniye hazırım. [If there are any messages you would like to give to the American public opinion, I am most willing to convey them].

Mustafa Kemal Paşa's Answer

[**French**]: "*Javais expliqué à tous les américains avec lesquels j'avais été en contact l'inclination et les sentiments pleins de sincérité du peuple turc envers l'Amérique tels que je les sentais de près. L'un de ces américains a été le Général Harbord qui m'a dit être muni de pouvoirs étendus. Je croyais qu'il serait répondu d'une façon très positive à toutes mes explications.*

Mail il était dit qu'en politique à la place des sentiments humanitaires et des inclinations des peuples nous rencontrerions les initiatives des hommes politiques basées sur toutes sortes de calculs.

C'est pourquoi prenant en considération cette pénible impression reçue par le peuple turc je n'oserai rien ajouter en son nom tant que je n'aurais pas observé la réalisation de son attente relative à une attitude plus humaine à son égard."

[**English**]: "So far, I have expressed the sincerity and the good feelings the Turkish nation possesses for the Americans to every single American I made contact with. One of these was General Harbord. I assumed this was to become manifest in positive responses.

However, it is said that in political spheres, it is predestined to see nations act not according to their personal and sincere inclinations but according to other calculations by their politicians.

That is why, taking into consideration my nation's grief, I cannot say much until I see them enjoying benefits that they had been waiting for."

Türkiye Büyük Millet Meclisi Reisi [President of the Grand National Assembly of Turkey]

Mustafa Kemal

Hamiş [Postscript]:

Bu suallerin cevaplarını lütfen Fransızca olarak verirseniz Zati Samilerine karşı ayrıca minnettar olacağım efendim. [If Your Excellency could provide the answers to these questions in French I would be most grateful].

Clarence K. Streit, *Public Ledger* - Philadelphia

Moustafa Kemal [Mustafa Kemal]

Président de la Grande Assemblée Nationale de Turquie [President of the Grand National Assembly of Turkey]

Le 26 *Février* 1921 [February 26, 1921]

Pour copie conforme [Certified true copy]:

Le Directeur de la Section Politique du Commissariat du Peuple aux Affaires Etrangères [Director, Political Section, People's Commissariat for Foreign Affairs]

Note: As the reader has undoubtedly discerned there are numerous gaps, spelling errors and mistakes in the published version of the French answers which were supplied to Clarence Streit by Mustafa Kemal [**Appendix IV.**: pp. 195-209 above]. Unfortunately, as the following statement by Streit indicates, his copy of the original document was lost:

> According to what I was told there [Ankara], I was the first western correspondent to attend sessions of the Grand National Assembly, and to interview its President. First I sent him a rather comprehensive list of probing questions. He sent back his answers in French; one could not ask for a more clear-cut, straightforward response, without hint of evasion. (Later I loaned the original of this precious historical document to Charles Crane, head of a U.S. Commission of Inquiry into Turkey...who lost it, to my continuing regret, even though I have a copy). Kemal Pasha then invited me to see him at his office --the modest small cottage near the railway station of the pre-war Station Master. We had a couple of hours alone, the talk all in French, with nothing 'off the record,' if memory serves. He was in civilian attire. He impressed me strongly as a far-sighted statesman, a general, of simple, democratic manners, dedicated to the vast undertaking of transforming a decadent, despotic, theocratic Moslem government and largely illiterate but intelligent people into a westernized Republic, based on Bill of Rights, civil law, separation of Church and State. In short, he struck me as being, truly, a great man indeed [**Streit Papers II:** 75; Folder 4].

Among the Streit materials preserved in the Library of Congress is a six-page typed French document [**Streit Papers II:** 75; Folder 5], with a note in his handwriting reading: "*Février 1921- les premier trois pages étaient les réponses écrit*[*es*] *les autres en conversation*" ("February 1921 – the first three pages consisted of the written responses; the others, responses given in conversation"). This document appears to be what Streit was referring to when he wrote about Charles Crane having lost the original and added: "*even though I have a copy.*" It is a combination of the written responses he received and Mustafa Kemal's answers when he interviewed him in person.

A comparison of the contents of this document with those provided in the version published by the Turkish Ministry of Culture in 1992, establishes that while there is general agreement among the two texts, there are differences in wording between them. In addition, several of the questions submitted by Streit, and Mustafa Kemal's written answers, do not appear in the first three pages of Streit's six-page French document, i.e., among what he termed "*the written responses.*" Among these are what appears in the 1992 Ministry of Culture book as questions/answers #7 and #8 [See: **Appendix IV** above, pp. 201-203], on the Armenian war-time deportations and the reports of atrocities being perpetrated then by Greeks and Armenians against the Turkish inhabitants of Anatolia. This despite the fact that the list of questions Streit had submitted in Ottoman Turkish [**Appendix IV** above: pp. 193-194], clearly contained these queries.

It appears that having lost the original written answers supplied by Mustafa Kemal, Streit 'reconstructed' them on the basis of his notes taken in the course of his interview with the Nationalist leader and his translation of numerous lengthy quotations from them which he had used in the stories he dispatched to the Philadelphia ***Public Ledger*** in the Spring of 1921. Given this fact, I chose to use the Ministry of Culture's published version as the only actual (albeit flawed by poor French and missing words) copy of the written answers provided Streit by Mustafa Kemal Paşa [HWL].

APPENDIX V: CLARENCE K. STREIT'S ARTICLE IN THE PHILADELPHIA *PUBLIC LEDGER* (MARCH 28, 1921) BASED ON THE ANSWERS TO QUESTIONS HE SUBMITTED TO MUSTAFA KEMAL PAŞA[231]

Turkish Nationalist Put Peace Up To Allies

Mustafa Kemal Declares for Self-Determination and Just Settlement in Comprehensive Review of Near East Problem

By Clarence K. Streit, Special Correspondent

Copyright, 1921, by Public Ledger Co.

Angora, Feb. 27 – An official statement going in detail into nearly every angle of the complex Near East situation was given the *Public Ledger* correspondent yesterday by Mustafa Kemal Pasha, president of the Great National Assembly in Turkey, in written answers to questions submitted to him. From my own observation I can say he speaks with the authority of a leader who knows his people and enjoys enormous prestige among them. The text of the questions and answers follows:

What is your attitude toward the London conference?

"*We've sent our delegates to the London conference in order to show every one, our people as well as our enemies, that we do not wish to let any chance for peace, no matter how feeble, escape. If our enemies, by violating once more the principles for which the Entente declared they fought for more than four years and by taking no account of promises they made us before the conclusion of the armistice, reject our moderate and just conditions, they will assume all responsibility for the blood which will continue to flow as well as for the grave crises which the continuation of war in the Levant will provoke in the whole universe. Our peace conditions are contained in our National Pact of January 28 last year.*"

What are your relations with Soviet Russia?

"*Our relations with Soviet Russia are based on actual comprehension of our aspirations, rights and interests, and are most cordial.*"

Have you signed an alliance with Russia?

Studying Conditions in Russia

"*An important Turkish mission headed by Youssouf Kemal Bey has just arrived in Moscow, and its duty is to study with the Russian Government all eastern questions, those of the Caucasus as well as those of all Asia, and to decide upon the future conduct of the two peoples in the solution of great world questions.*"

---

[231] [LC: Streit Papers II: 75 – Folder 1].

Do you expect to settle the Dardanelles question without consulting Russia?

"The clause in our national pact relative to the straits question has been recognized by Soviet Russia as just, and constituted Article VI of the treaty signed last summer by the delegates of the two governments."

The clause referred to, which is Article VI of the part, reads: "*The security of the city of Constantinople, which is both the seat of the Caliphate and the capital of the Ottoman empire, and likewise the security of the sea of Marmora, ought to be guaranteed against all aggression, with this one condition, the decision which will be taken in common accord between us and all interested states relative to the opening of the straits of the Black sea and the Dardanelles to world commerce and transportation will be valid.*"

What is your attitude toward communism and internationalism?

Nationalists, Not Communists

"Communism does not exist in Turkey. All the world considers us Nationalists, and we are, in so far as we are defending the independence, rights and interests of our nation. If by inter- nationalism you mean respect for the independence and rights of all peoples, then, yes, we are also internationalists. Moreover, I do not see how communism, in so far as it is opposed to the national and religious spirit, can find a field of application here. It is only in case an attack begun against the Turkish people succeeds that this eventuality could come about."

What is your attitude toward America?

"We greatly desire to enjoy the friendship of America. We have never considered ourselves at war with the American people and are astonished that they have not yet resumed the usual diplomatic relations with us. We are ready to resume diplomatic relations with the United States on the basis of our national pact, independently or our political situation; vis-à-vis other powers. We already have presented this matter to your government.

I believe American aid would be precious for developing our natural resources for the greatest profit of our people and of all humanity."

Do you desire any unofficial American technical advisers?

"Any aid offered to facilitate our economic restoration will be accepted with gratitude, and we would be the more happy to have help from American experts since the United States has never had any territorial desires in any part of our country."

What is your attitude toward American schools and relief work in Anatolia?

American Relief Welcome

"All benevolent enterprises which lighten human suffering without distinction as to race or religion are welcome here as long as they pursue no immediate for remote political ends."

What solution do you propose for the problem of non-Moslem peoples in Turkey?

"***The answer to that question is contained in our national pact.***" [Article V of the national pact to which he refers reads: "*In order to assure the Moslem population in the neighboring countries identical rights we will recognize and guarantee minorities in Turkey the same rights as those contained in arrangements concluded between the Entente powers, their enemies and several of their associates.*"]

What is your policy while war lasts toward the Greeks and Armenians in Anatolia?

"***We make no distinctions between Musselman and non-Musselman citizens of Turkey. Consequently Greeks and Armenians have nothing to fear as long as they do not conspire with the enemy.***"

What is the official viewpoint of your government toward the Armenian deportations and massacres during the world war?

"***After making allowance for the enormous exaggerations always made by those who accuse their enemies, the Armenian deportation affair reduces itself to this – the Armenian-Dashnak committee, then in the service of the czar, had caused the Armenian population behind our troops to revolt when the Russian army began its great 1915 offensive against us.***"

Attacked by Armenians

"***Obliged to retreat before the superior numbers and material of the enemy, we found ourselves constantly between two fires. Our convoys of supplies and wounded were pitilessly massacred, roads and bridges destroyed behind us and terror reigned through the Turkish countryside. The bands which committed these crimes, and which included in their ranks Armenians able to bear arms, were supplied with arms, munitions and provisions in Armenian villages, where, thanks to the immunities accorded in the capitulations, certain foreign powers had succeeded during peacetime in establishing enormous stocks for this purpose. The world which regards with indifference the fashion in which England in peacetime and far from the battlefield treats the Irish nation cannot in all justice complain of the resolution we were obliged to take relative to Armenian deportations. Contrary to calumnies spread against us the deportees are alive and many of them would have returned to their homes if the Entente had not forced us to recommence war.***"

What information can you give regarding the reported massacres of Turks by Armenians and Greeks?

U.S. General a Witness

"***It would be too long to go into detail as to the atrocities committed by the Armenians and Greeks against the Moslem population during the world war and after the armistice. The massacres and devastation caused by Armenian bands while the Russians were evacuating our eastern provinces are sufficiently known. The American general, Harbord, with whom I talked at Sivas and who after having visited these regions and having made edifying observations on the conduct of the Armenian bands, wrote to tell me that all I had told him was true, is a witness from whom American opinion can usefully inform itself. The Dashnaks, moreover, continued their crimes in the zone of Kars and Olti until the conclusion of the Alexandropol treaty.***

The Greeks on their side have committed such crimes during the Smyrna occupation that the interallied investigation commission itself, although constituted of Greeks and Allies, severely criticized the Greek authorities in its report made after visiting this province in the autumn of 1919. In the zone of occupation of the Greeks tens of thousands of Turks of all ages and both sexes have been massacred, all livestock has been taken to Greece and several unfortunate refugees in our zone are altogether destitute."

What is your attitude toward Pan-Islamism, Pan-Turanism and Pan-Turkism?

For Self-Determination

"Pan-Islamism, in so far as it means the union of all Moslems under Turkish domination, and Pan-Turkism, in so far as it means union of all countries of the Turkish race under Turkish domination, are bugaboos which the English imperialists use to lead their people in a perpetual crusade against us. We have no intention nor desire to conquer have of the globe as have the English, who launch their ridiculous accusations against us, have done and are continuing to do each day. Our national pact, furthermore, is explicit on this point. On the contrary we are convinced that only a sincere application of the principle of self-determination of peoples for all nations, including the Moslems, can save humanity from the catastrophe to which the perpetuation of wars is leading it."

What is your policy in religious affairs with special regard to holy wars, the holy law and the separation of church and state?

"I think each individual as each people ought to enjoy absolute liberty of conscience. This principle unfortunately is trampled upon by our enemies who believe our people, because it is Moslem, has not the right to independence. What is going on now in Syria, Mesopotamia and Anatolia is the best proof of my statement. Our religion is Mohammedanism, which, considered in its undogmatic part, is at bottom only a political social system based on the greatest tolerance and forms a mean between individualism and communism."

What are your relations with and policy toward other Moslem countries?

Cordial to All Moslems

"We are naturally maintaining extremely cordial relations with all Moslem states. An important Turkish military mission called by the Emir of Afghanistan should soon go to join at Kabul, the Turkish officers already working there to make the Afghan army an instrument for modern war. I have said above, my most ardent desire is to see the right of self-determination granted to all Moslem peoples."

What is your attitude toward Georgia with special regard to the question of Batum?

"Our relations with Georgia are good. I desire that the question of Batum may receive, through understanding, a peaceful solution conforming to the wishes of its population and our legitimate rights as well as to the interests of the Caucasian peoples."

What are your relations with Soviet Armenia and what is your opinion of the Wilsonian boundaries of Armenia?

"*Armenia in the last few days has fallen into the hands of the Dashnak party. Any Armenian government which sincerely applies the Alexandropol treaty can count on our friendship. I find Mr. Wilson's project, tending to place several million Turks under the domination of several thousand Armenians, simply ridiculous.*"

What is your opinion on the society [sic. league] of nations?

League a British Instrument

"*I think the society of nations at present is one more instrument in the hands of England.*"

What is your policy toward the Mosul oil fields?

"*It is evident that the enslavement of a people in order to appropriate the natural resources of a country is contrary not only to the spirit of the century but also to the most elementary principles of humanity. I think the Mosul oil riches, which, moreover, are within the frontiers defined by our national pact, ought to be exploited freely for the common benefit of the region's population and all humanity, without monopoly of any sort.*"

What are your hopes and plans for the future of Turkey with special regard to the form of government, the position of the sultan and caliph, public instruction, position of women, and economic development?

"*The present and future Turkish regime is and will be based on the absolute sovereignty of the people. The existence and power of the Turkish people are the true sources of strength of the caliphate and the sultanate. We already have begun to make great efforts for popular instruction and will give it a new impulse when we have peace. We attach equally great importance to the education of women. When untrammeled by the capitulations which now enchain us we will work feverishly for our economic rehabilitation, as soon as we have peace. We eagerly ask from all advanced peoples, the aid of their capital and specialists.*"

What statement do you wish to make regarding the Izzet Pasha mission?

"*The Izzet Pasha mission undertook its trip to Anatolia with excellent intentions but ignorance of the real situation, both interior and exterior, and only became acquainted with this situation after having crossed the frontiers of the Turkish great national assembly's government. Because this mission had come with the resolution to serve the interests of the country and nation they have accomplished the duty commanded by the public good, as well as by their conscience, in joining themselves with the people. However, they are free in their actions, that is to say, they can remain here if they wish or return to Constantinople for any private affair. At bottom this mission had no connection with the true work we are accomplishing.*"

Have you anything else you wish to say to the American public?

"I have explained to all Americans whom I have met the sentiment, full of sincerity, of the Turkish people toward their government as I from intimate knowledge, felt that to be. One of these Americans was General Harbord, who told me he had been given wide powers. I thought the American people would respond in very positive fashion to all my explanations. But it has been said in politics instead of humanitarian sentiments and sympathies of people, we have to deal with the moves of politicians, based on all sorts of calculations. That is why, taking into consideration this painful impression received by the Turkish people, I shall not dare add anything in its name until I have seen a realization of its desire for more humane attitude toward it."

Appendix VI.: Streit's dispatch to the *Public Ledger* following his March 3, 1921 interview with Mustafa Kemal Paşa[232]

Note: Untitled Story on Streit's Interview with Mustafa Kemal Paşa, in the Philadelphia ***Public Ledger***, March, 1921. I have been unable to find copies of the ***Public Ledger*** for the date it appeared. On the typewritten copy which is preserved in his papers, Streit wrote: '*Very important document. cks.*' [HWL].

Mustapha Kemal Pasha, who is one of the most democratic of men, received me informally in his study, furnished in western style, in the small house formerly occupied by the railway division superintendent in Angora, in which he now lives. In true Turkish fashion, he offered me coffee and cigarettes. He talked freely with me for nearly two hours, speaking good French in a slow, measured tone. He is not a dictator -I know of no western parliament which exercises as much real power as does the National Assembly of Turkey today- but, because of his prestige as the organizer and leader of the nationalist movement and because of his ability and personality, he is easily the most influential man in Turkey. From my own observation I can say that he speaks with the authority of a leader who is loved and trusted by his people.

As the London Conference was then in session, I asked him what he expects to result from it.

"***Frankly,***" he replied, "***I do not believe it will accomplish any real results. The Allies talk as if this were simply a territorial question between us and Greece. But territorial matters are of secondary importance – what is essential is our complete economic as well as political independence. That we must have. Before the war our development was throttled by foreign interference, by the capitulations and other privileges which foreign powers held in Turkey.***

Since then the Entente has tried to carry this enslavement even further. The Treaty of Sevres could be applied only to a herd of cattle – not to a nation of men. It must be abolished completely before any peace can be made.

As for the Greeks, they have refused to agree to a Commission of Investigation for Smyrna, which as you know we accepted. We saw no need of the investigation, for the Allies have already made one, but we are so sure of the sentiments of the people that we are willing that another inquiry be made, if the Greeks are required first to evacuate the territory. If they should remain, the investigation would be a farce. The English, very likely, may say that they can't force the Greeks to withdraw. It seems to me that the question between us and Greece may be most easily settled on the battlefield – by our driving them from Turkey."

[232] [LC: Streit Papers II: 75 – Folder 5].

What are your views on Thrace?

"*We must have the frontier drawn as it was after the second Balkan war, with the line adjusted to protect Adrianople by returning to Turkey the small salient taken by Bulgaria. For western Thrace there should be a plebiscite.*"

To what settlement of the Straits question would you agree?

"*We are perfectly willing that the Straits be made free, that we remain neutral there. We are willing to destroy all the fortifications along the Dardanelles and Bosporus. Our one condition is that Constantinople --our capital—be protected. It should be possible to do that by international agreement. We are perfectly willing that this question be settled by an International conference, if in that conference the States along the Black Sea are represented. This question concerns them rather than England, which desires control of this waterway apparently because she wants to control the route to the Baku oil fields.*"

Your National Pact giving your peace terms speaks of the Armistice line as the southern boundary which you claim. Could you show me just where that line ran?

I offered him my map and he drew a line beginning at about Ourdou on the west, running just south of Aleppo to the Euphrates, following it to Ed Deir, and thence going almost straight east to the Persian frontier.

"*That is approximately the boundary we ask,*" he explained. "*We are willing to let the rest of the Ottoman Empire go. We think, however, that the peoples inhabiting it ought to have the right to decide their fate for themselves by a plebiscite. If they vote to join us, of course we will have to accept them. I was in command at Aleppo when the war ended. The population of that city has given me many proofs of its desire to be with us. However, we are willing to accept a plebiscite there and also in Ed Deir, but not for Mosul. We have made no definite line for the latter, but we consider that the vilayet belongs to Turkey. The Suleiman and Gerguk districts are unquestionably ours. There are Arabs and Kurds in the vilayet, but the majority is Turkish.*

We held Mosul when the war ended. The English agreed to let it remain with us. They then asked us to allow one of their generals to come there on a friendly visit. He brought troops with him; more came later, and thus, despite the Armistice agreement, the English occupied the district, making Ihsan Pasha, who commanded there, a prisoner. A friendly English call-----" and he smiled.

Is it true (as it was then reported) that the English are evacuating the Mosul district?

"*I think that the English very probably will be leaving Mosul this spring, though they are still there at this time. They are not fighting against us alone, you know, but the Arabs, too. An Arab government has been constituted in the desert between Bagdad and Basra – naturally not near any city or where the English can reach it. These Arabs have told me that they wished to join us and have asked me to send them some representative.*"

Is it true, as the London press reports, that you are sending them the fourth son of Sultan Abdul Hamid?

"*No, there is no foundation for that report. We have no princes here,*" – and he smiled. "*I am sending them some of our own men who can represent us better. Perhaps my friend the Grand Sheik of the Sunussi may be the man who will lead them. We became friends during the war with Italy in Tripoli. Recently he paid me a visit here and he is now at Diarbekir en route for Arabia.*"

When I asked Mustapha Kemal Pasha about the San Remo oil agreement, I found that apparently he had not seen a copy of it. He laughed at the idea, and said:

"*It is all very well to divide on paper the natural resources of other countries, but it is best first to be sure of having them to divide.*"

If you regain the Mosul oil fields, are you willing to have them exploited by foreign capital?

"*Yes. But we do not want English capital there. The English have a peculiar habit in their commercial dealings: First they invest capital in a country, then, on the pretext of protecting their investments they invade the country with troops and install themselves permanently.*

We are most favorable to American capital being invested in Mosul and in all parts of Turkey as well, for we know that you have no desire for any part of our territory and have no aims incompatible with Turkish independence. Naturally, we will need a great deal of aid in building up our country and we are especially desirous of obtaining both material and technical help from America in preference to any other country."

According to the fundamental law which the Assembly has passed, both executive and legislative powers are vested exclusively in it. How is that going to affect the future position of the Sultan?

Mustapha Kemal Pasha smiled:

"*He will have to accept our fundamental law – or get out. It will be easy to find another sultan who will be amenable to our wishes.*"

Is it true that the capital of Turkey in the future will be situated in Anatolia?

"*Constantinople is, of course, our traditional capital, and such it must continue to be. But we have had an experience in this war which has taught us a lesson. The sultanate and caliphate will remain in Constantinople, but the seat of the real government, the National Assembly and the cabinet, should be situated here in Anatolia – in the center of the country where it will be better protected than at Constantinople. The Assembly, of course, can go from time to time to Constantinople, but the permanent seat of government should not be there. The question has not been decided definitely, but it is being discussed. We are considering Kaisarieh, Sivas and Yozgad as possible sites. We will send a commission to survey this central area for the best capital site. It should have groves of trees, a stream – in a word, natural beauty.*"

In answer to my request that he explain in more detail his attitude toward religious affairs and toward the Holy War, he laughed again, and said:

"*I am not very well acquainted with religious matters, but from what I have heard, the Caliph has the right, when Islam is in danger, to call upon all Moslems to wage a Holy War of defense. The Sultan during the Second Balkan War, I believe, made such an appeal, but as you know it met with no success. Here we do not believe in mixing religion with political affairs. We make war with only the material forces at our command, without calling to our aid religious sentiment. The Turks are not fanatics. Of course, there are hodjas -priests- among us, as in every country, who try to stir up the people, but we must and we will keep them in hand.*"

A confident smile accompanied his last words.

Would you say that there is a tendency here to separate the Church from the State?

Mustapha Kemal Pasha assented:

"*For instance,*" he said, "*at Constantinople the Sultan as Caliph names the Sheik ul Islam, who acts for him as head of the Church, controls religious affairs and stands next to the Grand Vizier in the government. Here we have no such sheik. It is true that we have a Commissar for Religious Affairs in place of him, but he is concerned only with spiritual questions and is a deputy elected by and subject to the Great National Assembly, like any other Commissar.*"

APPENDIX VII.: ROBERT STEED DUNN'S JULY 1, 1921 INTERVIEW WITH MUSTAFA KEMAL PAŞA AT HIS ANKARA (TRAIN STATION) RESIDENCE[233]

A) Dunn's Impressions Based on Interview with Mustapha Kemal Paşa (Angora, July 1, 1921):

I met the Nationalist leader by appointment at 4 p.m., in his 'Winter Palace' at the railway station. Mr. Heck had seen him in the morning and reported him cold and unresponsive, with the attitude that no business could be done with the Nationalists without establishing a political appui first. He had made Heck talk with him in Turkish and only smiled once during the interview. It was not satisfactory.

I went with Miss. Allen[234] to interpret. All sorts of civil and uniformed functionaries lined the way from the gate to the council room upstairs in the little stone house under the lime trees. Mustafa Kemal Pasha was waiting in a large room with a baize covered council table, many chairs, a sofa and an alcove. He met me standing just inside the door, nervously dangling a chain of pink coral conversation beads with a pink silk tassel. He seemed to have been waiting for me rather nervously. He wore a dark slate blue lounge suit, very natty and evidently not made in Angora, or even Turkey, a white pique shirt with soft front, and a small black bow tie with soft collar. I did not notice his feet or cuff buttons. He wore no fez or kalpac [kalpak], and his thinnish light hair was brushed straight back like a college student.

His youthfulness struck you: the high cheek bones, somewhat hollow cheeks, small reddish and very trim mustache, steel blue eyes. His face was immobile -and he always tried to keep it so- suggesting, oddly, that of the well-trained and very superior waiter. The key to the man was his brow, above very narrow slitted eyes, which kept giving quick, furtive glances. As if almost against his will the waiter-like face would leap into that of a clever, ugly customer. Throughout he tried to conceal this sensitive automatic facial expression, but succeeded in only limiting it to raising and lowering his straight eyebrows.

These were very straight and grew close to the narrow eye-cavities. With his out-sloping, sharp pointed temples they were the main features of his remarkable brow: not intellectual but subtle and mercuric. He had two small nubs just above his nose. He raised or lowered his eyebrows in either direction to express amusement or disapproval. You could not tell which was intended until you noticed whether the corners of the straight slits of his mouth were slightly drawn up or not. The chin was pointed and prominent, although small. His facial motions gave you the impression of fluttering, although his eyelids hardly moved. You got a sense of concentration in the brain behind, with immense possibilities of inexorability, cruelty even, yet of completed realization of all points at issue and a broad outlook.

I said I had called upon him immediately upon arriving in Angora and had been here a week without his even acknowledging the visit. I purposely gave the impression that I considered that his manners had been at fault. He expressed conventional surprise, but made no apologies. As an opening, I told

---

[233] These documents are taken from the U.S. National Archives: Record Group 84: Correspondence, U.S. Embassy - Turkey, 1921. Volume 16 - 800 Turkey. Herein are presented: a) Dunn's impressions based on July 1, 1921 interview with Mustafa Kemal Paşa; b) A series of fourteen (handwritten) questions submitted by Dunn to Mustafa Kemal in the course of their July 1, 1921 meeting, and c) Mustafa Kemal's written answers to Dunn's Questions.

[234] Lowry, 1986: pp. 209-252.

him of having passed him in 1919 between Erzurum and Erzinjan [Erzincan], when I met his staff in an automobile on the road while he was on horseback in the hills. His face expressed incredulity; and seemed to express almost annoyance when I told about my trip from Batoum [Batum] to Kars last winter and dwelt on my personal intimacy with Kasim Karabekir Pasha [Kazım Karabekir Paşa] and Bekir Sami Bey. I detailed my arrest by Armenian Bolsheviks at Karaklis [Karakilis] and he almost laughed when I quoted a slurring remark of Bekir Sami Bey's about Moscow. It was easy at anytime to change his grimacing into a veiled smile, but to do so you always had to switch quickly from the serious subject in hand to a lighter one.

Youssouf [Yusuf] Kemal Bey, Minister of Foreign Affairs came in evidently by appointment. He wore a black kalpak and sat at the long table. There was a pause, neither of them introduced the object of my visit, or led the conversation toward it; so I was forced to do so myself, rather abruptly. I went into further details, in re the breaking of relations between Turkey and the United States, how no state of war even existed, that we could not distinguish between the Constantinople and Angora governments; that I was here unofficially to look the ground over and considered personally that any initiative in reestablishing political relations must come from his government rather than ours. I even suggested that their parliament might pass a resolution declaring the Constantinople act severing relations with the U.S. as void. Both Youssouf and Mustapha Kemal appeared struck and pleased by this, nodded and signified "it could be done," as at a happy thought breaking upon a situation, before wholly unrealized and obscure to them.

Throughout, their interest and questions centered on the attitude of Washington toward resuming political relations. This kept me constantly emphasizing two points: 1) the general lack of interest in the U.S. toward the Near East owing to distance, etc., 2) that we in Constantinople had no expression on or opinion from the government regarding the resumption of relations, and that in order to get any such expression, we considered it our duty and initiative to send Washington the true facts regarding the situation in the Near East, in order to stimulate their attention. The attitude of the pair continued very formal. By now I saw that conversation and oral questions could not break their inscrutable air, so I produced the written memorandum which I had prepared for such a necessity [See: pp. 224 - 227 below]. They at once seized on this method of conference, as if they had been about to suggest it themselves. Miss Allen and Youssouf Kemal together orally translated the questions and statements into Turkish for the Pasha. I reminded them that some of the questions might seem impertinent but that I would not resent their refusal to answer any of them.

Several of the questions were informally discussed after being read. Regarding the anti-Near East Relief propaganda I agreed that much of it as printed was too true for me to deny, thus stealing the fire of any argument which they might make; but I insisted that this propaganda was not news and it seemed to me ill-timed and undiplomatic to allow it to be printed in newspapers.

Regarding Bouillon, I related how General Gourard's representative at Constantinople had told be confidentially about Bouillon's visit to Angora, and that I was sure that now the visit was ended, I would be given the facts about it, were I in Constantinople. Both Youssouf and the Pasha smiled and nodded grimly but did no enlightening. They agree to answer all my questions in writing, but called attention to how searching they were, and how 'unusual' it was to present them. I remarked that one never gets results without going to the limit of his demands. Also that I could expect in return nothing worse than a 'No,' which was often quite as satisfactory as admissions. The inscrutable smile broke forth on the Pasha's face.

Immediately two points were made, the first by the Pasha, that he would like equally to submit to me similar political questions regarding America. I eagerly acceded to this, saying I would answer all of them within my knowledge as we had nothing to conceal [No such questions were submitted to me during the ten days more that I stayed in Angora]. The second, Youssouf Kemal said that whereas I might speak to him unofficially, anything that Mustapha Kemal Pasha said or wrote would be considered as official. I did not agree to this point of view, but stated that I considered that any response to statements made unofficially by me should be considered as equally unofficial but no less reliable. Youssouf Kemal may not have the subtler mind of the two, but he expressed himself more keenly than did the Pasha and continuously dove deep to fish up the logical and sticky point.

Refreshments were being served by an attendant who always backed out of the room, first coffee, then purple fruit ices, and last iran [sic. ayran]. Both the Pasha's and my ices melted before we got around to eating them.

Every lead in the talk as usual led up to the so-called 'National Pact.' Several references were made to the report of the Harbord Commission and the Pasha was interested to know whether it had been placed before Congress. I said I supposed that it had been submitted to the War and State Departments, but could not say if the Foreign Relations or Military Committee of Congress had seen or acted on it. The Pasha spoke as if Harbord had made promises to him when they met at Sivas in 1919, which have not been carried out. I got the same impressions from Miss Graffum at Sivas. The Pasha's chief interest was in our relations with the Entente Powers at Constantinople, and I went into great detail in explaining them: how we were not parties to the armistice and that the American High Commissioner did not attend the meeting of the European High Commissioners; how our relations were very friendly personally but officially not confidential. I remarked that once some British officers had reproached us for not backing their policies in the Near East, to which I replied that Americans could not be expected to back policies of which they disapproved. I also explained at his request our relations with the Constantinople government, for he seemed to have an idea that we dealt with them directly. I told him that we did deal with some Turkish officials directly but quite unofficially as we did also with the Allied High Commissioners, this being one advantage of a Military High Commission. I dwelt particularly on our rather anomalous position of not being at war with Turkey or having been in a state of war, as Greece was during the Great War when Turkish and Greek forces were close to one another in the field.

Miss Allen stated later that she considered the interview, which lasted exactly one hour, a great success. She said that it was a great concession that the Pasha should have so willingly consented to answer my submitted questions at all. She has conferred with him several times before and had often found his manner much more cold and reserved than he was with me.

B & C) Dunn's Handwritten Questions & Written Answers Provided by Mustafa Kemal Paşa[235]

Dunn's Question #1: What political parties exist in the Angora Government, and in what way are their views and principles opposed to one another?

Mustafa Kemal Paşa's Answer: "*Political factions do not exist in the Great National Assembly of Turkey. The whole of the Assembly concentrates its foreign and internal policy in the National Pledge* [Pact]. *The Assembly has vowed to work as a block to secure the terms of the National Pledge. It is true that at different times groups such as: 'The Independence Group,' 'The Reformation Group,' 'Defense of Rights' and other such factions were formed to facilitate the work of the Assembly of which the members are numerous. At present the 'Anatolia and Roumelia* [Rumeli] *Defense of Rights Group' has replaced all these different groups. As the name implies, this group is based upon the 'Anatolian and Roumelian Defense of Rights' organizations. Members of the Assembly considered from a general point of view show two inclinations: Liberal and Conservative. The 'Anatolian and Roumelian National Defense' group which is the one that has organization and forms the majority, is Liberal.*"

Dunn's Question #2: What authority decides in detail and principle on the present deportation of Greek and Armenian employees of the Near East Relief and American Tobacco Companies from the Black Sea Coast? Who is held responsible for the correct execution of the deportation orders? What body supplies evidence against deportees who are ordered away for political reasons?

Mustafa Kemal Paşa's Answer: "*Greeks on the Black Sea coast -especially in Samsoun* [Samsun]*- are trying to establish a Greek government which they propose to call the Pontus Government. This secret organization is directed from and by Athens. This secret organization tries to bring about the ruin of Turkey, and to help the Hellenic Army which has occupied the Smyrna* [İzmir] *region. By bombarding Ineboli* [İnebolu] *the Hellenic government is helping and encouraging these treacherous people. The Hellenic government is landing soldiers at Samsoun from time to time, and is making propaganda to the make the Greeks cooperate with them. The government has sufficient documents to prove this activity of the Greeks and the atrocities they commit, such as killing the Turks and burning Turkish villages. Some of these documents are still before the tribunal. Greeks who have been armed by the Commission, disguised under the name of the Greek Cross, are up to this day committing atrocious crimes in the hills against the Turks.*

The Pontus Committee is trying to bring thousands of Greeks from Russia and from the Caucasus, so as to be strong for the work of securing their treacherous purpose. Greeks who are Ottoman subjects have sent their sons to the Hellenic army. These we meet on the Smyrna front. There are such men among the prisoners we have taken. The Great National Assembly of Turkey takes all measures necessary to preserve its existence without hesitation. Armenians who are found to follow harmful policies are punished. Turks who do the same are treated in exactly the same way. Severest measures have been taken against the Moslems who with this anxiety of independence have gone through a wrong road. But the barbarism and the atrocities of the Greeks have continued for such a long time now and nobody has thought of saving the poor Moslems. Greeks have committed these crimes against the Moslems before the eyes of Europeans and the Americans."

[235] Lowry, 1986.

Dunn's Question #3: What is the present financial status of the Angora Government? Amount of exports and imports? Amount received from all taxes? External and internal debt, loans, etc.?

Mustafa Kemal Paşa's Answer: "*The position of the Great National Assembly of Angora is such that it is sure of the realization of the national purpose and desire. Our import and export is about to balance. The present customs and duties meet our expenses. The government of the Great National Assembly of Turkey has not yet felt the necessity of making a loan. Consequently we have no external or internal debt.*"

Dunn's Question #4: Why does the Government allow, after accepting American relief and charitable institutions in Anatolia, after taxing them, and allowing a representative at Angora, the present press propaganda against these institutions and the Americans connected with them?

Mustafa Kemal Paşa's Answer: "*We gladly welcome the humanitarian and philanthropic activities of the A.C.R.N.E. on condition that these activities are in accord with our laws. But we regret to say that investigations have proved that some of these institutions such as those in Mersiphoum* [Merzifon] *and Caesarea* [Kayseri] *have been means to treacherous purposes. The complaint made by the press is nothing more than the publishing of these facts. It must not be forgotten that the press with us is free as it is everywhere.*"

Dunn's Question #5: Why does the Government allow, after expressing a desire for close commercial relations with America, seek to close down the largest American commercial undertaking in Turkey -the Samsoun Tobacco interest -which bring $14,000,000 a year into Turkey- by deporting its workers, whom it is incredible to think have any connection with the Pontus sedition?

Mustafa Kemal Paşa's Answer: "*The government of the Great National Assembly of Turkey has already helped to facilitate the work of the American Tobacco companies in Samsun and is still helping. Measures taken against the workmen of these companies are very natural if one considers the fact that these men who are armed may help our enemies. These measures which are taken for the just cause of self defense must in no way be considered as a step to close these institutions. The government is ready to do any further help these companies may want.*"

Dunn's Question #6: What are the exact political and military relations between Angora and Moscow?

Dunn's Question #7: Has any Russian-Turkish treaty been signed or ratified (with dates) since the March Treaty? Have any proposals or requests been made by either government on the other, since the signing of that Treaty, and what was the nature of such proposals and requests (with dates)?

Mustafa Kemal Paşa's Answer [**Note**: to Questions # 6 & #7]: "*Relations between Moscow and the Government of the Great National Assembly of Turkey are in accordance with the principles laid down by the treaty dated March 16, 1921. These relations are pleasant.*"

Dunn's Question #8: Would the Angora Government allow a resumption of diplomatic relations with the United States which did not demand abolition of the capitulations?

Mustafa Kemal Paşa's Answer: "*The Government of the Great National Assembly of Turkey wants with pleasure to enter into relations with America. But the national government hopes that the American* *government does not insist for the continuation of the capitulations which deprive Turkey of its absolute independence. The absolute independence which necessitates the annulling of the capitulations is the governing principle of the Great National Assembly."*

Dunn's Question #9: What is the present state of negotiations with the French for peace in Cilicia? What new propositions from the French did Mr. Bouillon bring to Angora, and what Turkish proposals did he take away with him?

Mustafa Kemal Paşa's Answer: "*Being ready to come to an understanding which is in accord with the National Pledge with France, just as with all countries, we tried to find a means of stopping the war between the two countries.*"

Dunn's Question #10: What negotiations, if any, are going on between British representatives and the Angora Government looking toward peace with Greece, and settlement of the Smyrna and Eastern Thrace questions? Have French or Italian representatives any participation in such negotiations?

Mustafa Kemal Paşa's Answer: "*Nothing can be said on this subject as yet.*"

Dunn's Question #11: What are the maximum and minimum terms regarding Smyrna and Thrace on which the Grand National Assembly would probably consider making peace with Greece?

Mustafa Kemal Paşa's Answer: "*The conditions for coming to an understanding in regards to the Smyrna and the Thrace questions are clear and absolute in the National Pledge. The condition is: Their remaining under Turkish supremacy without any condition.*"

Dunn's Question #12: What evidence is there beside letters which Mustapha Saghir received in Turkey, and his confession, that he was sent here to prepare the ground for assassination of Mustapha Kemal?

Mustafa Kemal Paşa's Answer: "*It is proved that besides the documents discovered, and confessions made by Mustapha Saghir, he has tried to influence some of the commanders of the guards around Moustafa Kemal Pasha. Moustafa Saghir has further tried to influence Moustafa Kemal Pasha's janitor.*"

Dunn's Question #13: Is there any evidence that the British were negotiating to send Talaat Pasha to Angora from Berlin for political purposes just previous to Talaat's assassination?

Mustafa Kemal Paşa's Answer: "*That the British have come into touch with Talaat Pasha is a fact. But we have no document in hand which shows that these communications were in any way related to Talaat Pasha's desire to come back to his country.*"

Answers by Youssouf Bey, Minister of Foreign Affairs, Angora, 3 July 1921

Regarding deported Tobacco employees at Samsoun. Forwarded to Alston Tobacco Co., Samsoun.

Lieutenant R. S. Dunn:

Sir:

1. Tobacco specialist workmen who do not infringe the rules and regulations and who do not abuse confidence are allowed to continue their work.

2. Permanent written permission will be given to the three directors of the American commercial houses to travel between Constantinople and this city. These permissions are not transferable to other persons.

APPENDIX VIII.: STREIT'S FIRST DISPATCH FROM ANATOLIA (SENT FROM SAMSUN), FEBRUARY 3, 1921[236]

TURKISH NATIONALISTS DETHRONE CHURCH LAW

Purely Moslem Code Subjected to That of State, Removing Clause of 'Capitulations'- Caliphate and Sultanate Ignored

By Clarence K. Streit

Special Cable Dispatch

Copyright 1921, by Public Ledger Co.

Samsun, Asiatic Turkey, Feb. 3 via London, Feb. 6. - A summary of the law passed by the great national assembly at Angora January 20 establishing a new form of government for Turkey was given your correspondent today by Ibrahim Edhem Bey, governor -Mutessarif-of the Samsun district. The greatest fundamental changes made are subjection of the church law to that of the state, and administrative decentralization with a large measure of local autonomy and full parliamentary sovereignty. Both the sultanate and caliphate are absolutely ignored in the report received here of the law, the wording of which, however, clearly indicates that these offices, if they continue to exist, are shorn of all power.

The provision in the statute bringing application of the holy law under the jurisdiction of the national assembly is evidently a move by the Turks to remove the cause for the capitulations treaties with foreign powers which give them the right to settle in their consular courts all legal cases in which their nationals in Turkey are concerned. Under the old system the sultan as caliph is head of the church, but his religious powers are exercised through the Sheik ul Islam who is a member of the cabinet standing next to the grand vizier and whose functions are more judicial than spiritual. The importance of his position from the fact that all disputes among Ottoman subjects are settled on the basis of the holy law drawn from the Koran and the sayings of Mahomet [Prophet Muhammed] as interpreted by the Mullahs. To escape Moslem ecclesiastical law foreigners obtained the capitulations, the abolition of which the Kemalists demand as a peace condition.

Summary of New Law

The summary follows:

"***Sovereignty belongs exclusively to the nation and legislative and executive power exclusively to the great national assembly. Thus the Turkish state will be governed by the assembly under whose jurisdiction are the fundamental sovereign rights, as well as application of the holy law, amendments to the constitution legislation, treaty making, declaring war and making peace. Members of the cabinet are called executive***

236 "Turkish Nationalists Dethrone Church Law: Purely Moslem Code Subjected to That of State, Removing Cause of 'Capitulations' - Caliphate and Sultanate Ignored," in the Philadelphia ***Public Ledger***, February 7, 1921.

commissioners and all are to be elected by the members of the assembly who are elected by various districts. The life of each assembly is two years, but in accordance with the law passed September 5, the present assembly holds office until the peace aims are attained.

The Turkish state is to be divided into districts and sub districts according to geographical and financial necessities and legal and moral units. Except for foreign, interior, judicial, religious and political questions and some taxation, district councils will administer the public works, health, instruction, agriculture, finances and endowment schools, these councils to be chosen by the people of the district for two year terms. The national assembly will be represented in each district by a governor whose duty will be to look after matters concerning the district and nation. The districts then will be grouped together in zones under general inspectors who will keep permanent control over the carrying out of the financial policies in which the districts have a common interest.

The sub districts are to be divided into communes, considered independent moral units having a council elected by the people which in turn selects its executive committee and president."

Kemalists to Build Railway

Plans for constructing a railway in the spring from Samsun to Sivas, a distance of 280 miles, were considered here yesterday at a meeting of local merchants with the provincial governor. The railroad is to be under national control, but hope is expressed that capital will become interested and furnish the necessary material. A French company had the concession before the war and completed the grade and tunnels, forty miles from Samsun, but no steel was laid.

A representative of this company, who arrived here a few weeks ago to look after its interests, was politely ushered out of the country. The railroad is much needed as Samsun is the Black sea terminus for caravan routes from the interior of Anatolia and does a heavy commerce now with only camels and wagons for transportation.

Appendix IX.: Clarence K. Streit's dispatch of March 25, 1921 predicting defeat of Greek invasion of Anatolia

FAILURE OF GREEKS IN WAR FORSEEN[237]

Odds Early in Campaign in Anatolia Gave Turks an Alarming Advantage

SLIM CHANCE FOR VICTORY

Turkish Army and Population Confident and Equipped for a Long Contest

By Clarence K. Streit

Special Correspondent

Copyright, 1921, by Public Ledger Co.

Constantinople, March 25. - While the Greeks report successes in their double offensive [for Afioun Karahissar and Eski-Shehr] on the Ouschak and Brusa fronts there is virtually no chance of their obtaining the decisive results they expect. Even if they should take Angora they have by no means finished with the Turks.

Though loss of the first two cities would be a serious blow to the Turks, it would not be decisive. Turkey is not to be compared to highly organized western states where the capture of railroads and cities means victory. It is more like a segmented worm - chop it in pieces and each piece continues to live.

The only way in which the Greeks can crush the Turk is to sweep through Anatolia to the eastern frontiers, garrisoning every town as they go and preparing for military occupation for years to come. They have neither the men nor the money with which to do this-as it is, they cannot pay the Government employees their full salaries.

The best they can possibly hope to do is reach Angora, which would simply drive the Turks closer into the arms of the Russians and would most probably result in a Red army coming to the rescue. Then, too, the Turks have large supplies of munitions and artillery in the eastern provinces taken from the Armenians and they have troops concentrated in the Diarbekir region. Meanwhile the Greeks would be far from their base of supplies with bad communication lines, for the Turks most assuredly will destroy bridges and railroads if they have to retreat, and have a hostile armed population to deal with.

---

237 This story appeared in the Philadelphia ***Public Ledger***, Sunday Morning, April 17, 1921[LC: Streit Papers II: 75 - Folder 1].

The French know what that means. For months they had to fight against the civilian population in the streets of Aintab before they captured the city and now they have had to give up the Cilician venture as a bad job. As Ismet Pasha, chief of the general staff and commanding the Brusa front, put it in my conversation with him and as I had occasion to observe: "*The greatest strength of Turkey lies in the sentiment of the people that they absolutely must defend themselves.*"

And the Greeks must count on an even more bitter popular resistance than the French encountered, for the Turks and Greeks are old enemies. The present Greek offensive impresses me, after having been in both Anatolia and Greece, as a more than useless waste of blood. Constantine assumed a grave responsibility in launching the attack and it may cost him dear. Whatever success the Greeks may obtain will be temporary and in the end will mean at best that they have retarded the growth of a movement which holds the greatest promise in history for democracy to progress in Turkey and that they have set the clock back years as far as their own development is concerned.

But this is assuming that the Greeks will gain their objective, which is assuming far more than the strength of the Turkish army, as I saw it while in Anatolia, warrants. Turkish strategy, as Feyzi Pasha, people's commissar for national defense, explained it to me, is to carry on a war of attrition. They are on their own soil, they have plenty of food and munitions everywhere, they have a united population behind them and they are sure that they can hold out longer than the invading Greeks can. If the Greeks have made as easy an advance as they report it is due to this defensive policy of the Turks, who may have fallen back on prepared positions in the hope of enticing the Greeks, already over-confident, into a trap.

The Turks have been preparing for months for this attack, though the Greeks still outnumber them and have the advantage in motor transportation and supplies. The Turks during the winter succeeded in disbanding irregular forces and have a regular army all along the Greek front. Last year they called five classes to the colors and, while these conscripts still are pouring into camps, they already have had time to organize an army of perhaps 60,000 to 70,000 against 90,000 Greeks.

I have seen their troops at Angora and Eski-Shehr. At the latter place Colonel Nadji Bey, chief of staff, held a special review of infantry, cavalry and a battery of artillery for me and I inspected the troops with him. The soldiers are fully equipped, well drilled and disciplined. They are well clothed-most of them clad in American or British uniforms and overcoats, many garments still retaining their original buttons. All through the country I saw Turks wearing uniforms sold by the A. E. F. in France, and either resold by the French and Italians to the Turks or obtained from the Armenians after the Turks defeated them. The cavalry was mounted on small but sturdy horses, was armed with sabers as well as rifles and was accompanied by mounted machine-gun squads.

The artillery I saw were 120-caliber German guns, with British locks, range-finders and other parts. The Turks themselves have succeeded in making missing parts in their railway machine shops-no small accomplishment considering the means at their disposal-and it is supposedly ruined artillery, and not Italian and Russian guns, which they are using against the Greeks. I have seen about twenty different parts for cannon which they have had to make and the tool work is of good quality.

They have airplanes-I saw four at Eski Shehr-and plenty of skilled aviators. I talked with several of their pilots, many of whom were trained in Germany during the war. Once, Captain Midhat, received his pilot's brevet in France nine years ago; another, Lieutenant Fadil Bey, flew over London several times during the war with the Germans. The Turks also have established aviation repair shops, have towner factories scattered through Anatolia and apparently have no lack of arms and munitions. I saw cartridges, rifles and revolvers for sale cheap in various towns. Most of their munitions were hidden in Anatolia after the war or have been smuggled in from Constantinople. Smuggling still is going on, as a British officer here told me. "*It is impossible to prevent it, for the whole Turkish population is Nationalist at heart.*" They also have received some supplies from Russia, more from Armenia and probably some from Italians, though I saw no direct evidence of the latter, and statements made to me on the subject were conflicting. In any case, the Italians and Bolshevists, as far as munitions go, have not helped the Turks nearly as much as the world imagines.

It is purely a Turkish army-I saw no evidence whatever of German, Italian or Bolshevist officers who have been continually reported as directing the Turkish Army. There was one Austrian prisoner of war from Russia working in the aviation shops, but that is all. The Turks, after the experience they had with Germany during the war, would never accept foreign supervision of their army.

The Turks are not entirely lacking in motor transport-in Eski Shehr, where I was given a tour of the city in one of the Benz touring cars of the general staff, I saw a long line of German camions they have repaired ready for use in case of emergency. The railroads are in good shape from Biledjik beyond Konia and from Eski-Shehr to Angora, with a narrow-gauge going fifty miles further east. They have a weekly express train from Angora to Konia and a fair amount of rolling stock for troop movements. Though they have no coal and use wood ordinarily for fuel, they have seven powerful oil-burning locomotives which they are holding in reserve, together with a considerable supply of crude oil left over from the war.

The morale of the troops and population I found everywhere to be excellent. Time after time I heard Turk troops lustily singing Nationalist songs as they marched-sometimes with a good military band at their head. The soldiers receive $10 a month, and none of those with whom I talked complained of not being paid. There is very little desertion now. As to the morale of the population, while the people long for peace, they are evidently determined to fight it out to the bitter end. And the Turks come from fighting stock, as the remark made to me by Mustafa Mayor of the peasant village of Djerid Muminli indicates.

"*Yes my son was wounded in the World War. They took him to a hospital at Constantinople and informed me. Oh, I longed to go see him-but I could not let the village people think a Turkish father could not bear to have his son wounded.*"

Appendix X.: Miscellaneous documents & photographs related to Streit's trip

Note: As has been noted throughout this study, Clarence Streit wrote handwritten 'labels' on the back of many of the photos he took in Anatolia. Below [**Plate 119**] is the label from his photograph of the Staff of the Bolshevik Embassy in Ankara [See: **Plate 50**, p. 62 - fn. 96] [HWL].

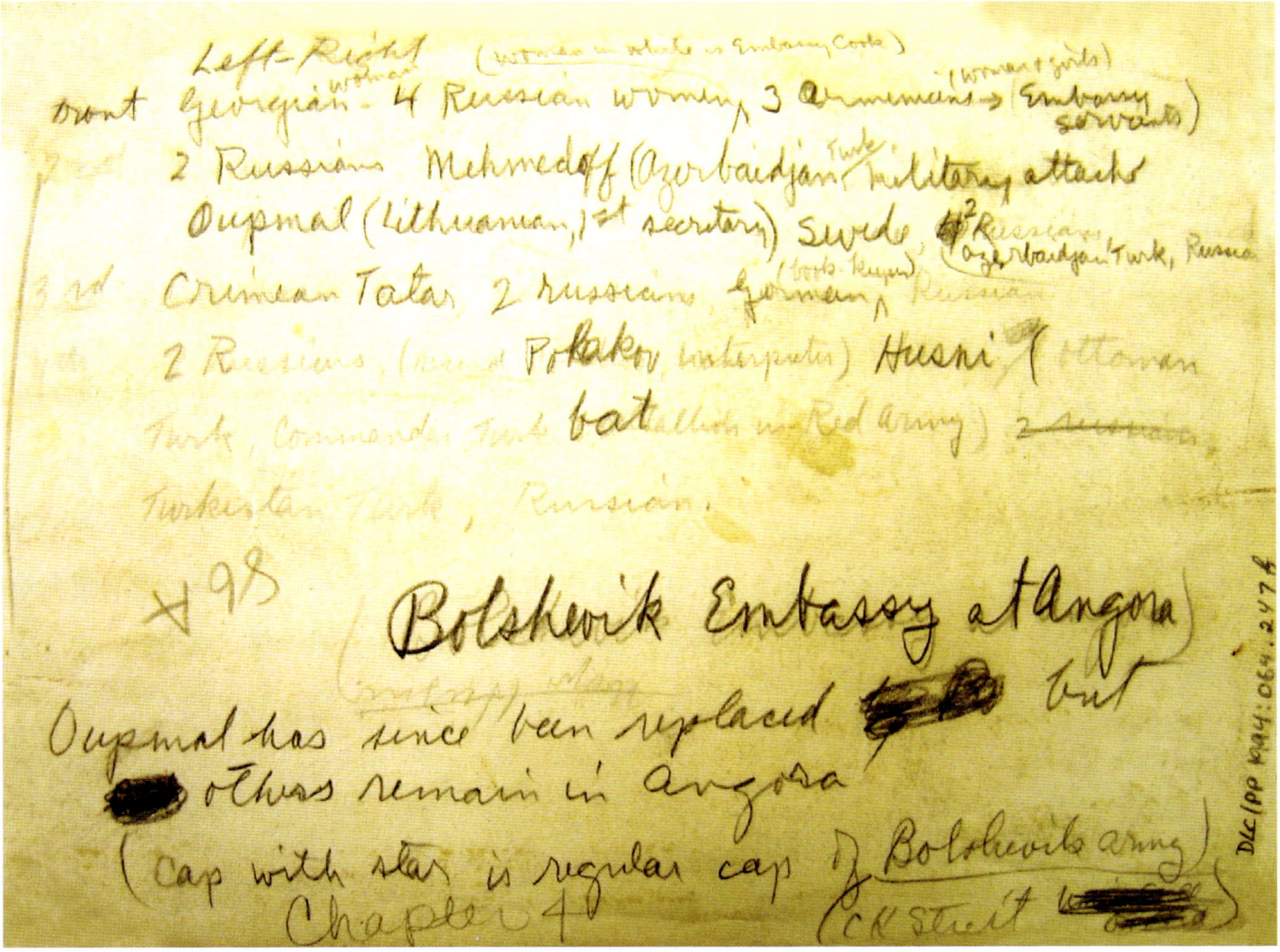
Left-Right (woman in white is Embassy Cook)
front Georgian woman - 4 Russian women, 3 Armenians (women & girls) (Embassy servants)
2 Russians Mehmedoff (Azerbaidjan Turk, military attaché)
Oupmal (Lithuanian, 1st secretary) Swede, 2 Russians (Azerbaidjan Turk, Russian
3rd Crimean Tatar, 2 russians, German (book-keeper) Russian
2 Russians, (...) Polakov interpreter) Husni (Ottoman
Turk, Commander Turk battalion in Red Army) 2 russians,
Turkestan Turk, Russian.
X 98
Bolshevik Embassy at Angora
Oupmal has since been replaced [redacted] but
[redacted] others remain in Angora
(Cap with star is regular cap of Bolshevik army)
Chapter 4
CK Streit [redacted]

Plate 119: Streit's Handwritten Note on Back of **Plate 50: p. 62 - fn. 96** Identifying Bolshevik Embassy Staff.

Note: As the careful reader has doubtlessly realized, many of the photographs used in this study are taken from a photograph album which Streit compiled after his visit. As the page presented below [**Plate 120**], which is a typical example taken from his 'Red Album,' illustrates, the actual size of his photos are often quite small. As the negatives of his photographs have not survived, it has been necessary to use this unique source material in the form it is preserved in [HWL].

Plate 120: A Typical Page from Streit's 'Red Album'[238]

[238] LC Catalogue #: DLC/PP 1994: 064 Red Album: Turkey 1920 - 1921 by C.K. Streit.

Note: The extent of the impression left by the hospitality Streit experienced in the village of Ceritmüminli (while enroute to Ankara), is attested to by this receipt [**Plate 121**]. Dated October 6, 1923, it is for the shipping costs involved in his sending two steel plows to the villagers of Ceritmüminli. At the bottom of the receipt is Streit's handwritten note reading: "*Bill for shipping 2 plows I gave to village of Djerid Muminli where I spant a night in 1921.*"

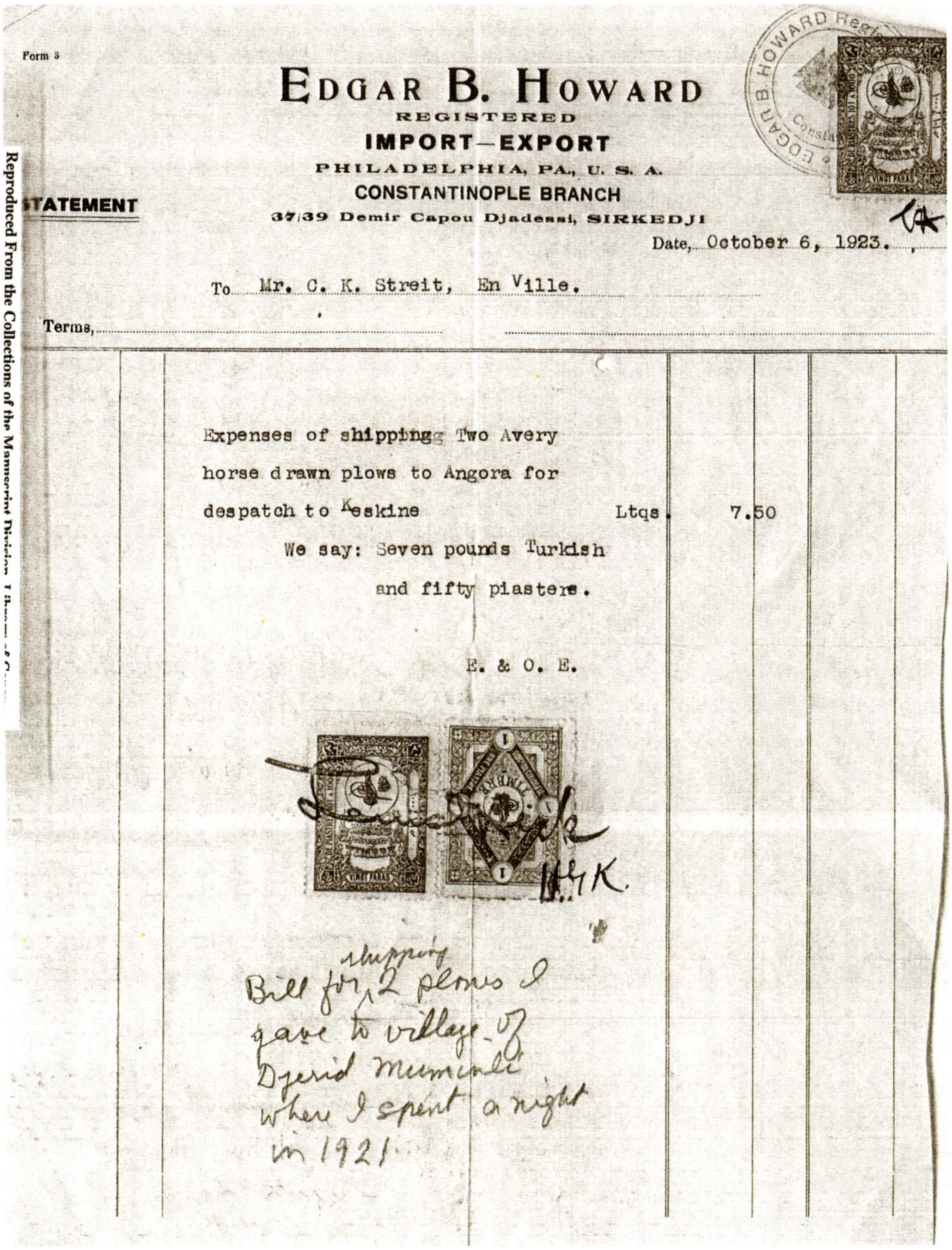

Form 3

EDGAR B. HOWARD
REGISTERED
IMPORT—EXPORT
PHILADELPHIA, PA., U. S. A.
CONSTANTINOPLE BRANCH
37/39 Demir Capou Djadessi, SIRKEDJI

STATEMENT

Date, October 6, 1923.

To Mr. C. K. Streit, En Ville.

Terms,

Expenses of shipping Two Avery horse drawn plows to Angora for despatch to Keskine — Ltqs 7.50

We say: Seven pounds Turkish and fifty piasters.

E. & O. E.

Bill for shipping 2 plows I gave to village of Djerid Muminli where I spent a night in 1921

Plate 121: Streit's shipping receipt[239]

239 LC Manuscript Division: Streit Papers II: 75 - Folder 8.

Turks Find Lausanne Treaty Requires Hanging of Kemal

Amazing Joker Makes Angora Rather Glad Ismet Was Not Stampeded Into Signing. British and French Continue Bidding

By CLARENCE K. STREIT
Public Ledger Foreign Service
Copyright, 1923, by Public Ledger Company

Constantinople. March 1. — (By Cable.)—The Turks have discovered a really amusing joker in the Lausanne treaty.

Hidden in the long document is an innocent-appearing sentence which binds Angora to ratify all measures taken since the occupation of Constantinople by the Sublime Porte in agreement with the Allies. As one of those measures was the condemnation of Mustafa Kemal and Adnan Bey, now Governor of Constantinople, with his famous wife, Halide Hanoum, and other Nationalist leaders to be hanged as rebels, Ismet in signing the treaty would have signed their death warrant.

Only the most suspicious Turks, however, think the Allies inserted the clause for this "Shylockian" purpose—and it is not only that which makes them glad Ismet was not stampeded into accepting the treaty at Lausanne.

Bidding continues to go on merrily between the English and French for Turkish favor. The French, not to be outdone by the conciliatory British gesture at Smyrna, have taken the initiative themselves in officially telling the Turks that "Since we were unjustly accused of preventing peace by our economic and financial demands we will prove what good fellows we are by agreeing to postpone the settlement of these questions for six months. Now let us sign the remainder of the treaty."

Prepare Counter-Proposals

The Turks tell the news to the British who answer, "Wait a minute. You want a definite settlement now and so do we. Why postpone these important matters? We are willing to consider your propositions now." And the Turks now are preparing their counter-proposals, but will not forget to take plenty of time so as to give the French an opportunity to make another bid.

Constantinople does not care how long Angora debates the treaty since the discussion already has diverted the deputies from carrying out their intention to begin enforcing the "dry" law here. Protests from thirsty citizens of all races and religions, including Turks, have so flooded Governor Adnan Bey that he has asked Angora for detailed instructions.

The fatal day has arrived, but the instructions have not, and until they do Adnan has decided not to deport John Barleycorn. It is more and more probable that Constantinople may definitely escape the Turkish drought, for the argument that America is unable to enforce prohibition in the big coastal cities, such as New York, is gaining the local "wets" much support.

Plate 122: Streit's March 1, 1923 dispatch[240]

Note: This story, which appeared in the Philadelphia ***Public Ledger*** on March 1, 1923 [**Plate 122**], was filed by Streit after his return to Turkey in 1923. It is reprinted here as an example of his writing from that period and also due to the fact that it deals with two little known, albeit, interesting events: a) the fact that as originally proposed the wording of the Lausanne Treaty, contained a clause guaranteeing the ratification of all measures adopted by the İstanbul government of the Sultan during the period of the occupation. Had this version of the text been adopted (İsmet Paşa did not sign it), it would have mandated the execution of Mustafa Kemal and several of his closest associates whom the Sultan's government had condemned to death as rebels; and, b) it touches on what at the time were the unsuccessful attempts of the Ankara government to enforce the strict prohibition against the making, selling or consumption of alcohol in İstanbul. While this legislation had been in effect throughout those areas of Anatolia controlled by Ankara since its adoption by the Grand National Assembly on 1 *Murarrem* 1339 (September 15, 1920), it had of course never been implemented in the capital which was under the control of the British-French occupying forces. This legislation is referred to by Streit as the "*dry*" law, and its attempted implementation in İstanbul as the deportation of "*John Barleycorn*" (an American name for whiskey). Public opposition (Streit's "*wets*") in İstanbul (with its large non-Muslim population), was such that the Governor, Adnan [Adıvar] Bey had chosen not to implement it on the stipulated day, preferring instead to ask Ankara for further instructions.

In ***The Unknown Turks***, while describing his 1921 visit to Ankara, Streit, as earlier had Paul Williams [See: **Appendix III** - p.192], commented on the prohibition of alcoholic beverages in the Nationalist controlled regions of Anatolia [See: p. 43 above], where he correctly describes the legislation as one of the first acts adopted by the Grand National Assembly [HWL].[241]

---

[240] LC Manuscript Division: Streit Papers II: 75 - Folder 8.

[241] For this legislation, known in Turkish as: *Men'i müskirat kanunu* (Prohibition of Alcohol Legislation), see: *T.B.M.M. Zabıt Ceridesi, Devre*: I, *Cild*: I, *İctima Senesi*: 1 – pp. 5 & 114; & *Cild* 4, pp. 134 - 154 (where the actual debate and results of the vote are given). The legislation was adopted on a day when Mustafa Kemal Paşa was not in attendance. The original vote was: 71 in favor, 71 opposed. The deciding vote was cast by the acting President of the Assembly, Ali Şükrü Bey (Trabzon). This is the same deputy who was assassinated on on March 27, 1923 by Topal Osman Ağa, the commander of Mustafa Kemal Paşa's bodyguards. My thanks to Necdet Tekin, a former Turkish Minister of Education, for his assistance in locating copies of these documents.

Bibliography

BIBLIOGRAPHY

Chronological List of Clarence K. Streit Dispatches & Articles (1921-1924)

Note: The following list of dispatches and drafts of articles written by Clarence K. Streit and dealing with Turkey, is in no way intended to be comprehensive. I have been unable to locate a complete run of the Philadelphia ***Public Ledger*** for the period he was in Turkey, and consequently the following list is compiled from 'clippings' of his stories which are preserved in the collection of his papers in the Library of Congress, supplemented by back issues of the ***Public Ledger*** for the months of January-March 1921, which I was able to obtain through the good offices of Princeton University's Interlibrary Loans Department [HWL].

January 6, 1921

"*Smyrna Convinced King Will Recall Venizelos*: *Athens Reports Say Constantine Now Is Negotiating Secretly to Have Ex-Premier Head Cabinet -Winter Halts War on Turks - Spring Drive Planned,*" in the Philadelphia ***Public Ledger***, January 6, 1921 [LC: Streit Papers II: 12 - Folder 1]. **Note**: On this story Streit wrote: "*My first dispatch as a war correspondent. - cks*" [HWL].

February 7, 1921

"*Turkish Nationalists Dethrone Church Law*: *Purely Moslem Code Subjected to That of State, Removing Cause of 'Capitulations' - Caliphate and Sultanate Ignored,*" in the Philadelphia ***Public Ledger***, February 7, 1921.[242]

March 17, 1921

"*Turkish State in Asia Strong and Efficient: Public Ledger Correspondent, First in Angora in 8 months, Finds Government Running Smoothly and Making Remotest Districts Safe,*" in the Philadelphia ***Public Ledger***, March 17, 1921 [LC: Streit Papers II: 75 - Folder 5].

March 27, 1921

"*Turkish Nationalists Put Peace Up to Allies*: *Mustafa Kemal Declares for Self-Determination and Just Settlement in Comprehensive Review of Near East Problem,*" in the Philadelphia Public Ledger, March 27, 1921 [LC: Streit Papers II: 75 - Folder 1].

[242] **Note**: When no Library of Congress [LC] reference is given, the articles cited were not found in the Streit Papers, rather they were copied from actual issues of the ***Public Ledger*** [HWL].

March-April, 1921

"*Untitled: Story on Streit's Interview with Mustafa Kemal Paşa,*"[243] in the Philadelphia ***Public Ledger***, March-April [?], 1921 [LC: Streit Papers II: 75 - Folder 5].

April 17, 1921

"*Failure of Greeks in War Foreseen,*" in the Philadelphia ***Public Ledger***, April 17, 1921 [LC: Streit Papers II: 75 - Folder 1].

April 23, 1921

"*Victor of Eskishehr: Mustapha Kemal Pasha,*" in ***The Illustrated London News***, April 23, 1921 with four Streit photos [LC: Streit Papers II: 75 - Folder 1].

April 24, 1921

"*U.S. Missionaries Warned by Turks: Trouble Feared if They Continue to Become Involved with Greek Population - Marsivan Incident Cited: American College Harbored Band of Political Plotters, Turk Authorities Point Out,*" in the Philadelphia ***Public Ledger***, Sunday, April 24, 1921.

Note: Philadelphia ***Public Ledger*** Pictorial Section (Sunday, April 24, 1921): Three photos: a) Mustafa Kemal dressed as 'Arabian Shiek; the caption reads: "*Mustapha Kemal Pasha, the leader of the Turkish Nationalist forces fighting the Greeks in Angora, photographed in the costume of an Arabian shiek. An unusual picture of the firebrand of the East presented by him to the* ***Public Ledger*** *staff correspondent in Angora*;" b) Mustafa Kemal Pasha with glasses. Caption reads: "*The Turkish Nationalist Leader in European Attire. A new and unusual picture of Mustapha Kemal Pasha*;" and, c) a signed picture of Halide Edib Hanım on horseback. The caption reads: "*An autographed picture of the Turkish authoress and military leader who may become Ambassador to America. Halide Edib Hanoum, now in charge of the military intelligence section of the Turkish General Staff in Angora. Her husband is Dr. Adnan Bey, first vice president of the Turkish Assembly at Angora, and her two sons are students at the University of Illinois.*" [HWL].

May 25, 1921

"*Mustafa Kemal and the New Turkey,*" in ***The New Oxford***, May 25, 1921. pp. 5-8.

October 16, 1921

"*Armenian's Pistol Upset British Plans For Turkey: Talaat Pasha Was Being Groomed as London's Secret Emissary to Angora When He Was Assassinated, Declares American Intelligence Officer* [Robert Steed Dunn][244] *in Near East,*" in the Philadelphia ***Public Ledger***, October 16, 1921 [LC: Streit Papers II: Microfilm - Reel 1].

[243] **Note**: This is the article based on Streit's Ankara interview with Mustafa Kemal Paşa. I have been unable to find copies of the Public Ledger for the time it appeared. On the typewritten copy which is preserved in his papers, Streit wrote: '*Very important document. cks.*' [HWL].

September 23, 1922

"*All Turkish Claims Conceded by Allies; Early Parley Urged,*" in the Philadelphia ***Public Ledger***, September 23, 1922 [LC: Streit Papers II: 75 - Folder 1].

May 17, 1922

"*Turkish Atrocities Charge is Political Move, Italians Say: British Playing a Losing Game in Asia Minor Trying to Influence Western Opinion, Officials Assert. Trouble Brews in Islamic World*" in the Philadelphia ***Public Ledger***, May 17, 1922 [LC: Streit Papers II: Microfilm - Reel 1].

June 14, 1922

"*British Policy Worries Turks: Nationalists Fear Ruin of Army's Morale if Peace is Offered Sultan,*" in the Philadelphia ***Public Ledger***, June 14, 1922 [LC: Streit Papers II: Microfilm - Reel 1].

October 9, 1922

"*Kemal Envoy Asks for World Inquiry: Trip to Smyrna Would Show What Greeks Have Done to Turkey, He Says,*" in the Philadelphia ***Public Ledger***, October 9, 1922 [LC: Streit Papers II: Microfilm - Reel 1].

November 9, 1922

"*Mustafa Kemal As Caliph Suggested By Egyptians: Would Strengthen Turkish Prestige - Moslem Opposition Could Be Overcome by Delegating Temporal Power to Turkish People,*" in the Philadelphia ***Public Ledger***, November 9, 1922 [LC: Streit Papers II: Microfilm - Reel 1].

November 13, 1922

"*Parley Delay 'Unjustified;' Turks Angered: Delegates Arrive Without Notification - Insist Mudania Agreement Observed,*" in the Philadelphia ***Public Ledger***, November 13, 1922 [LC: Streit Papers II: Microfilm - Reel 1].

November 21, 1922

"*Lausanne Envoys Shout Peace, Then Scramble for Oil: Turks Dangling Bait Before Italy and U.S.,*" in the Philadelphia ***Public Ledger***, November 21, 1922 [LC: Streit Papers II: Microfilm - Reel 1].

[244] **Note**: Robert Steed Dunn (the U.S. High Commissoner in Constantinopoli (İstanbul) Admiral Bristol's intelligence officer), is quoted in this October 16, 1921 story as saying: "*Lieutenant Dunn believes that the present Greco-Turk war will end in the near future with virtually complete Turkish victory, entailing Greek withdrawal from Symrna and the reopening of the Thracian question. He declares that the Greeks, exhausted by their recent defeat, are at the end of their resources and now eagerly are seeking any way to save their face.*" Once again Dunn's prescience is apparent [HWL].

November 21, 1922

"*Plan to Muzzle Lausanne Envoys Balked by Ismet: Refuses to Pledge Secrecy With Allies; Warns He Will Speak Publicly,*" in the Philadelphia ***Public Ledger***, November 21, 1922 [LC: Streit Papers II: Microfilm - Reel 1].

"*Ismet Presents Turkish Demands; Tempts Bulgarians,*" in the Philadelphia ***Public Ledger***, November 21, 1922 [LC: Streit Papers II: Microfilm - Reel 1].

November 22, 1922

"*Mussolini Finds Ally In Soviets Lausanne Envoy: Their Turkish Policies One, Vorovsky States,*" in the Philadelphia ***Public Ledger***, November 22, 1922 [LC: Streit Papers II: Microfilm - Reel 1].

"*Turks Hostility Denied By Child: Report of Attitude Toward U.S. at Lausanne False, Says Ambassador,*" in the Philadelphia ***Public Ledger***, November 22, 1922 [LC: Streit Papers II: Microfilm - Reel 1].

"*New Balkan War Looms In Parley; Crisis Due Today: Turks Find Allies, Rumanians, Greeks, Jugoslavs and Bulgars Arrayed Against Them,*" in the Philadelphia ***Public Ledger***, November 22, 1922 [LC: Streit Papers II: Microfilm - Reel 1].

November 26, 1922

"*Kemalists Aiding American Trade, Bristol Reports: Those Visiting Angora Favorably Impressed by Regime of Mustafa Kemal,*" in the Philadelphia ***Public Ledger***, November 26, 1922 [LC: Streit Papers II: Microfilm - Reel 1].

"*Turks 'Open Door' To Americans Only: British Expected To Lose Mosul Fields With Kemal Declaring Oil Is Not for Them and Eager to Tempt United States Capital,*" in the Philadelphia ***Public Ledger***, November 26, 1922 [LC: Streit Papers II: Microfilm - Reel 1].

November 28, 1922

"*Angora Welcomes American Schools: Turks Never Interfered With Institutions Because They Were Foreign, Says Ismet,*" in the Philadelphia ***Public Ledger***, November 28, 1922 [LC: Streit Papers II: Microfilm - Reel 1].

November 29, 1922

"*Oil-Pact Approval Halts Mosul Issue: Equal Division of Rights Between Turkey and Anglo-Franco-American Group,*" in the Philadelphia ***Public Ledger***, November 29, 1922 [LC: Streit Papers II: Microfilm - Reel 1].

December 2, 1922

"*Turks And Allies Deadlocked; Talk of Ending Parley: Unyielding Views on Capitulations Create Serious Situation at Lausanne,*" in the Philadelphia ***Public Ledger***, December 2, 1922 [LC: Streit Papers II: Microfilm - Reel 1].

December 3, 1922

"*Russians Deliver Ultimatum After Talk With Ismet*: *Refuse to Be Bound by Decisions at Lausanne if Not Admitted*," in the Philadelphia ***Public Ledger***, December 3, 1922 [LC: Streit Papers II: Microfilm - Reel 1].

December 4, 1922

"*Russians Resume Old Battle With British On Straits*: *Tchitcherin Arouses 'Monsieur' Curzon's Ire in Pleading Cause of Angora*," in the Philadelphia ***Public Ledger***, December 4, 1922 [LC: Streit Papers II: Microfilm - Reel 1].

December 5, 1922

"*Turks To Demand U.S. Take Part In Straits Control*: *Allies Alone Not Trusted if International Commission Plan is Accepted*," in the Philadelphia ***Public Ledger***, December 5, 1922 [LC: Streit Papers II: Microfilm - Reel 1].

December 7, 1922

"'*War' Is Mussolini Warning to Turks*: *Premier Announces Complete Italian-British Accord at Lausanne*," in the Philadelphia ***Public Ledger***, December 7, 1922 [LC: Streit Papers II: Microfilm - Reel 1].

December 7, 1922

Manuscript: Untitled Interview With İsmet Paşa at Lausanne - Compared with Streit's February 1921 interview with Mustafa Kemal Paşa. Dated: December 7, 1922 [**Note**: Presumably this appeared around this date in the Philadelphia ***Public Ledger***. However, I have been unable to locate the published version of this story? HWL] [LC: Streit Papers II: Microfilm - Reel 1].

December 8, 1922

"*Lausanne Envoys Reach Agreement On Straits Issue*: *Compromise on Turkish Sovereignty and Free Passage of Merchant Vessels*," in the Philadelphia ***Public Ledger***, December 8, 1922 [LC: Streit Papers II: Microfilm - Reel 1].

December 9, 1922

"*Turkey Warned Against Placing Trust In Allies*: *British Duping Ismet to Split Angora and Moscow, Says Tchitcherin*," in the Philadelphia ***Public Ledger***, December 9, 1922 [LC: Streit Papers II: Microfilm - Reel 1].

December 10, 1922

"*Irish Executions Shake Turks Faith*: *Kemalists See Parallel in British Compromises With Dublin and Angora*," in the Philadelphia ***Public Ledger***, December 10, 1922 [LC: Streit Papers II: Microfilm - Reel 1].

December 11, 1922

"*Soviet Menacing On Strait Issue*: *Will Arm Immediately Should Warships Enter Black Sea, Tchitcherin Warns,*" in the Philadelphia ***Public Ledger***, December 11, 1922 [LC: Streit Papers II: Microfilm - Reel 1].

December 12, 1922

"*Turks May Adopt U.S. Plan To Help Levant Minorities*: *Favor Idea of Territorial Refuges - Exchange of Peoples Defended,*" in the Philadelphia ***Public Ledger***, December 12, 1922 [LC: Streit Papers II: Microfilm - Reel 1].

December 13, 1922

"*British Demands Menace Lausanne*: *Curzon Accused of Trying to Break Up Parley - United States Seeks Compromise,*" in the Philadelphia ***Public Ledger***, December 13, 1922 [LC: Streit Papers II: Microfilm - Reel 1].

December 14, 1922

"*Turks End Crisis*; *Embrace League With Reservation*: *Peace and Mosul First*; *Then They Will Come In, Ismet Adds; Ousting of Patriarch Still Insisted Upon*; *Constantinople Declared No Place for Head of Christian Greek Church,*" in the Philadelphia ***Public Ledger***, December 14, 1922 [LC: Streit Papers II: Microfilm - Reel 1].

December 15, 1922

"*Religious Issue Upsets Lausanne*: *France and Italy Support Turks in Fight to Expel Greek Patriarch*; *British Split on Question,*" in the Philadelphia ***Public Ledger***, December 15, 1922 [LC: Streit Papers II: Microfilm - Reel 1].

December 16, 1922

"*Britain Resumes Mosul Oil Fight*: *Offer to Give Turks All of Territory Except Oil-Yielding Areas,*" in the Philadelphia ***Public Ledger***, December 16, 1922 [LC: Streit Papers II: Microfilm - Reel 1].

December 18, 1922

"*Three Solutions Of Straits Issue Swamp Lausanne*: *Allies Offer League Guarantee*; *Tchitcherin Terms Body 'Organized Impotence,'*" in the Philadelphia ***Public Ledger***, December 18, 1922 [LC: Streit Papers II: Microfilm - Reel 1].

December 19, 1922

"*Allies Insist Turks Yield Or Quit Parley: Curzon Declares Limits of Concessions on Straits Has Been Reached,*" in the Philadelphia ***Public Ledger***, December 19, 1922 [LC: Streit Papers II: Microfilm - Reel 1].

December 20, 1922

"*Sidetrack U.S. Note In Secret Deal On Straits*: *Game of Double Cross A Dual One At Lausanne,*" in the Philadelphia ***Public Ledger***, December 20, 1922 [LC: Streit Papers II: Microfilm - Reel 1].

"*Tension Relaxes As Envoys Steer Toward Compromise,*" in the Philadelphia ***Public Ledger***, December 20, 1922 [LC: Streit Papers II: Microfilm - Reel 1].

December 21, 1922

"*Envoys Row, Say What They Think*: *Venizelos-Riza Bey Altercation Breaks Up Meeting At Lausanne,*" in the Philadelphia ***Public Ledger***, December 21, 1922 [LC: Streit Papers II: Microfilm - Reel 1].

December 22, 1922

"*Open Diplomacy Is At Last In Use, But Only By Turks*: *Ottoman Delegates Report On Everything; Peace Likely When Powers Realize They Are Dealing With Sovereign Assembly,*" in the Philadelphia ***Public Ledger***, December 22, 1922 [LC: Streit Papers II: Microfilm - Reel 1].

December 23, 1922

"*Lausanne's Game Is To Dupe Public*: *Both Allies and Turks Utilizing Surface Clashes to Sway Opinion,*" in the Philadelphia ***Public Ledger***, December 23, 1922 [LC: Streit Papers II: Microfilm - Reel 1].

December 27, 1922

"*Lausanne Crisis Forced By British*: *Turks Say Stand On Mosul Makes Treaty With English Impossible,*" in the Philadelphia ***Public Ledger***, December 27, 1922 [LC: Streit Papers II: Microfilm - Reel 1].

December 28, 1922

"*Warning By U.S. Inspires Turks; Checks Rupture*: *Their Parley Reply on Minorities and Capitulations Today to Have Saving Loophole,*" in the Philadelphia ***Public Ledger***, December 28, 1922 [LC: Streit Papers II: Microfilm - Reel 1].

December 29, 1922

"*Turks Adamant On Mosul Claims*: *Simultaneously Allies Give In on League Commissioners as Guard for Minorities,*" in the Philadelphia ***Public Ledger***, December 29, 1922 [LC: Streit Papers II: Microfilm - Reel 1].

December 30, 1922

"*Americans Urge Armenian Home*: *Turks See Ulterior Motive in 'Observers' Plea - British Think Day Saved,*" in the Philadelphia ***Public Ledger***, December 30, 1922 [LC: Streit Papers II: Microfilm - Reel 1].

December, 1922

"*The Flower of Islam,*" in ***The Forum***. New York City, December, 1922. pp. 1044-1051 [LC: Streit Papers II: 75 - Folder 1].

January 3, 1923

"*Turks Adhering Rigidly To Pact*: *Kemal's Demands of 1921 Now Being Reiterated At Lausanne,*" in the Philadelphia ***Public Ledger***, January 3, 1923 [LC: Streit Papers II: Microfilm - Reel 1].

January 17, 1923

"*Lausanne Climax Sought By Curzon*: *Two Months Enough of Near East Parley for Pessimistic British,*" in the Philadelphia ***Public Ledger***, January 17, 1923 [LC: Streit Papers II: Microfilm - Reel 1].

January 23, 1923

"*Turks Threatened With League Club*: *Curzon to Denounce Them at Geneva for Refusing Mosul Arbitration,*" in the Philadelphia ***Public Ledger***, January 23, 1923 [LC: Streit Papers II: Microfilm - Reel 1].

January 25, 1923

"*Allies to Leave if Turks Fail to Sign Treaty in Week*: *Agree to Reassemble if Kemalists Yield. Balkans Reported Arming Feverishly. Powers Military Position Weak,*" in the Philadelphia ***Public Ledger***, January 25, 1923 [LC: Streit Papers II: Microfilm - Reel 1].

March 1, 1923

"*Turks Find Lausanne Treaty Requires Hanging of Kemal*: *Amazing Joker Makes Angora Rather Glad Ismet Was Not Stampeded Into Signing*. in the Philadelphia ***Public Ledger***, March 1, 1923 [LC Manuscript Division: Streit Papers II: 75 - Folder 8].

April 6, 1923

Manuscript: Streit story on Kiazim Karabekir Pasha - Dated April 6, 1923. [**Note**: Presumably this appeared around this date in the Philadelphia ***Public Ledger***. However, I have been unable to locate the published version of this story. HWL] [LC: Streit Papers II: Microfilm - Reel 1].

April, 1923

"*Blind Forces at Lausanne,*" in ***ASIA*****: *The American Magazine of the Orient***, April, 1923. pp. 282-286 [LC: Streit Papers II: 75 - Folder 1].

November 22, 1923

"*Mustapha Kemal Pasha*: *'Purified Perfection,*" in the Philadelphia ***Public Ledger***, November 22, 1923 [LC: Streit Papers II: 75 - Folder 1].

1923-1924

Undated Manuscripts: Four columns written by Clarence K. Streit entitled: '*If I Were A Turk.*' These are clearly the English drafts for the columns he contributed in 1923 to the İstanbul daily newspaper ***Vatan*** which was edited by Ahmet Emin [Yalman], who describes them in his memoirs.

March 3, 1924

"*Turk Assembly Votes End of the Caliphate,*" in the Philadelphia ***Public Ledger***, March 3, 1924 [LC: Streit Papers II: 75 - Folder 8].

March 4, 1924

"*Caliph Spirited Out of Turkey; Sent Westward,*" in the Philadelphia ***Public Ledger***, March 4, 1924 [LC: Streit Papers II: 75 - Folder 1].

Primary Sources Cited

In addition to the manuscript of Clarence Streit's '***The Unknown Turks***' which was given to me by the author in 1983 (together with a revised version he had prepared in the previous year), I have used the following collections housed in the Library of Congress in Washington, D.C.:

a) **Clarence K. Streit A Register of His Papers in the Library of Congress - Part I**: Prepared by Connie L. Cartledge in 1989. Manuscript Division, Library of Congress;

b) **Clarence K. Streit A Register of His Papers in the Library of Congress - Part II**: Expanded and revised by Connie L. Cartledge with the assistance of Sherralyn McCoy in 1994. Manuscript Division, Library of Congress;

Both of the above are 'Finding Aids' to the materials preserved in the collection known as the: **Clarence Streit Papers.** The materials in Part I were given to the Library of Congress by his wife, Jeanne Defrance Streit, in 1987-1988; while those in Part II were given between 1991-1994 by Jeanne Defrance Streit and by Ira Straus (Director of the Association to Unite the Democracies). Copyright to the unpublished writings of Streit reverted to the public on September 8, 2007.

The Streit photographs which were included with this collection were transferred to the Prints and Photographs Division of the Library of Congress. The cataloguing of the photographs is a work in progress, for which a preliminary 'Finding Aid:' **Container List for Streit (Clarence K.) Papers: PR 13 CN 1994:064** is available.

In the preparation of the following work, I have examined the following materials:

a) **Part I.: Container Nos. 9-14;**

b) **Part I.: Container & Microfilm Reels Nos. 1-3;**

c) **Part II.: Container Nos. 2-6 (Diaries);**

d) **Part II.: Container Nos. 6-9 (Notebooks);**

e) **Part II.: Container Nos. 12-13 (Newspaper Correspondent Files);**

Note: In addition, I examined and took photos of all of the Streit photographs taken during his 1921 travels in Anatolia, as well as a number of photos he took (or acquired) during his second stay in Turkey (1923-1925) [HWL].

Other Works Cited

Akbulut, Erdem & Tuncay, Mete: *Türkiye Halk İştirakiyun Fırkası (1920-1923).* İstanbul (Sosyal Tarih Yayınları), 2007. pp. 332-340].

Aydemir, Şevket Süreyya: *Tek Adam: Mustafa Kemal (1919-1922).* Volume II. İstanbul (Remzi Kitapevi), 1967.

Bodurgil, Abraham: *Kemal Atatürk: A Centennial Bibliography (1881-1981).* Washington, D.C. (Library of Congress), 1984.

De Groot, Alexander H.: *The Netherlands & Turkey: Four Hundred Years of Political, Economical, Social and Cultural Relations.* İstanbul (The ISIS Press), 2009.

Dunn, Robert Steed: *World Alive: A Personal Story.* New York (Crown Publishers), 1956.

Ellison, Grace: *An Englishwoman in Angora.* London (Hutchinson & Co.), 1923.

Erdinç, Erol Şadi (Ed.): *Ahmed Emin Yalman: Yakın Tarihde Gördüklerim ve Geçirdiklerim.* Cilt I (1888-1922). İstanbul, 1997.

Halide Edib: *The Turkish Ordeal.* New York (The Century Co.), 1928.

Lord Kinross: *Ataturk: A Biography of Mustafa Kemal, father of modern Turkey.* New York (William Morrow and Company), 1965.

Lowry, Heath W.: "Richard G. Hovannisian on Lieutenant Robert Steed Dunn," in *Osmanlı Araştırmaları* [Journal of Ottoman Studies], Volume 5 (İstanbul, 1986), pp. 209-252.

Mango, Andrew: *Atatürk.* London (John Murray), 1999.

Shaw, Stanford J.: *From Empire to Republic: The Turkish War of National Liberation.* 5 Volumes. Ankara (Türk Tarihi Kurumu), 2000.

Şimşir, Bilal: *Dış Basında Atatürk ve Türk Devrimi.* Cilt I. (1922-1924) *Bir Laik Cumhuriyet Doğuyor* [Atatürk & the Turkish Revolution in the Foreign Press. Volume I (1922-1924) The Birth of a Secular Republic]. Ankara (Türk Tarihi Kurumu), 1981.

T.C. Kültür Bakanlığı (Republic of Turkey - Ministry of Culture): *Atatürk'ün Milli Dış Politikası.* 2 Volumes (Ankara, 1992).

George E. White: *Adventuring with Anatolia College.* Grinnell, Iowa (Herald-Register Publishing Company), 1940.

Williams, Paul: "Wilson's 14 Points Or War - Kemal Pasha." Chicago *Daily Tribune.* Chicago, Ill.: May 4, 1920. p. 3.

Williams, Paul: "Kemal Unmasks London Squeeze Play on Turkey: Nationalist Chief Evaded Trap." Chicago *Daily Tribune*. Chicago, Ill.: May 8, 1920. p. 3.

Williams, Paul: "Kemal's Fear of Allies' Aims Like Prophecy." Chicago *Daily Tribune*. Chicago, Ill.: May 12, 1920. p. 10.

Williams, Paul: "Secret Treaty Forced Turks to War - Kemal: Says Allies Had Pledged Porte to Russia." Chicago *Daily Tribune*. Chicago, Ill.: May 13, 1920. p. 7.

Williams, Paul: "Turk Victims of Stage Setting, Kemal Charges: Says Allies Show Them in Worst Light." Chicago *Daily Tribune*. Chicago, Ill.: May 15, 1920. p. 6.

Williams, Paul: "Free Turkey or Dead Turkey is Hope of Kemal: Cuts Adrift from Porte for Heeding British." Chicago *Daily Tribune*. Chicago, Ill.: May 16, 1920. p. 4.

Index

A.C.R.N.E [American Committee for Relief in the Near East], 225
A. E. F. [Allied Expeditionary Force], 232
Abdülhak Adnan [Adıvar], 108-109, 120, 124, 174
Abdülhak Hâmid [Tarhan], 125 (fn. 174)
Abdülhalim Çelebi Efendi (Mevlevi Postnişin & Parliamentary Deputy), 83 (fn. 120)
Abdülhamid II [Sultan], 84, 89, 112 (fn. 158), 121, 125, 219
Abraham [Prophet], 23, 44
Adalia [See: Antalya]
Adrianople [See: Edirne]
Afghanistan, 52, 97, 205, 214
Afioun Karahissar [See: Afyonkarahisar]
Afyon, 157-158
Afyonkarahisar, 157, 166, 188, 231
Agricultural Bank, 133, 154
Ahmed (Streit's yaylı driver), 31, 34
Ahmed Chukri [See: Ahmet Şükrü Bey]
Ahmed Emin Yalman, 163
Ahmed Ferid [Tek] Bey, 119 (fn. 165), 135
Ahmed Mouhtar Bey [See: Ahmed Muhtar Bey]
Ahmed Muhtar Bey, 110 (fn. 154), 133, 172 (fn. 211)
Ahmed Ruchdi Bey [See: Ahmed Rüşdi Bey]
Ahmed Rüşdi Bey (Samsun Régie Tobacco Plant's Turkish Director), 12
Ahmet Şükrü [Esmer], 73 (fn. 113)
Aidin [See: Aydın], 157
Aintab, 192, 232
Akbulut, Erdem, 62 (fn. 96)
Alaca, 25-26, 165
Aladja [See: Alaca]
Albania, 112, 140
Aleppo, 218
Alevi, 42-43
Alexandrapol Agreement/Treaty, 203, 206, 213, 215
Ali (Halide Edib's son), 121
Ali Fethi [Okyar], 176
Ali Kazim Bey [See: Ali Kâzım Bey]
Ali Kâzım Bey, 65 (fn. 99), 79
Ali Kemal Bey, 141-142
Ali Şükrü Bey, p. 106 (fn. 145)
Allah, 18, 20, 31, 46, 144-145
Allen, Annie, T., 105 (fn. 138), 221-223
Allied High Commissioners, 223
Allied Investigating Commission, 203
Allies, 3-4, 11, 52, 58, 68, 80, 87-88, 113, 124, 126, 133-134, 147, 190, 203, 211, 214, 217
Alpay, Hande, xviii
Alpay, Ziya, xviii
Alston Tobacco Co, 227
America, 4, 7, 11-12, 38, 55-57, 69, 112, 119, 121, 126, 140-141, 146, 150-151, 191, 208, 212, 219, 223, 225
American, 3-8, 19-20, 22, 38, 41, 43, 53, 55-59, 61, 68, 72-74, 79, 105, 119-121, 123-124, 126- 127, 141-143, 147, 149, 152, 154, 163, 165, 191, 199-201, 203, 208-209, 212-213, 216, 219, 223-225, 227, 232
American Chamber of Commerce, 4
American High Commission, 121, 223
American Mandate, 191 (fn. 229)
American Tobacco Companies, 224-225
Amsterdam Algemeen Handelsblad (Dutch newspaper), 75 (fn. 116)
Anatolia, 55, 198, 204, 208
Anadolu Ajans [See: Anatolia Agency]
Anafarta, 113
Anatolia Agency, 55, 88, 198
Anatolia & Roumelia [Rumeli] Defense of Rights Group, 224
Anatolia College, 19, 165
Anatolian Stage Society, 63
Ancyra [See: Ankara]
Andros (Russian assistant driver), 17-18
Anglo-Arab troops, 113
Anglo-Russian Agreement, 198
Angora [See: Ankara]
Ankara, 3, 8, 51, 55, 60-62, 73, 75, 79, 97, 107, 114 (fn. 162), 122-123, 127-128, 140, 173, 189-190, 208, 211, 217, 221-227, 229, 231-233
Ankara Government, 224-226
Ankara Kalesi [Fortress], 51
Ankara Military School/Academy, 127 (fn. 175), 128 (fn. 176)
Ankara Nationalists, 74
Antalya, 42, 75, 108, 139, 157-160, 166
Apaydın, Zekai, 108 (fn. 151)

Arab, 33, 42, 52, 105, 125, 143, 154, 218
Arabia, 219
Arabs of Mesopotamia, 52
Arbor Day Custom, 65
Ardahan, 86, 205-206
Ari Bournou [See: Arıburnu]
Arıburnu, 113
Armenia, 22, 87, 191, 206, 215, 233
Armenians, 4, 7-8, 12, 20, 33, 42, 56, 61-65, 73, 75, 83, 87-88, 112, 117, 133-134, 145-146, 187, 192, 201-203, 206, 213, 215, 222, 224, 231-232
Armenian Bolsheviks, 222
Armenian (prostitutes in Eskişehir), 146
Armenian Republic, 4, 206
Armistice, 11, 59, 113, 121, 143, 218
Army Intelligence Service (France), 4
Artvin, 86, 206
Artwin [See: Artvin]
Asia, 8, 51-52, 56, 80, 82, 139, 157, 159, 189-190, 192, 197, 211
Asia Minor, 8, 51-52, 56, 80, 82, 139, 157, 159, 189-190, 192
Asiatic Turkey, 3, 5, 7, 42, 52, 61, 83, 117, 135, 145, 229
Aşık atmak (knucklebones), 72 (fn. 110)
Atatürk, ix, 97 (fn. 134) [See: Mustafa Kemal Paşa]
Athens, 43, 56, 148, 224
Atlantic Federalism, xi
Austria, 113
Austrian, 233
Austrian armies, 40
Aydin, 157
Azerbaijan, 61, 133-134, 172, 191
Azerbaijani Turks, 62, 134-135

Baba, 43, 165
Ba-Ba [See: Baba]
Badlands of Montana, 31
Bagdad, 218
Baki Bey (Lieutenant in Eskişehir), 142, 144, 146, 157
Baku, 59, 134, 191, 218
Baku Congress of Oriental Peoples, 134 (fn. 178)
Balkan, 40, 69, 95, 112, 126, 139-140, 144, 163, 183, 218
Balkan War, 69, 95, 112, 126
Barker (American Destroyer/Dreadnought), 5-6, 165
Basra, 218
Basri Bey [Hasan Basri Aytöre], 141(fn. 187), 142
Batoum [See: Batum]
Battle of Kosova, 139
Batum, 4-6, 205-206, 214, 222
Bayezid I [Sultan], 52
Bekir Sami [Kunduh] Bey, 60 (fn. 92), 86 (fn. 123), 222
Belgian, 69
Belgrad, 112
Belgrade [See: Belgrad]
Berlin, 112, 141, 148, 226
Beyoğlu, 186
Biledjik, 233
'*Bir Amerikali Olsaydım*' ('Had I been an American'), 163
'*Bir Türk Olsaydım*' ('Had I been a Turk'), 163
Bitlis, 113
Black Sea, 4, 7, 74, 106, 134, 218, 224
Boğazlar, 196, 198
Bolsheviks, 11-12, 58-62, 88, 117, 133-135, 172, 190-191, 235
Bolshevik Embassy, 58, 61-62, 134, 235
Bolshevik Envoy, 60
Bolshevik [Gold] (given to Ankara Government), 117, 134,
Bolshevism, 8, 135, 169, 198, 233
Bosporus, 4, 68, 121, 218
Bouillon, [Franklin], 222, 226
Bourdour [See: Burdur]
Brest-Litowsk Agreement, 203
Britain, 191, 202
British, 3, 7, 11, 58, 69, 80, 89, 95, 113, 117, 119, 124, 134, 142-143, 191-192, 198, 204, 206, 215, 223, 226, 232-233
British troops, 11, 124
Brusa [See: Bursa]
Bulgaria, 140, 165, 218
Bulgarian, 5, 68-69, 142
Burdur, 158, 160, 166
Bureau of Accounts, 118
Bureau of Information of the R.S.F.S.R, 11

Bursa, 68, 135, 145, 231-232
Büyükerşen, Yılmaz, xvii, 141 (fn. 186)
Büyük Millet Meclisi [See: Grand National Assembly]

Caboul [See: Kabul]
Caesarea [See: Kayseri]
California, 39
Caliph, 80-81, 88-89, 95, 220
Caliphate, 81, 89, 207, 212, 229
Cambridge University, 147
Catholic, 89, 114
Caucasus, 4, 133, 191, 197, 206, 211, 224
Caucasian, 113, 191, 214
Caucasian Moslems, 191
Celal Bey [Mahmud Celal(eddin) Bayar], 135 (fn. 175), 165
Celaleddin Arif Bey, 108 (fn. 151)
Cemal (Boy Soldier), 65, 69-72
Cemal Bey (Commander in Green Army), 69, 72
Ceritmüminli, [Village of], 35-40, 63, 83, 165, 233, 237
Cettinge [See: Çetince]
Cevat Bey, 74 (fn. 115)
Cevat [Ünügür] (son of Hasan Bey), 152-154
Cevdet Bey (Nationalist Captain in Eskişehir), 143
Chatopski, Prince (Bolshevik Consul General in Ankara), 61, 135
Chevrolet, 105, 109
Chicago ***Daily Tribune*** (Chicago newspaper), 58, 123, 189-90
Chicago, 144
Chicherin, [Georgy Vasilyevich], 87 (fn. 124), 133, 198
Christ, 23, 36, 65
Christian, 4, 9, 12, 20, 32, 36, 40, 43, 53, 57, 65, 83, 88, 108, 117-118, 146, 187, 189-190
Christian Deputies (absence of), 83
Christian Ottomans, 118
Christianity, 8, 41, 65, 141, 145
Church, 65, 95, 220, 229
Cilicia, 173, 226, 232
Commissaire du Peuple [See: People's Commissar]
Commissar, 8, 82-84, 86-87, 95, 108-109, 119-120, 127, 135, 147, 165, 169-174, 220
Commissar for Finances, 119-120, 135
Commissar for Foreign Affairs, 86, 110, 133, 172
Commissar for Public Economy, 109, 135, 169
Commissar for Public Instruction, 108, 147, 170-171
Commissar for Religious Affairs, 95, 220
Commissar for the Interior, 53, 86, 173-174
Commission of Investigation for Smyrna, 217
Committee of Union and Progress, 84, 125,
Communism, 133, 198-199, 212
Communist, 61, 133-135, 172, 212
Constantine I, King (Hellenic Kingdom of Greece), 56 (fn. 85), 106, 232
Constantinidi, Th. (Samsun Regie Tobacco Plant Manager), 12
Constantinople, 3, 40, 53-54, 58, 121, 174, 183-184, 186, 189-192, 208, 212, 215, 218-220, 222-223, 227, 231, 233
Constantinople College [for Girls], 121
Constantza [See: Köstence], 165
Constitution, 53, 55, 81, 88, 165
Constitution Hotel (Ankara), 53, 55, 165
Coombs, Colonel J.P., 7 (fn. 16)
Corona (typewriter), 38
Corporal Edhem Tchavoosh (Çavuş) [See: Edhem Çavuş]
Council of Commissars, 82, 84
Crane, Charles, 210
Crimea, 62, 154
Crook, Clive, xviii
Crusaders, 52, 108
Czar, 61, 86, 134-135, 202

Çelebi Efendi [See: Abdülhalim Çelebi Efendi]
Çelik Alay (Iron Regiment), 184 (fn. 223)
Çetince, 112
Çoban Mustafa Paşa, 145 (fn. 193)
Çorum, 17, 20-24, 40, 57, 165

Damascus, 112
Dardanelles, 112, 212, 218
Dashnak [Armenian Committee], 202-203, 206, 213, 215
De Groot, A., 116 (fn. 116)
Derna (Libyan town), 112

Diarbekir [See: Diyarbakır]
Dinar, 157, 166
Diyarbakır, 219, 231
Djelal Bey [See: Celal Bey = Mahmud Celal(eddin) Bayar]
Djelal Eddin Arif Bey [See: Celaleddin Arif]
Djemal [See: Cemal (boy soldier)]
Djemal Bey [See: Cemal Bey (Commander in the Green Flag Army)]
Djerid Muminli [See: Ceritmüminli]
Djevad [See: Cevat]
Djevdad [See: Cevdet Bey (Captain)]
Doğan, Uğur, xi
Doruk Han, 18, 20, 165
Dunn, Robert Steed, 105 (fn. 138), 106, 221, 224-227, 241 (fn. 243)
Dutch, 73, 75

Ebu Bekir Hâzım [Tepeyran] Bey, 55 (fn. 83)
Eceabat, 113
Ed Deir (Syrian Town), 218
Ede Bali [See: Şeyh Edebâlî]
Edhem Bey, İbrahim (Samsun Mutasarrıf), 7-8
Edhem Bey (Çerkez), 68 (fn. 103)
Edhem Çavuş (Gendarme Corporal), 31, 165
Edib Bey, 121
Edirne, 69, 218
Egypt, 52, 142
Eliot, George, 124
Ellison, Grace, 107 (fn. 147)
El-Müşir (Field Marshal) El-Gazi Mustafa Kemal Paşa, 107
Emir of Afghanistan, 52, 97, 205, 214
Encyclopedia Britannica, 47
Engheri = *en geri* (Ankara), 53
England, 12, 80, 121, 190, 213, 215, 218
English, 4, 7-8, 11-12, 19, 41, 52, 58, 61, 63, 68-69, 73-74, 88, 95, 111, 113, 117, 119-121, 124- 125, 141-142, 147, 154, 157, 160, 192, 195-209, 214, 217-219
Enkara = *en kara* (Ankara), 53
Entente Powers (Great Britain, France and Russia), 3, 114, 195-196, 202, 211, 213, 217, 223
Enver Paşa 73, 84, 93 (fn. 131), 113, 192
Epifani, Signor Luigi, 58
Erdinç, Erol Şadı, 163 (fn. 205)
Ergin, Canan, xviii
Erzincan, 222
Erzinjan [See: Erzincan]
Erzurum, 80, 84, 188, 195, 222
Erzurum Congress, 84
Eski Shehr [See: Eskişehir]
Eskişehir, 24, 53, 56, 60, 69, 139-151, 153-154, 157, 166, 179-181, 232-233
Eskişehir Primary School (children waltzing), 148-149
Esat Nedim [Tengizman], 60-61 (fn. 94), 110, 174, 179, 180
Essad Nedim [See: Esat Nedim]
Es-Sayyid Es-Şerif, al-Şeyh Ahmad Sennusi, 52,107-108 (fn. 148), 219
Es-Sultan Selâhaddîn-i Eyyûbî el-Kebir, 107
Eşrefoğlu Rûmî, 145 (fn. 193)
Eunu [See: İnönü], 112
Euphrates [River], 218
Europe, 22, 41, 113, 126, 147, 190, 192
European High Commissioners, 223
European Powers, 57, 119
European Turks, 82
Evans, Mary Anne [See: Eliot, George]

Fadil Bey, Lieutenant (Nationalist pilot), 233
Fago, Dr. Vincenzo, 58
Faizie School [See: Feyziye School]
Falkenhayn, [Marshall Erich von], 113 (fn. 161)
Fatma [Seher] Hanım, 188 (fn. 188)
Federalism, 163
Federated Socialist Republic of the Soviets of Russia, 11
Ferid [Ferit] Bey (Lieutenant), 141-142, 152
Ferit Paşa, 74,
Fetih [Okyar] Bey, 176
Fetiy [See: Ali Fetih (Okyar)]
Fevzi [Çakmak] Paşa, 11 (fn. 24), 84 (fn. 121), 127-128 (fn. 175), 232
Feyzi Pasha [See: Fevzi (Çakmak) Paşa]
Feyziye School, 147
Florence Hotel (Missoula, Montana), 25 (fn. 41)

Foreign Affairs, 8, 60-61, 87, 118, 169, 172, 209
Foreign Relations, 223
France, 86, 112, 121, 142, 149, 151, 197, 226, 232-233
French, 4, 7-9, 11-12, 19, 55, 58, 61, 68-69, 73, 87-88, 93, 95, 111-112, 117, 120, 124-125, 135, 139-142, 144, 146-147, 149, 160, 163, 169, 192, 195-209, 217, 226, 230, 232
French military, 112
Frenchman, 4, 59
Fundamental Law, 88

Galata Köprüsü (Galata Bridge), 184-85
Galatia, 51
Galicia, 40
Gâlip Hoca, 135 (fn. 179) [See: Celal Bey = Mahmud Celal(eddin) Bayar]
Gallipoli, 106, 113, 183
General Staff, 84, 112-113, 121, 124, 127, 141-143, 178
Georgia, 4, 58-60, 86-87, 96, 111, 191, 205, 214
Georgian, 59-62, 86
Georgian Ambassador, 60, 86
Gerguk [See: Kerkuk]
German, 12, 58-59, 61-62, 93, 113, 124, 141-144, 146, 148-149, 154, 158, 192, 232-233
Germany, 113, 140-141, 192, 232-233
God, 65, 112-113, 141, 144-145, 148
Godfrey de Bouillon, 52
Gourard (French General), 222
Graffum, Miss (American missionary in Sivas), 223
Grand National Assembly (*Büyük Millet Meclis*), 43, 52, 65, 68, 73, 79-83, 85, 87-89, 93, 95, 110, 113-114, 124, 127, 133, 139, 147, 165-166, 174, 176-177, 189, 195-196, 209, 211, 217, 219-220, 226, 239
Grand Rue de Pera (İstiklal Caddesi), 186-187
Great National Assembly of Turkey, 79 (fn. 118), 85 (fn. 122), 93, 110 (fn. 155), 127 (fn. 175), 211, 220, 224-226
Great War, 126, 223
Greece, 20, 106-107, 118, 140, 203, 214, 217, 223, 226, 232
Greek, 3-4, 7-9, 11-12, 20, 33, 40, 42-43, 51-53, 55-56, 64-65, 68-69, 73, 75, 84, 88, 96, 107-108, 112, 117, 124, 133, 139, 141-142, 144-147, 154, 159-160, 165, 179, 187-188, 192, 201-203, 213-214, 217, 223-224, 231-232
Greek Kingdom, 11
Greek Pontus Republic, 11
Greek priests, 11
Greek War, 12
Green [Flag] Army, 69 (fn. 106),
Güneysucu, Arman, xviii
Gürcistan [See: Georgia]

Hacı (Streit's gendarme), 31, 35, 73, 165
Hacı Bayram Camii (Ankara Mosque), 73 (fn. 112)
Hadji [See: Hacı]
Hafız Kerun, 148
Hakimiet Millieh [See: ***Hâkimiyet-i Milliye***]
Hâkimiyet-i Milliye ('National Sovereignty' – Ankara Newspaper), 87 (fn. 127)
Halıcı, Şaduman, xvii, 141 (fn. 186)
Halide Edib Hanım, 3, 57, 60 (fn. 92), 61, 74, 108-109, 120 (fn. 168) 121-124 (fn. 172), 125, 157, 160, 174, 189, 200
Halideh Edib Hanoum [See: Halide Edib Hanım]
Halk Komisar [See: People's Commissar]
Hamburg, 141
Hamdullah Suphi [Tanrıöver], 61 (fn. 93), 108 (fn. 150), 124, 147, 170, 171
Hamlet, 63-64
Hanioğlu, Şükrü, xvii
Harbord, General J. G., 22 (fn. 40), 203, 208-209, 213, 216, 223
Harbord Commission, 223
Harem, 9, 23
Hasan (Halide Edib's son), 121
Hasan Baba, 43-44
Hasan Bey (Eskişehir Landowner), 151-152 (fn. 199), 153-154
Hasan Dede, [village of], 42-43, 165
Hasan Deh-Deh [See: Hasan Dede]
Hasif Bey (architect), 65 (fn. 99)
Hassan Bey [See: Hasan Bey]

Hassan [See: Hasan (Halide Edib's son)]
Havza, 18-19
Hazim Bey [See: Ebu Bekir Hâzım Tepeyran Bey], 55
Hedjaz [See: Hicaz] Railway
Hellenes, 56, 89
Hellenic Army, 224
Hellenic Government, 224
Hicaz [Railway], 47, 113
Hikmet [Bayur] Bey, 60-61 (fn. 93)
Hoca Fatin Efendi, 74 (fn. 115)
Hoja Fatin Effendi [See: Hoca Fatin Efendi]
Holy War, 95, 220
Hotel Anatolia (Çorum), 22, 24, 165
Husni [See: Hüseyin Hüsnü Alibeykov]
Hüseyin Hüsnü Alibeykov (Commander Turk Battalion Red Army & Ankara Bolshevik Embassy translator), 62 (fn. 96)
Hüseyin Hüsnü Emir [Erkilet] (Kurmay Albay), 184 (fn. 223)

Ihsan [See: İhsan]
Ihsan Pasha [See: İhsan Paşa]
Iliave (Second Bolshevik Ambassador in Ankara), 135
Imperial Ottoman Bank, 8, 117
Independence Group, 224
India, 52, 69
Indian, 52, 68, 157
Ineboli (İnebolu), 224
Ingall, Valdemar, 11
Intelligence Section, 141-142, 146
International Institute of Agriculture, 151
Iraq, 205
Irish, 202, 213
Islam, 8-9, 23, 41, 43-44, 52, 65, 80-81, 89, 95, 97, 107, 133-134, 141, 148, 190-191, 205, 220
Islamic, 23, 40, 52, 93, 108
Ismid [See: İzmid]
Istanbul [See: İstanbul]
Istiklal [See: İstiklâl] ('Independence' - Eskişehir Newspaper), 188 141
Italian, 58, 117, 144, 158-160, 166, 226, 232-233
Italian Catholic Mission, 158
Italian Colonial, 58
Italian Consul, 158, 166
Italian Foreign Office, 58
Italian High Commissioner, 158, 166
Italy, 86, 108, 112, 159, 197, 219
Izzet Pasha Delegation [See: İzzet Paşa Heyeti]
Izzet Pasha [See: İzzet Paşa]

İbrahim Edhem Bey (Samsun Mutasarrıf), 7 (fn. 17), 229
İbrahim Refet [Bele] Paşa, 173
İhsan (Streit's Gendarme), 17, 22-23
İhsan Paşa, 218
İnönü (Battle of), 139
İslâm, 204, 205
İslâm Birliği (Pan İslâmizm), 204
İsmail, 23, 111
İsmet Bey, 139
İsmet [İnönü] Paşa, 68, 84, 139 (fns. 180 & 181), 166, 142, 232, 239
İstanbul, 3-5, 7-9, 24, 33, 39, 42, 52-53, 55, 58, 61-62, 64-65, 69, 73-75, 80, 82-85, 87, 89, 95, 105-107, 112-114, 117-121, 124-125, 134-135, 142-143, 147, 152, 158-160, 163, 165-166, 176, 183, 185, 187, 196, 208
İstiklâl ('Independence' - Eskişehir Newspaper), 188 141
İstiklal Caddesi (Independence Boulevard), 186
İzmid, 69, 188
İzmir, 58-59, 75, 106, 124, 135, 192, 203, 214, 224, 226
İzzet Paşa [Ahmed İzzet Furgaç Paşa] (ex-Grand Vezir), 3 (fn. 10), 74, 208, 215
İzzet Paşa Heyeti, 208

Jelal Bayar [See: Celal Bayar]
Jerusalem, 107-108
Jewess (prostitutes in Eskişehir), 146
Jewish, 106, 112, 117, 145
John D. Edwards (American Destroyer/Dreadnought), 5-7, 165
Judaism, 41, 145

Kabul, 52, 97, 205, 214
Kadınlar Dünyası ('Women's World' - İstanbul Magazine), 120

Kaisarieh [See: Kayseri]
Kalaba (Ankara village), 61 (fn. 93), 124
Kamal Raza [See: Kâmil Riza Bey]
Kâmil Riza Bey, 63 (fn. 98), 64
Kara Fatma (Black Fatma) [See: Fatma (Seher) Hanım]
Karakilis, 222
Karaklis [See: Karakilis]
Kars, 203, 213, 222
Kasim Karabekir Pasha [See: Kazım Karabekir Paşa]
Kayseri, 114, 219, 225
Kazım Karabekir Paşa, 175, 222
Kemalist, 3-4, 80, 109, 229-230
Kerkuk, 218
Keskin Mümünlü [See: Ceritmüminli (Village of)]
Khavsa [See: Havza]
Kızıl Irmak (River), 42, 46, 165
Kizil Irmak River [See: Kızıl Irmak]
King Constantine I (Hellenic Kingdom of Greece), 56 (fn. 85), 106
Konia [See: Konya]
Konya, 83, 139-140, 166, 233
Konya Express Train, 140
Koran [See: ***Qu'ran***]
Köstence, 5, 165
Krennikoff, Georges, 17-18, 20-21
Kuneralp, Sinan, xvii
Kurds, 218
Kutahia [See: Kütahya]
Kütahya, 144

Latin, 52, 72
Lausanne Peace Conference, 139 (fn. 181), 242-246
Laze (Laz), 68
Levant, 75, 211
Levantines, 75
Liberty Hotel (in Ankara), 53, 165
Library of Congress, xvii, 210, 252
Libyan, 107-108
Lipton, Sir Thomas, 53-54 (fn. 79)
Lithuanian, 61, 62
London, 58, 86-87, 107, 141, 148, 192, 195-197, 211, 217, 219, 229, 233
London Conference, 86-87, 195-197, 217
[Lowry], Demet, xviii
Lowry, Heath W., xiii, xviii, 106 (fn. 138)

Mc Dowell, Robert (Samsun Director of Near East Relief), 12
McLachlan, Dr. Alexander (President, International College in İzmir), 59 (fn. 88)
Madan [See: Maden]
Maden, 35, 41-42, 165
Mahmud Celal(eddin) [Bayar], 109, 135, 169
Mahmud Chevket Pasha [See: Mahmud Şevket Paşa]
Mahmud Şevket Paşa, 112 (fn. 159)
Mahomet [See: Muhammed (Prophet)]
Maidose (Madytos = Eceabat) [See: Eceabat]
Malta, 80, 89, 117, 176
Manchester School, 119
Mangal (charcoal brazier for heating), 33, 53
Marash [See: Maraş]
Maraş, 192
Marmara, Sea of, 212
Marmora, Sea of [See: Marmara]
Maubert, Henry (Henri), 117 (fn. 164), 118
Mdivani, [Polikarp] Boudou (Bolshevik Ambassador in Ankara), 59 (fn. 89), 60-61, 134-135
Mdivani, Simon (Georgian Menshevik Ambassador in Ankara), 59 (fn. 90), 60 (fn. 92)
Meddah (professional storyteller), 23
Mediterranean (Sea), 159
Mehmed (Çorum hotel owner's son), 24
Mehmed Ali [Mehmedoff],4-12, 17-18, 23, 27, 31, 37-38, 44, 53-54, 57, 69, 152, 157-158, 166
Mehmed Inaayet [See: Mehmed İnayet]
Mehmed İnayet, 65, 68
Mehmed Selâmi (electrical engineer in Eskişehir), 140
[Mehmed] Talât Bey [See: Talât Bey/Paşa]
Mehmed V, [Sultan], 113
Mehmed VI, [Sultan Vahdettin], 3, 89 (fn. 129), 113
Mehmedoff (Azerbaijani Turk - Ankara Bolshevik Embassy Military Attaché), 62 (fn. 96)
Men'i Müskirat Kanunu, 239
Menshevik, 58-60
Menteşe, 177
Mersiphoum [See: Merzifon]
Mersivan [See: Merzifon]
Merzifon, 17-20, 26, 34, 165, 225
Merzifon American College, 19
Mesopotamia, 97, 204, 214,

Mevlevi, 83
Michigan Agricultural College, 4
Midhat, Captain (Nationalist Pilot), 232
Military Committee of Congress, 223
Military High Commission 223
Minister of Foreign Affairs, 3, 222, 227
Missouri Meerschaum, 144
Mohammedanism, 214
Montana, 25, 31
Moore, Laurence (American teacher and businessman in İstanbul), 4-5
Moscow, 58, 61, 86, 133-134, 197, 211, 222, 225
Moslem, 189-191, 197, 213-214, 220, 224, 229
Mossoul [See: Mosul]
Mosul, 119, 207, 215, 218-219
Mouhiddin [See: Muhittin Bey]
Moustapha Reis [See: Mustafa Reis]
Moustapha Saghir [See: Mustafa Sagir]
Muffide Hanoum [See: Müfide Ferid Tek]
Muhammed V, [See: Mehmed V (Sultan)]
Muhammed (Prophet), 229
Muhittin [Birgen] Bey, 87 (fn. 126)
Mullahs, 229
Munir Kiamil [See: Münir Kâmil]
Murad I, [Sultan], 139
Musa Kâzim Karabekir, 175
Mush [See: Muş]
Muslim, 4, 8-9, 11-12, 23, 27, 31, 36, 40-42, 51-52, 57, 64-65, 83, 88, 93, 95-97, 107-108, 110-112, 114, 117-118, 121, 125, 133-134, 144-145, 147-148, 150, 172, 201, 203-205, 213
Muslim Arab, 125
Mustafa Kemal Paşa, xi, 3, 6-8, 11, 20, 22, 44, 52, 58, 61, 65, 68-69, 75, 80-84, 86-87, 89, 93-114, 120-121, 123-124, 126-129, 134, 144, 146, 165-166, 170, 173-175, 178-181, 184, 189-190, 193, 195-209-211, 217, 219-226, 239
Mustapha Reis [See: Mustafa Reis]
Mustapha Kemal Pasha [See: Mustafa Kemal Paşa]
Mustafa Reis, 36-40, 157
Mustafa Saghir [See: Mustafa Sagir]
Mustafa Sagir, 69 (fn. 105), 226
Musul [See: Mosul]
Müfide Ferid [Tek], 120
Müftüoğlu, Dr. Asuman (granddaughter of Hasan Bey in Eskişehir), 152 (fn. 199)
Münir Kâmil, Lieutentant (Samsun), 9-10
Muş, 113

Naci Bey [Ahmet Naci Tınaz] (Colonel), 84, 142-143 (fn. 189), 146, 149, 157, 232
Nadji Bey [See: Naci Bey (Colonel)]
Nakie [See: Nakiye Hanım]
Nakiye [Elgün] Hanım, 147 (fn. 194)
Namık İsmail Bey, 111 (fn. 156)
Natanson, Barbara Orbach, xvii
National Assembly [See: Grand National Assembly]
National Pact, 95, 126, 195-198, 200-201, 204, 206-207, 211, 218, 223
Nationalist, 3-4, 8-9, 24, 36, 42, 47, 49, 51-53, 55, 57-59, 61, 63, 65, 67, 69, 71, 73-75, 80, 83-84, 86-89, 93, 95-96, 103, 105-106, 108, 111, 117, 119-120, 123-124, 128, 134-135, 139-140, 150, 154, 157, 165-166, 169, 171, 173, 175, 177, 179, 181, 183, 185, 187-188, 221, 233
Nationalist Army, 24, 36, 188
Nationalist Commissar for Public Instruction, 124
Nationalist General Staff, 139, 166
Nationalist guerilla, 105
Nationalist President, 112
Nationalist troops, 128, 187
Nationalist Turkey, 3, 75, 87-88, 106
Nationalists, 3-4, 7, 21, 26, 42, 53, 58, 61, 68, 75, 79-80, 84, 86-89, 95, 107, 114, 117, 120, 124, 134-135, 143, 150, 178, 190-191, 199, 212, 221, 229
Nazilli, 188
Nazim Hikmet [Ran], 63 (fn. 98), 87 (fn. 126)
Near East, 3-4, 7-8, 12, 17, 19, 40, 73, 106, 120, 126, 133, 165, 183, 211, 222-224
Near East Relief [Commission], 3, 7-8, 12, 17, 19, 120, 165, 224
New Testament, 23, 145
New Turkey, 84, 89, 125, 157
New York, 7-8, 21, 53-54, 60, 64, 106, 169
Nypels, George, 73-75 (fns. 116 & 117)

Office of the Presidency, 118
Old Testament, 23, 145

Olti, 203, 213
Omar Khayyam, 31
Oral, Haluk, xvii
Ordu, 218
Orient, 9, 23, 41, 44, 93, 133, 139, 195
Orient Express, 139
Oriental, 4, 23-24, 31, 38, 53, 61, 63, 84, 158
Oriental Carpet Company (Italian firm in Burdur), 158
Osman, Sergeant (boy soldier), 65-66, 68-69
Osman Ferid Bey (agriculture official in Eskişehir), 151-152
Osman Gâzi, 145
Osmanlı, 106, 112, 141, 145, 150
Osmanlı Hotel (hotel in Eskişehir), 141
Otelo Kâmil [See: Kâmil Rıza Bey]
Ottoman, 3-4, 47, 52, 55, 61-62, 65, 79-81, 89, 93, 106, 113-114, 117-118, 135, 145, 159, 206, 212, 218, 224, 229
Ottoman Christians, 80
Ottoman Empire, 3, 61, 93, 113-114, 117, 145, 218
Ottoman Government, 206
Ottoman Greeks (Antalya), 159
Ottoman Public Debt Administration/Commission, 117-118, 206
Ottoman Turks, 52, 135
Ouchak [See: Uşak]
Oupmal (Bolshevik official in Ankara), 62 (fn. 96), 134
Ourdou [See: Ordu]
Ouschak [See: Uşak]
Oxford, 41, 147
Oyunlarım Üstüne (Nazim Hikmet article), 63 (fn. 98)

Özbey, Faruk, xviii

Pan-Turanism, 95, 204, 214
Pan-Islamism, 95, 204, 214
Pan-Turkism, 204, 214
Paris, 40, 54, 73, 119, 141, 144, 148, 189
Parisian, 12, 124
Pasha Hanım [See: Halide Hanım]
Payen, Fernand, xv
People's Commissar, 8 (fn.18), 135, 169
Persia, 5, 41, 135
Persian, 4-5, 8, 12, 42, 52-53, 61, 68, 125, 135, 218
Persian Shiites, 42
Philadelphia ***Public Ledger*** (Philadelphia newspaper), xi-xiii, xv, 4, 8, 20, 40, 55, 93, 139, 163, 183-184, 193, 209-211, 217, 229, 231, 239-247
Piaster, 117 (fn. 163), 119, 146
Polakov (Ankara Bolshevik Embassy interpreter), 61-62 (fn. 96), 134
Pomeroy, Dr. G.T. (American doctor in Samsun), 7-9, 11, 57
Pontus, 7, 11, 20, 51, 224-225
Pontus Agitation, 11
Pontus Committee, 224
Pontus Government, 224
Pontus Greeks, 11
Pontus Republic, 7, 20
Press Pass (*Duhul Fırkası*), 79
Prince Chatopski (Bolshevik Consul General in Ankara), 61, 135
Prohibition Law [in Nationalist Turkey], 43, 85, 192
Propaganda and Press, 118
Public Economy, 118, 169
Public Health, 82, 108, 118, 174
Public Health and Acting Commissar, 108
Public Health and Social Aid, 118
Public Instruction, 118
Public Ledger [See: Philadelphia ***Public Ledger***]
Public Works and Religious Affairs, 82, 118

Qur'an, 23, 31, 36, 41, 80, 133, 145, 148, 229

Rakı, 43
Red Album [Streit's photograph album], 5-6, 10, 13, 17-21, 26, 33, 36, 39, 41-44, 46-47, 54-56, 59, 66-67, 70-72, 97, 106, 109, 151, 158-159, 171, 173, 236
Red Crescent Society, 143
Red Wheat, 142, 144
Reed, Howard A., 59 (fn. 88)
Refet Pasha [See: Refet (Bele) Paşa]
Refet [Bele] Paşa, 173
Reformation Group, 224
Régie Tobacco Plant (Samsun), 12-13
Reo (truck), 17, 165
Republic of Georgia, 59, 86

Robert College, 4, 73, 141, 174
Rome, 51-52, 54, 114, 148, 151
Royal College in London, 141
Royal, Lieutentant (Executive Officer of the John D. Edwards), 7
Rue, Larry, 58 (fn. 87)
Rumania, 140, 165
Rumanian port of Constantza (Constanta), 5
Russia, 11-12, 58, 60, 62, 88, 133-135, 190, 197-198, 211-212, 224, 233
Russian, 5, 17, 19, 59-62, 84, 86, 113, 120, 133-134, 142, 145-146, 197, 202-203, 211, 213, 225, 231-232
Russian Bolsheviks, 84, 120
Russian Government, 211
Russian refugee, 17
Russian (prostitutes in Eskişehir), 146
Russo 133, 135, 198
Russo-English Trade Agreement, 198
Russo-Turkish, 133
Ryak (Syrian town), 113

S.S. Milano (Italian Steamship), 42, 160, 166
Saadet (Samsun schoolgirl), 9-10
Sabri Sefi [See: Sabri Seyfi]
Sabri Seyfi, 140
Salih Bey, Dr. (Director of Military Hospitals in Eskişehir), 149
Salih Bozok [Omurtak], Major, 178-181
Salih Pasha [See: Salih Paşa]
Salih Paşa [Salih Hulusi (Kezrak) Paşa] (ex-Grand Vezir), 74 (fn. 114)
Salonika [See: Selânik]
Sami Bey (Eskişehir Mutasarrıf), 143, 146
Samsun, 3-5, 7-8, 11-13, 17, 20-21, 26, 55, 61, 120, 127, 135, 140, 160, 165, 224-225, 227, 229-230
San Francisco, 21
San Remo Pact, 190, 219
Sanders, General Otto Liman von, 113 (fn. 160)
Sandıklı (village of), 157, 166
Sandykly [See: Sandıklı]
Scott, John, xviii
Second Balkan War, 106, 183, 220
Sekili (village of), 32-34, 36-38, 165
Selânik, 106, 112, 190
Seljuk Turks, 52
Senussi [See: Es-Sayyid Es-Şerif, al-Şeyh Ahmad Sennusi]
Sèvres Agreement, 195
Shakespeare, 63-64
Sharp, Captain Alexander, 6-8
Sheik [See: Şeyh]
Sheik ul Islam [See: *Şeyhülislâm*]
Sherif Roumi [See: Eşrefoğlu Rûmî]
Sherii [See: Şeriat]
Shiite, 42
Shoukri Naili Pasha [See: Şükri Naili Paşa,Commander]
Shuster, Morgan, 41 (fn. 65)
Signor Tuozzi [See: Tuozzi, Signor]
Sinop, 11
Sinope [See: Sinop]
Sivas, 17, 44, 47, 114, 140, 163, 165, 195, 203, 213, 219, 223, 230
Sivas Congress, 163, 195
Smyrna [See: İzmir]
Sofia [See: Sofya]
Sofya, 112
Soviet, 59, 87, 197-198, 206, 211-212, 215
Soviet Armenia, 206, 215
Soviet Russia, 59, 197-198, 211-212
Spor Alemi ('Sports World' - İstanbul magazine), 73
State Department [U.S.], 223
Streit, Clarence K., xi, xv, 8, 55, 75, 122-123, 154, 163-164, 183, 193-211, 229, 231, 235-239
Sublime Porte (office of the Grand Vezir or Prime Minister), 3-4, 84
Suleiman (district in Iraq), 218
Sultan Osman [See: Osman Gâzi]
Sultanate, 81, 89, 207, 229
Sungurlu, 25
Sunnite, 42
Sunussi [See: Senussi]
Swedish, 61
Swiss, 69
Switzerland, 144
Syria, 97, 113, 204-205, 214

Şeriat (Holy Law), 81
Şeyh, 52, 84, 219-220, 229
Şeyhülislâm, 84, 95, 220, 229
Şeyh Edebâlî, 145 (fn. 192)
Şükri Naili [Gökberk] Pasha, Commander, 183 (fn. 222)

Tagore, Rabindranath, 40 (fn. 63)
Talât Bey/Paşa, 112 (fn. 157), 226
Tallat Pasha [See: Talât Bey/Paşa]
Tambour [See: *tanbur / tambur*]
Tanbur / tambur (type of lute), 23
Tarık Yahut Endülüs'ün Tarihi [stage play by Abdülhak Hâmid], 125 (fn. 174)
Taşhan (Ankara hotel), 54
Tchelebi Effendi [See: Çelebi Efendi]
Tchitchérine [See: Chicherin, (Georgy Vasilyevich]
Tchorum [See: Çorum]
Teşkilât-ı Mahsûsa (Special Organization), 135 (fn. 179)
Tevfik (boy soldier), 44, 65, 67-69
Tevfik Rüştü [Aras]), 177
Tevfik Paşa, 196
Tewfik Paşa [See: Tevfik Paşa]
Thames River, 95, 204
The Rise of Women in the New Turkey [article by Halide Hanım], 125-126
The Unknown Turks [Clarence Streit's unpublished manuscript], xii, 93, 147 (fn. 195), 163, 239, 248
Thrace, 188, 218, 226
Time Magazine, 163
Timur, 52
Tobacco, 12, 225, 227
Tobacco Workers, 12
Topal Osman [Kayıkçi] Ağa, 105-106 (fn. 145)
Torook Han [See: Doruk Han]
Towfik [See: Tevfik (Boy Soldier)]
Trabzon, 61, 135
Treaty of Alexandropol (Tr.: Gümrü Antlaşması), 87 (fn. 125)
Trebizond [See: Trabzon]
Tree Association, 65
Tripoli, 112, 219
Tuozzi, Signor (Italian High Commissioner's Delegate for Asia Minor), 158, 166
Tuncay, Mete, xvii, 62 (fn. 96)
Turan Birliği (Pan Turanizm), 204
Turcoman, 61
Turkestan, 61-62, 93
Turkish Agricultural Bank (Eskişehir), 144
Turkish Armed Forces, 84, 178
Turkish Army, 231, 233
Turkish Assembly, 80
Turkish Conservatory, 63
Turkish Minister of War, 112
Turkish Nationalists, 3, 7-8, 11, 52-53, 75, 83, 85, 109, 117, 140, 159, 189, 211
Turkish (prostitutes in Eskişehir), 146
Turkish University of İstanbul, 147
Turko-Greek, 53, 188
Turko-Italian, 112
Turkophile, 8
Türklük Birliği (Pan Türkizm), 204

Umid [See: ***Ümid***]
Union Now (Clarence K. Streit book), xi, 11, 163
Unionist, 3, 84, 93, 112, 125-126
Unionist Party, 84, 125
United States, 4, 12, 20, 31, 57, 69, 119-121, 126, 140-141, 163, 172, 199-200, 212, 222, 225
University of Illinois, 121
Uşak, 173, 231

Ümid ('Hope' - İstanbul magazine), 65, 120

Varna (Bulgarian port), 5, 165
Vatan ('Fatherland' - İstanbul newspaper), 163
Venetian, 159
Venizelos, Eleftherios Kyriakou, 106-107 (fn. 146)
Victory Arch, 186
Vienna, 36, 40, 54, 113, 141
Virgin Mary, 65

War Department [U.S.], 223
War of Independence, 61, 68, 120, 163
Washington D.C., 54, 95, 97, 121, 148, 163, 172, 200, 222

Washington, George, 93
Webster's New World Dictionary Second College Edition, 117 (fn. 163)
Wells, H.G., 41(fn. 64)
White, George E., 19 (fn. 35)
Williams, Paul, 58 (fn. 87), 123 (fn. 171), 189-191, 239
Wilson, Woodrow, 22, 58, 189, 192, 206, 215
Winter Palace, 221
World War, 7, 22, 32, 39, 62, 68-69, 81, 93, 95, 113-114, 117, 146, 154, 183-184, 201, 203, 233

Yaili [See: *yaylı*]
Yahşihan, 44, 47, 165
Yakın Tarihte Gördüklerim ve Geçirdiklerim ('Things I Have Seen & Experienced in the Recent Past' – Ahmet Emin Yalman's memoir), 163
Yakshi Khan [See: Yahşihan]
Yalman, Mehmet Emin, 163 (fn. 205)
Yaylı (horse drawn covered spring wagon), 17, 23, 26-27, 31-32, 35, 42, 157-158, 160
Yeni Gun [See: ***Yeni Gün***]
Yeni Gün ('New Day' - Ankara newspaper), 87 (fn. 128)
Yeni Shehr [See: Yenişehir]
Yenişehir, 68
Yoğurt, 152
Young Turks, 65, 93, 112, 135, 146
Youssouf [See: Yusuf Kemal Bey]
Yozgat, 21, 22, 25-26, 32, 47, 114, 157, 165, 219
Yusuf Kemal [Tengirşenk] Bey, 197, 211, 222-223, 227
Yücel, Enver, xvii
Yozgat, 21
Yuzgad [See: Yozgat]

Zonguldak, 74
Zungouldak [See: Zonguldak]

Recent Related Titles from the Bahçeşehir University Press

Books in English:

Heath W. Lowry & İsmail E. Erünsal: *Remembering One's Roots*: *"Mehmed Ali Paşa of Egypt's Links to the Macedonian Town of Kavala* (*Architectural Monuments, Inscriptions* & *Documents*) İstanbul (Bahçeşehir University Press), 2011. pp. x + 271. Price: $45 [Includes Shipping & Handling]

Heath W. Lowry: *Historical Vestiges of Nîyazî Mısrî's Presence on the Island of Limnos* (*Niyâzî Mısrî'nin Limni Adası'nda Bulunan Tarihi İzler*) İstanbul (Bahçeşehir University Press: Occasional Papers in History #3), 2011. pp. ix + 143. Price: $12 [Includes Shipping & Handling]

Heath W. Lowry: *The Evrenos Family* & *the City of Selânik* (*Thessaloniki*): Who Built the *Hamza Beğ Câmii* & *Why*? / *Evrenos Ailesi ve Selânik Şehri*: *Hamza Beğ Câmii Niçin ve Kimin Tarafindan Yapıldı*? İstanbul (Bahçeşehir University Press: Occasional Papers in History #2), 2010. pp. viii + 102. Price: $10 [Includes Shipping & Handling]

Heath W. Lowry & İsmail E. Erünsal: *The Evrenos Dynasty of Yenice-i Vardar*: *Notes* & *Documents*. İstanbul (Bahçeşehir University Press), 2010. pp. ix + 184 + 90 Photos. Price: $40 [Includes Shipping & Handling]

Heath W. Lowry: *In the Footsteps of the Ottomans*: *A Search for Sacred Spaced* & *Architectural Monuments in Northern Greece*. İstanbul (Bahçeşehir University Press), 2009. xvi + 231 + 350 color photos. Price: $40 [Includes Shipping & Handling]

Heath W. Lowry: *Ottoman Architecture in Greece*: *A Review Article With Addendum* & *Corrigendum*. İstanbul (Bahçeşehir University Press: Occasional Papers in History #1), 2009. pp. viii + 79. Price: $10 [Includes Shipping & Handling]

Heath W. Lowry: *The Shaping of the Ottoman Balkans, 1350-1550*: *Conquest, Settlement* & *Infrastructural Development of Northern Greece*. İstanbul (Bahçeşehir University Press), 2008. pp. xii + 286 + 10 Maps + 220 Photos. Price: $40 [Includes Shipping & Handling]

Books in Turkish:

Heath W. Lowry ve İsmail E. Erünsal: *Aslına Dönüş: "Mısır Valisi Mehmed Ali Paşa'nın Kavala Kasabası ile Bağları: Mimari Eserler, Kitabeler ve Belgeler*. İstanbul (Bahçeşehir Üniversitesi Yayınları), 2011. s. x + 271. Fiyatı: 65 TL [Gönderi ücreti dahildir].

Heath W. Lowry: *Niyâzî Mısrî'nin Limni Adası'nda Bulunan Tarihi İzler* [*Historical Vestiges of Nîyazî Mısrî's Presence on the Island of Limnos*] İstanbul (Bahçeşehir Üniversitesi Yayınları: Occasional Papers in History #3), 2011. s. ix + 143. Fiyatı: 18 TL [Gönderi ücreti dahildir].

Heath W. Lowry: *Evrenos Ailesi ve Selânik Şehri: Hamza Beğ Câmii Niçin ve Kimin Tarafından Yapıldı?* [*The Evrenos Family & the City of Selânik (Thessaloniki): Who Built the Hamza Beğ Câmii & Why?*]. İstanbul (Bahçeşehir Üniversitesi Yayınları: Occasional Papers in History #2), 2010. s. viii + 102. Fiyatı: 15 TL [Gönderi ücreti dahildir].

Heath W. Lowry & İsmail E. Erünsal: *Yenice-i Vardar'lı Evrenos Hanedanı: Notlar & Belgeler*. İstanbul (Bahçeşehir Üniversitesi Yayınları), 2010. s. ix + 184 + 90 Photos. Fiyatı: 60 TL [Gönderi ücreti dahildir].

Heath W. Lowry: *Osmanlıların Ayak İzlerinde: Kuzey Yunanistan Mukaddes Mekânlar ve Mimarî Eserleri Arayış Yolculukları*. İstanbul (Bahçeşehir Üniversitesi Yayınları), 2009. xvi + 231 + 350 Renkli fotoğraf. Fiyatı: 60 TL [Gönderi ücreti dahildir].

Heath W. Lowry: *Osmanlı Döneminde Balkanların Şekillenmesi, 1350-1550: Kuzey Yunanistan'ın Fethi, İskânı ve Altyapı Gelişmesi*. İstanbul (Bahçeşehir Üniversitesi Yayınları), 2008. s. xii + 286 + 10 Harita + 220 Resim. Fiyatı: 60 TL [Gönderi ücreti dahildir].

These Books Are Available From: